AF867628

# *UNDERSTANDING STEEL DESIGN*

# *UNDERSTANDING STEEL DESIGN*

- - -

## AN ARCHITECTURAL DESIGN MANUAL

- - -

Terri Meyer Boake

With Technical Illustrations
by Vincent Hui

Birkhäuser
Basel

The author and the publisher wish to thank the Canadian Institute of Steel Construction Regions and Walters Group for their participation in this book.

EDITOR
Andreas Müller

GRAPHIC DESIGN & PRODUCTION
ActarBirkhäuserPro
www.actarbirkhauserpro.com
Barcelona - Basel

A CIP catalogue record for this book is available from the Library of Congress, Washington D.C., USA.

BIBLIOGRAPHIC INFORMATION PUBLISHED BY THE GERMAN NATIONAL LIBRARY
The German National Library lists this publication in the Deutsche Nationalbibliografie; detailed bibliographic data are available on the Internet at http://dnb.d-nb.de.

This work is subject to copyright. All rights are reserved, whether the whole or part of the material is concerned, specifically the rights of translation, reprinting, re-use of illustrations, recitation, broadcasting, reproduction on microfilms or in other ways, and storage in databases. For any kind of use, permission of the copyright owner must be obtained.

This book is also available in a German language edition (ISBN 978-3-0346-0271-6)

© 2012 Birkhäuser GmbH, Basel
P.O.Box, 4002 Basel, Switzerland
Part of ActarBirkhäuser

Printed on acid-free paper produced from chlorine-free pulp. TCF ∞

Printed in Spain

ISBN 978-3-0346-0269-3
9 8 7 6 5 4 3 2 1

www.birkhauser.com

DISTRIBUTION

ActarBirkhäuserD
Barcelona – Basel – New York
www.actarbirkhauser.com

Roca i Battle 2
E-08023 Barcelona
T +34 93 417 49 43
F +34 93 418 67 07
salesbarcelona@actarbirkhauser.com

Viaduktstrasse 42
CH-4051 Basel
T +41 61 5689 800
F +41 61 5689 899
salesbasel@actarbirkhauser.com

151 Grand Street, 5th floor
New York, NY 10013, USA
T +1 212 966 2207
F +1 212 966 2214
salesnewyork@actarbirkhauser.com

# CONTENTS

# *Preface*

Building construction is an increasingly complex subject of study and field of practice. There are numerous materials and systems from which an architect or engineer can select when designing the structure of a building. The basis of the idea behind this book lies in a firm belief in the benefits of recognizing the intrinsic connection between characteristics of materials and the design of buildings. Good building design responds to, incorporates and builds upon the potential of its materials. The selection of the primary structural material must occur at the beginning of the development of the *parti* to be integrated into the design and fine-tuned by the design intentions.

Although steel is inherently a very technical material, from its engineering to its detailing, it is a material whose characteristics have enormous potential for the creation of dynamic architecture. I maintain that it is more important for architects to have a good grasp of the nature and detailing of steel systems than it is for them to perform calculations. Much is to be gained by careful study of exemplary projects as a means to leverage a better understanding of the potential of steel. Architects must also appreciate the critical role that is played by the steel fabricator and erector in facilitating the design of more complex structural systems and articulated details.

I have been teaching building construction at the School of Architecture at the University of Waterloo, ON, Canada since 1983. My approach to teaching has been strongly based on the review of projects with a mind to understanding and learning from their ambitions, successes and failures. I have worked with the Canadian Institute of Steel Construction and the Steel Structures Education Foundation of Canada to document exemplary steel projects, including their construction, where possible. The construction process is a temporary phase. Once a building is complete and aspects of the construction process removed from view, the study of the building structure becomes difficult. The majority of architectural publications focus on the occupied building and seldom include exhaustive information about the construction process. Most architectural photography is commissioned of completed buildings. Construction documentation is a long process that can require a commitment of several years. Most construction images are taken by site personnel and are not intended for publication. It became my personal passion to undertake such documentation in order to both personally understand the process as well as share it with my students.

It was my privilege over the last decade to have the opportunity to document several projects, largely covering the entire span from groundbreaking to opening, designed by high-profile architects such as Foster + Partners, Frank Gehry, Studio Libeskind, Antoine Predock and Will Alsop. These local projects lend a Canadian flavor to several chapters, as they form a core reference for some of the more detailed fabrication and erection descriptions.

Thanks to the steel fabricators, Walters Inc., Benson Steel and Mariani Metal for providing tours of their fabrication plants and to the contractors, PCL Constructors, EllisDon Corporation, Vanbots and Ledcor for facilitating my access to the sites. Thanks to Kubes Steel for allowing me to tour their bending facility.

The large custom-fabricated connections at Heathrow Terminal 5 in London, England by Richard Rogers are the result of high-level collaboration between the architect, engineer, fabricator and constructor.

## THE APPROACH OF THIS BOOK

It is the intention of this book to provide architects with a different kind of information about steel, one that places them ahead in understanding the design potential of the material.

There is a transformative connection between historic developments in iron and steel technologies over the past 250 years and the evolution of Modern architecture. This connection forms the basis of the brief selected history of the evolution of iron and steel construction to the present time disbursed throughout the following chapters. The connection between early or precedent-setting innovations in iron and steel, and the evolution of these methods as they impact current design, fabrication and erection methods, will inform the approach to understanding each aspect of steel design in contemporary architectural applications.

This is not a case study text. Many of the projects and buildings used as examples will be broken apart and their particular aspects discussed in appropriate chapters. Some more detailed, project-based "Process Profiles" provide the reader with a more comprehensive understanding of the detailed design and construction workflow. In addition to straightforward concepts like concealed structural steel framing, a focus will be on the design of exposed steel systems, as extrapolations of standard practice, because these require much more aptitude on the part of the architect, who must now be involved in the detailed design of systems and connections.

### Photographs

The majority of the photographs were taken by the author (if no other photo credit has been assigned). Architecture is experiential and a building cannot be fully understood by looking at a single "classic" shot. It is hoped that readers will gain some new and different insights into steel construction through the range of projects (both obscure and renowned) and the varied views. Steel construction is about details, and the photos included will take you as close as possible so that you can begin to understand better the process and workings of steel design.

The book has been crafted around my first-hand experience of steel buildings. It is my preference to speak and write about places that I have visited, rather than interpret the experiences of others. The use of my own photographs also reflects a focus on specific aspects of projects that are not often included in the images of others. Although many of the photos for this text have been sourced from my personal teaching collection, a significant effort was put into widening my international database of images to better reflect the current state of steel construction around the world.

### Drawings and Illustrations

Steel requires quite detailed drawings to communicate information among team members about the structure and connection design. Many illustrations included in the book have been contributed by fabricators who have been involved in the realization of many of the projects. These illustrations demonstrate the variety of approaches to sharing information about the detailing of the steel and the integration of other systems. Where such drawings or photographs were not available, illustrations have been created by Vincent Hui to provide more detailed and sometimes technical information about a particular building or method of construction.

The illustrations of the various projects in this book are intentionally devoid of dimensional and material size references. They are intended to increase the conceptual understanding of the types of systems and connection details used in the buildings. Predominant technical terminology follows North American use. European terms have been incorporated where appropriate.

ACKNOWLEDGMENTS

This publication has been made possible through the generous support of Walters Inc. Steel Fabricators and the Regions of the Canadian Institute of Steel Construction.

Particular thanks to Vincent Hui and Sam Ghantous of Ryerson University for the production of the technical illustrations in the book.

The writing of this book brings to a state of focus the accumulation of about 30 years of study, investigation and experience in the design and construction of steel buildings. The journey began when I was a student of architecture in the late 1970s and early 1980s and had the opportunity to travel to Paris and experience the newly constructed Centre Pompidou. Interest in the High Tech movement, historical cast steel structures and the emerging exposed structural steel style led me along an interesting path in the acquisition of knowledge and images of noteworthy steel buildings. Over the years I have attempted to visit each project and document it on a personal level. Whereas I could not possibly take my students to visit each site, I tried to bring to them a more personal experience of the architecture - different than that available in common texts on steel and construction techniques. I have made an effort to share this visual experience with the architectural community.

In the late 1990s I commenced a research relationship with the Canadian Institute of Steel Construction and the Steel Structures Education Foundation. The funded research that I carried out provided further opportunity to more completely understand the implications of fabrication and erection on design and detailing, as well as to experience projects more closely. Many thanks to Mike Gilmor, Dave MacKinnon and Hugh Krentz for trusting me with these interactive educational projects.

Involvement in the AESS Committee and the production of the "CISC Guide for Specifying Architecturally Exposed Structural Steel" is responsible for fuelling some of the more detailed technical material included in this book. My understanding and experience of steel would be nowhere without the assistance of Sylvie Boulanger, Walter Koppelaar and Tim Verhey. Sylvie is my engineering counterpart and has willingly shared so much knowledge and insight with me. We both have a passion for what steel can help architecture to be, AESS in particular. Walter has always encouraged me and allowed me into his fabrication shop, and provided access to numerous job sites (OCAD, ROM, Leslie Dan, Guelph Science Building, Bow Encana and the Canadian Museum for Human Rights). Accessing construction sites is not easy. Without these detailed first-hand experiences of construction in process, my expertise would not have progressed beyond that of a standard instructor and my image bank would be substantially poorer. Tim Verhey was always willing to provide me with very detailed technical clarifications, many of which are included in this book.

Thanks as well to Rob Third and Ziggy Welsch of George Third and Son Fabricators, Steve Benson of Benson Steel, Vince Mariani of Mariani Metal and John Rogers of Kubes Steel. The information, images, shop tours and insights you provided also feature heavily in this book.

Thanks to the students and faculty at the School of Architecture, University of Waterloo where I have been teaching full-time since 1986. You have always been encouraging of my work. To Reinhold Schuster, my former structures professor, who mentored my interest in structural steel and teaching. To Ed Allen for the inspiration that teaching materials could be "more".

Thanks as well to my editor Andreas Müller for "seeing this book in me" and who has made the process of bringing the book to completion pure pleasure. Gratitude to Andreas and his wife Barbara for hosting me in Berlin during the documentation and editing phases of the book. Rein Steger has done marvellous work in laying out the book. Thanks to Steffen Walter for the German translation.

Lastly thank you to my family for enduring me for the last year while I "lived the book". It has been quite exhilarating, full of writing and travel. Appreciation to my daughters Alex and Sierra for accompanying me to Europe and China on photo gathering missions, and to my husband Brian for taking me to the UAE to see some spectacular buildings. Thanks to Elanne for tolerating many long absences of her mother.

*CHAPTER 1*

---

# *THE TRANSFORMATIVE NATURE OF STEEL CONSTRUCTION*

---

## *THE INTRINSIC CONNECTION BETWEEN HISTORIC DEVELOPMENTS IN STEEL AND MODERN ARCHITECTURE*

STEEL IS ABOUT TENSION

STEEL IS ABOUT INDUSTRIALIZATION AND MASS FABRICATION

STANDARD STRUCTURAL STEEL VERSUS ARCHITECTURALLY EXPOSED STRUCTURAL STEEL (AESS)

## *FROM TECHNIQUE TO TECHNOLOGY*

Oriental Pearl Tower. The skyline of Shanghai, China as seen from the Huangpu River. The change in architecture, which is due to the impact of the potential of steel, is clearly evident in a skyline that borders on the futuristic. Whether these buildings have structural steel skeletons, or their concrete relies on steel reinforcing, the potential of the materiality and the structural properties of steel are at the root of the architecture.

The developments in the conceptual base of architectural design over the past 300 years reveal an intrinsic link between the emergence of new materials, the technological advancement of existing materials, progress in environmental control systems, and resultant architectural form and theory. Little change has taken place that cannot be traced to the influence of new technologies.

The complete course of architectural history and building activity has changed as the direct result of transformations due to the incorporation of steel as a main building material. Almost every urban skyline and major building uses this material. Steel has changed the way that we design buildings. It has allowed architects to create structures that at one time were captives of the imagination and the property of "visionaries".

Yet many in the architectural profession have not been able to grasp the full potential of the material, nor understand and therefore exploit its detailed design – from concept through fabrication and erection. As structural steel has slowly emerged from its traditional concealed state, to one of exposure and expression, it has also slipped from residing mainly in the field of engineering, and placed itself in the domain of architecture.

The advent of iron construction in France and England in the 18$^{th}$ and 19$^{th}$ centuries coincided with the growing separation between the areas of expertise of Architect and Engineer, and additionally gave rise to divisiveness in architectural theory and education regarding the adoption and suitability for use of the material. The calculation and detailing of iron came to be part of the engineer's duties as the 18$^{th}$ century use of iron was at first typically found in the construction of bridges, mill buildings and arcade roofs, which were seldom designed by architects. There was much controversy surrounding this new material and as a result, iron was at the outset delegated as an industrial material. Even J.N.L. Durand of the École Polytechnique, a more technically driven architectural institution compared to the École des Beaux-Arts, rejected iron as a building material. However, Durand's textbook *Précis des Leçons* and its establishment of the "*mécanisme de la composition*" were paramount in setting forth a rationalized grid which, in addition to building upon the accepted lines of classical symmetry present in Beaux-Arts design, in future allowed for the industrialization and regularization of architecture, qualities that were well suited to iron and steel construction and mass/modular production in general.

## *THE INTRINSIC CONNECTION BETWEEN HISTORIC DEVELOPMENTS IN STEEL AND MODERN ARCHITECTURE*

Architectural design is closely linked to the materiality of the structure and the systems chosen to frame and clad the building, and the inherent strength and performance characteristics of that material. There is a deep intrinsic connection between the characteristics of the material chosen and the building to be designed. The selection of the material must be concurrent with the conception of the idea or *parti* for the project. Highly successful architectural projects are the result of this type of comprehensive thinking. The invention of iron, and subsequently steel, was responsible for completely changing both the process and the product of architectural design. Historically based changes still influence and inform the way that architecture, particularly (but not exclusively) steel architecture, is designed today.

### STEEL IS ABOUT TENSION

Each material behaves in a unique manner – and the technological development of architecture has been reliant on discoveries surrounding the capabilities of each material. Architecture prior to the advent of iron was based on compression. Steel is, by its nature, a material that performs exceptionally well in tension. No other common building material comes close to this structural benefit. There were no significant structural or architectural precedents or experimentation prior to early iron buildings that were designed to intentionally exploit tension. Architectural and engineering developments from the past 250 years have made a significant contribution to the way that we understand and design with steel.

The Bibliothèque Ste. Geneviève in Paris, France, designed by Henri Labrouste, reveals the new lightness of structure enabled by the introduction of industrialized cast iron. Labrouste's work characterized a new typology today referred to as "Structural Rationalism". The notion of mass-produced, assembled architecture was introduced here.

### STEEL IS ABOUT INDUSTRIALIZATION AND MASS FABRICATION

Iron and steel lend themselves to industrialized manufacturing processes and mass production. This has had significant impact on the design, fabrication and erection of buildings. It has required that architects become increasingly familiar with the finer details of the process of construction, much more so than other materials have required. Architects must understand methods of fabrication and erection in steel in order to be able to contribute to successful design in this material.

### STANDARD STRUCTURAL STEEL VERSUS ARCHITECTURALLY EXPOSED STRUCTURAL STEEL (AESS)

Steel in buildings can take two forms. It is either structurally concealed or architecturally exposed. Hidden steel must be economically designed and "keep the loads happy". Architecturally Exposed Structural Steel (AESS) must, additionally, be designed in a way that creates a dynamic and vital aesthetic for the building. Basic structural steel requires less involvement in its "Design" from the project team. AESS design requires that architects not only understand the structural aspects of load paths and framing types, but also that they have expertise in designing connections that are suitable for crafting. Architects must also appreciate the overall impacts of the resultant fabrication and erection processes on the constructability and economy of a project. These might be understood as "best practices".

## *FROM TECHNIQUE TO TECHNOLOGY*

For understanding the impact that iron and steel have on the current state of contemporary building design, it is appropriate to focus on the influence of the rapid technological progress subsequent to the early 1700s. Here we can cite the scientific divide between those structural and material inventions that were the children of "technology" versus "technique". The term technology must be differentiated from that of technique in order to understand its implications. Technology deals with the scientific study of a subject. Such studies have only largely come about since the onset of the Industrial Revolution with the advent of advanced mathematical, scientific and engineering studies. Through these means, science offers a testing ground for increasingly reliable predictions. Technology allows for increased confidence in the design of accurate building structures, and an accelerated speed of documentation and construction. Technique, on the other hand, provides us with knowledge based on trial-and-error methodology, through information gathered via unscientific experimentation. Technology is, however, indebted to technique as an initiative for study and a field of experience.

There are four key aspects that must be addressed in looking at the history of architecture as it relates to the transformative nature of iron and steel construction:

- → What were the inherent structural benefits of the material steel and how did these affect the creation of architecture in general?
- → How did the adoption of steel building techniques change the physical form, and thereby the style, of architecture?
- → How did the nature of steel construction change the way that we construct, and therefore also the way that we need to design buildings?
- → What are the key projects whose creation provided lasting references upon which to build the language of steel construction?

The methodology of framed elemental construction, and the language of connections displayed in 19th century Structural Rationalist buildings, and subsequently High Tech Architecture, continues to be developed, perfected and exploited as one of the desirable aesthetic characteristics of expressed steel structures. Its industrialized construction system is also responsible for providing steel with a competitive edge over site-cast systems.

Steel, as a structural material, became an icon for technology and modernity in the 20th century. As a new structural material with immense tensile capabilities, steel allowed for the creation of architecture conceived in lightness and suspension, an architecture requiring ballasting and mass to prevent it from taking flight. To speculate on the ramifications of the non-existence of steel would make us realize the continuation of an earthbound, compressive design language. It was, in fact, the tensile capabilities of steel that challenged design in reinforced concrete to aspire to free itself from its inherent compressive conceptuality – and resulted in the eventual creation of tensile reinforcement, prestressing and a structural language of pure fantasy.

One of the most exceptional features of steel, as a direct result of its unique capacity to resist tensile forces, is its ability to cantilever. The Graduate Residence at the University of Toronto, ON, Canada, designed by Morphosis Architects, uses the cantilevering capabilities of steel to suspend its signage over the adjacent street.

There are significant inventions in the recent history of steel construction that have resulted in shifts in design and subsequent theory. The British High Tech movement was able to make use of the invention of tubular material, whose form changed the articulation and expression of this new language of exposed steel connections. This movement was to evolve into contemporary Architecturally Exposed Structural Steel. This type of structural expression demands that architects become increasingly engaged in understanding the design, detailing and construction of steel structures, not only as a function of the engineering of such forms, but more the realities and promise to be found in their fabrication. If Mies said that "God is in the details", he may have been seeing well beyond the strict formality of early Modern steel buildings and forward to the wild range of expression in contemporary structures.

Iron, steel and glazing systems have interdependent connectivity through their concurrent historical development. Early exhibition building, arcade and galleria typologies relied on inventions in iron and steel framing systems to permit increasing use of glass to daylight structures. The invention of stainless steel spider connections, cable support structures and mullionless glazing systems for projects like the Serres at La Villette by Peter Rice and the Willis Faber Dumas Building by Norman Foster forever modified the concept and detailing of the Modernist "glass box" and its dependency on traditional curtain wall cladding systems. Likewise, the more recent development of steel lattice systems, such as those seen in the Milan Exhibition Center by Massimiliano Fuksas and the British Museum Courtyard roof by Norman Foster, have freed steel design from strict platonic geometries.

The lead ironworker works to complete the erection of a tight-fitting element of diagrid steel into the Addition to the Royal Ontario Museum, Michael Lee-Chin Crystal, Toronto, ON, Canada by Studio Libeskind.

Brookfield Place, Toronto, ON, Canada, designed by Santiago Calatrava, highlights the potential of Architecturally Exposed Structural Steel.

The Neues Kranzler Eck Building in Berlin, Germany, designed by Helmut Jahn, highlights the dynamic potential of the marriage of exposed steel and glass systems.

The Pritzker Pavilion in Chicago, IL, USA, designed by Frank Gehry, illustrates the expressive potential and construction challenges in the use of curved steel.

*CHAPTER 2*

---

# *THE MATERIALITY OF STEEL*

---

*STRUCTURAL PROPERTIES OF STEEL*

*HOT-ROLLED STEEL SHAPES*

*HOLLOW STRUCTURAL SECTIONS (HSS)*

ELECTRIC RESISTANCE WELDING (ERW) PROCESS

FORM-SQUARE WELD-SQUARE PROCESS

*ECONOMIES IN DETAILING AND SPECIFYING STEEL*

*DESIGN AND MODELING SOFTWARE*

There is a wide range of steel shapes in production.
The availability of members varies by geographic location.

# STRUCTURAL PROPERTIES OF STEEL

Each material behaves in a unique manner – and the technological development of architecture has been reliant on discoveries surrounding the best capabilities of each material. Steel is by its nature a material that performs exceptionally well in tension. No other common building material comes close to this structural benefit. There are no significant structural or architectural precedents prior to experimentation in early iron buildings that were designed to intentionally exploit tension. Architecture prior to the advent of iron was based on compression.

*A chart comparing the Ultimate strength of*

Regular carbon steel: 400 MPa | 60,000 psi
High-strength steel: 760 MPa | 110,000 psi
Stainless steel: 860 MPa | 125,000 psi
Steel prestressing strands: 1,800 MPa | 260,000 psi

Wrought iron: 234–372 MPa | 34,000 – 54,000 psi
Cast iron w/ 4.5% carbon: 200 MPa | 29,000 psi
Timber (pine): 40 MPa | 5,800 psi
Marble: 15 MPa | 2,200 psi
Concrete is noted as having no real tensile strength.

The strength of steel is based upon its "ultimate tensile strength" (UTS). This is the maximum stress that a material can withstand while being stretched or pulled before *necking*, which is when the specimen's cross section starts to significantly contract. The tensile strength is dependent on the carbon content of the steel as well as the inclusion of various alloys. The majority of structural steel framework is fabricated from regular carbon steel. This steel is able to be welded or bolted and is commonly used in both concealed structural and exposed structural applications. High strength steel is predominantly selected for long-span situations as a means to reduce the use of material (thereby reducing the dead weight to be supported by the member) and overall dimensions of the members. Stainless steel, although stronger, is more expensive due to the presence of alloys, and requires extra engineering and care during fabrication. It is normally reserved for use in highly exposed conditions.

Steel can be manufactured in an Integrated Mill using the Basic Oxygen Method or at a Mini Mill using an Electric Arc Furnace. The Electric Arc Furnace is able to use a higher proportion of recycled steel (see Chapter 14: Steel and Sustainability for more information). Both methods include an amount of iron ore in their processes. Both mills manufacture hot-rolled sections as well as plate and bar type materials.

Standard structural steel has no built-in resistance to corrosion and, if used in applications where it will be exposed to moisture or a harsh environment, must be protected. Both stainless steel and weathering steel have altered chemical properties that provide them with very different, but inherent, resistance to damaging corrosion (see Chapter7: Coatings, Finishes and Fire Protection for more detailed information).

# *HOT-ROLLED STEEL SHAPES*

The hot rolling process produces a set range of steel shapes that are classed in terms of their section properties – overall dimensions, web and flange thicknesses, weight per linear meter or foot. Mills around the world will stock a slightly different range of sizes as a function of demand, production capability and adherence to either Imperial or SI units. If working "out of country" it is important to verify the range of product available if exact sizing is critical to the job. The transportation of the steel elements from the mill to the fabricator, and from the fabricator to the site, has a great impact on the cost of the product. The importation of specialty steel shapes can exacerbate this situation and also add time delays to a project. Transportation will also impact "green rating systems", so proximity to the fabricator is of issue here as well.

Hot-rolled steel shapes are formed using rollers and for the purposes of fabrication it should be recognized that the inside "corners" where the web and flange join will be rounded.

*The naming, sizing and availability of hot-rolled sections varies worldwide. It is strongly suggested that you verify this information for your region.*

Left: The inside corner and outer edges of these equal leg angles are rounded.

Right: The rolling process associated with these beam sections has resulted in a slope on the flange members.

If structural members are required which exceed the rolling limits of the mill, then these will need to be fabricated from plate sections. The dimensional limits of the section will then depend on the available plate thicknesses. Continuous weld seams will be apparent where the plates have been joined.

This large member is being fabricated from multiple thicknesses of 150 mm / 6 in plate to achieve the desired dimensions.

# *HOLLOW STRUCTURAL SECTIONS (HSS)*

Hollow structural sections were not widely available until the latter part of the 1970s and have truly changed the appearance and detailing of structural steel – particularly exposed structural steel. Standard hollow structural sections are available in square, rectangular or circular proportions. Special elliptical shapes are now also available, although the range of sizes and the number of mills producing these are limited. The overall dimensions will vary as a function of the capabilities of the mill, as not all mills are tooled to produce very large sizes. Generally sections over 400 mm in diameter will need to be specially ordered. Sometimes these are manufactured using helical welds. This should be verified before ordering in case these welds are not aesthetically suited to the project.

Hollow structural sections are to be differentiated from mechanical pipe. HSS members are typically created by rolling/forming and welding a flat plate (producing a continuous seam) while mechanical pipe is extruded and therefore has no seam. Mechanical pipe is made from different steel, resulting in altered structural and welding properties. Pipe is also only available in round cross-sectional shape. Mechanical pipe has a different surface than carbon steel, so that using mixed materials in an exposed application might negatively affect the appearance, as the differing surface characteristics will be visible through standard paint applications. The finish on pipe is more in keeping with the texture of cast steel and is therefore often chosen for use with castings (see Chapter 10: Castings). Pipe cannot be used in seismic locations.

There are three ways to form hollow structural shapes, the two most common of which are the basic Electric Resistance Welding Process and the Form Square Process.

<u>Electric Resistance Welding (ERW) Process</u>
HSS shapes are created from large coils of sheet material. The coils are unwound and pass through a series of rollers that form the sheet into a circular cross-section. The tube runs past equipment that creates a continuous weld along the seam. The strip edges are heated by either high-frequency induction or contact welding and then forged together by weld rolls to create a continuous longitudinal weld without the addition of filler metal. Once formed into a welded circular shape, the tubes will then pass through additional sets of rollers to create rectangular or square shapes. These are then cut into the required lengths and bundled for shipping to fabrication shops. The width of the plate will determine the maximum perimeter of the tubular shape. Before including very large tubular shapes in a design it is best to verify the maximum size that is locally available.

Left: Rolls of plate are used to create HSS shapes. The width of the plate will determine the perimeter measurement of the tube.

Right: The round primary HSS shape is formed by passing through a series of rollers prior to the welding of the seam.

The walls of these rectangular HSS shapes are quite thick, which means that the corners of the shape will have a larger radius than would result with the use of thinner plate. The weld seam can be seen on the interior of the shape and it should be noted that it is located asymmetrically. The position of the weld seam will vary because the base shape from which these are formed is circular, which makes it difficult for the seam to be uniformly oriented as the shape passes through the rollers. Some manufacturers are able to more accurately position the weld seam in a consistent manner. It is wise to ascertain this when you are sourcing material.

## Form-Square Weld-Square Process

This method is used exclusively for square members. The member starts as a long flat plate. In the weld mill, driven forming dies progressively shape the flat strip by forming the top two corners of the square or rectangular tube in the initial forming station. Subsequent stations form the bottom two corners of the shape. As the member is shaped the seam will be formed along the center top of the member. The shape's seam is welded by high-frequency contacts when the tube is near its final shape and size. The welded tube is cooled and then driven through a series of sizing stations which finalize the tube's dimensions.

As tubular shapes are created from plate, the wall thicknesses are consistent on all sides. HSS shapes are manufactured in a variety of weights with consistent exterior dimensions, as these are controlled by the setting of the shaping rollers. For visual consistency it is possible to maintain a uniform appearance of size while varying the wall thickness of the members to suit the loading requirements.

The weld appearance of the seam is partially removed from the exterior of the section but is still apparent on the product. It will be important, when using these sections in exposed conditions, to include the orientation of the weld seam in the design specifications. It is reasonable to ask that the weld seam be oriented consistently and away from view to improve the visual appearance of the finished steel.

There are many benefits to using HSS material over standard structural shapes. Although HSS sections are slightly more expensive than standard structural shapes, there are savings that result from a decrease in exterior surface area for finishing. Although HSS sections are generally used more in exposed applications, material costs can be reduced when these are used as unbraced or bi-axially loaded columns and beams.

The benefits of using HSS members specifically include:

- an aesthetic appeal due to the visual lightness of the members and cleanliness of the shape
- the reduced weight of the steel over standard structural shapes due to their relative structural efficiency
- HSS is good at resisting torsion effects due to eccentric loading.
- Tubular sections are efficient in compression due to their reduced slenderness in buckling situations.
- Tubular sections can be more efficient than a standard wide-flange beam if the member needs to be unrestrained throughout its length.
- Tubular sections are better with combined bending and torsion, which is of particular benefit for curved members in plain view.
- Coating costs are reduced as long as the interior is not required to be coated (as will be required in galvanized processes).

## *ECONOMIES IN DETAILING AND SPECIFYING STEEL*

The cost of steel to a project varies greatly from project to project. There are many variables that affect the cost of steel. The base cost of steel as a raw material fluctuates with the economy, supply and demand. As steel can use a high proportion of recycled material and avoid extraction and processing of raw ore, recycled content can result in decreased costs. If there is a local shortage of recycled steel due to high demand, this can drive up the cost of the steel. Energy costs associated with the production of shapes will also impact the cost of the steel. Generally, the cost of standard structural steel for a project is based roughly on tonnage, with some inflection as a result of the shape. W shapes, angles and channels generally cost less than hollow shapes, as the latter have higher production costs. HSS uses the steel more efficiently in some design circumstances, hence might cost less overall, as less tonnage may ultimately be required.

Fabrication costs for steel will be significant in Architecturally Exposed Structural Steel projects, where the steel becomes the expression of the architectural design. The connections in these projects tend to be more articulated and less regular and will cause additional costs that may range from 20 to 250% above standard costs (see Chapter 6: AESS: Design and Detailing Requirements for further discussion on this issue). Modular designs and repetitive components will benefit even the most articulated designs, as jigs can be constructed to assist with alignment and shop welding to a high level of consistency.

Shop labor is typically less expensive than site labor. The more elements can be fabricated and prefinished in the shop, the lower the costs. The shop provides a controlled atmosphere and access to overhead lifting equipment that adds efficiency. It will be important to predetermine the maximum size of element that can be prefabricated in the shop as a function of the shop size, size of exit doors from the shop, crane capacity, trucking capacity and the road and bridge overpass clearance between the shop and the site. The distance elements must be shipped directly impacts delivery costs.

The complexity of the building and its structural system will impact erection costs. Complexity normally infers additional time for erection and this translates quite directly into the cost of labor. Additional costs will result if a site is large and might require multiple cranes to orchestrate the lifts. Sometimes the crane can be located centrally and the pieces can be designed and sized to be lifted by a single crane. Regular geometries can be erected more quickly as it is more straightforward to predict the lifting points and the pieces tend to be assembled with ease. Diagrid buildings or those with eccentric geometries can require additional erection time. In some instances it is not unusual for the ironworkers to need more than one attempt to install oddly shaped or unbalanced pieces.

For specialty or advanced structures such as AESS, tensile structures, diagrids, curved elements and composite structures using wood and glass, extra costs should be budgeted for specialty engineering, shop drawings, mock-ups and potential scheduling delays arising from unforeseen erection or fitting problems.

For standard projects today, the cost of the material is around 25% of the cost of the installed and finished steel. The proportion of labor and engineering costs can be significantly higher on projects that expose the steel.

# *DESIGN AND MODELING SOFTWARE*

**The migration to Building Information Modeling (BIM) systems has offered some cost savings to the detailed design of a wide range of structural steel applications. The majority of steel projects now make use of specialized BIM detailing software, regardless of the complexity of the project.**

In Modeling mode this detailing software can:

→ view the structural models
→ create and modify grids
→ model parts and bolts
→ create welds
→ add loads to a model
→ create assemblies of steel parts
→ create levels of assembly hierarchy
→ create detailed steel connections
→ create automatic preset connections to multiple parts
→ create erection sequences
→ view model information in 4D (simulated schedule)
→ mark/number parts automatically

In Output mode this BIM software can:

→ create general arrangement drawings (plan, section, erection, etc.)
→ create single-part and assembly drawings
→ print and plot drawings and reports
→ create reports (assembly lists, part lists, etc.)

The software enhances cooperation among the members of the project team by allowing them to:

→ work simultaneously on the same model with several users
→ interface with other tools and disciplines
→ exchange data
→ export and import data
→ interface with Structural Analysis and Design software for data exchange
→ import and export graphic 2D and 3D data

**The incorporation of this new modeling software has given rise to great streamlining of the design and detailing process and has facilitated the creation of a wide range of projects with increasingly complex geometries.**

A typical digital model created using specialized BIM steel detailing software. It shows the steel foundation of the Bow Encana Tower in Calgary, AB, Canada, designed by Foster + Partners and Zeidler Partnership. The color coding allows for ease of differentiation among systems and can also be used to denote construction sequencing.

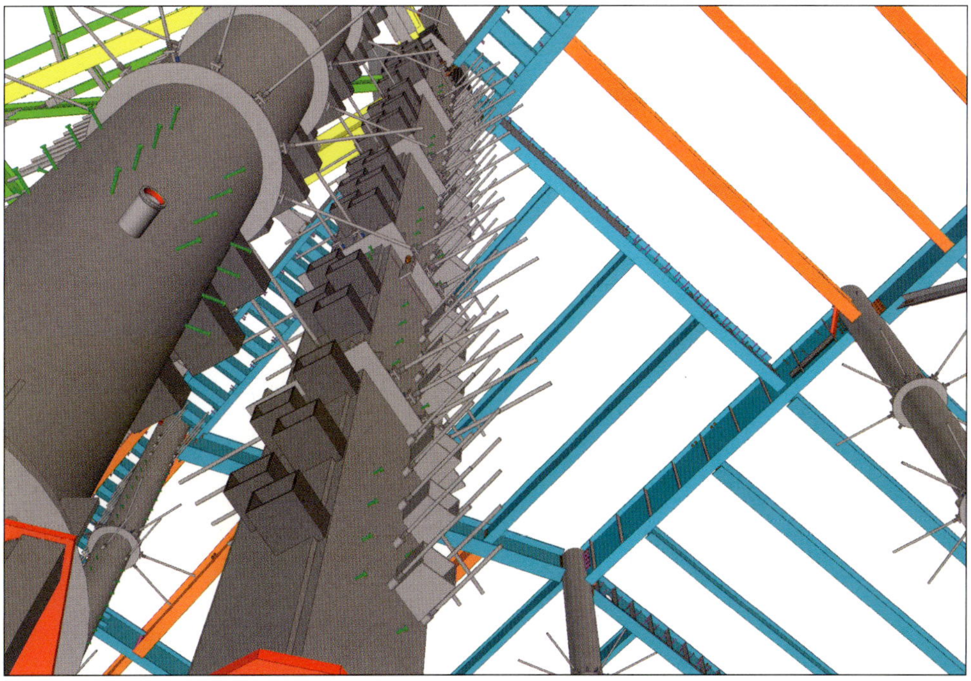

*CHAPTER 3*

---

# *STEEL CONNECTIONS AND FRAMING TECHNIQUES*

---

## *THE IDEA BEHIND FRAMING*

## *BASIC CONNECTION STRATEGIES*

## *FRAMED CONNECTIONS*

### BEAM-TO-GIRDER CONNECTIONS

### GIRDER OR BEAM-TO-COLUMN CONNECTIONS

### COLUMN CONNECTIONS

### PIN CONNECTIONS

## *FLOOR SYSTEMS*

## *BRACED SYSTEMS*

## *TRUSS SYSTEMS*

### PLANAR TRUSSES

### THREE-DIMENSIONAL TRUSSES

The tubular steel structure at the Friedrichstadtpassagen Quartier 206 Shopping Mall in Berlin, designed by Pei Cobb Freed and Partners, makes predominant use of welded connections to achieve a clean appearance in resolving the intersection of the large round members. The smaller members that support the skylight use a combination of welded and bolted connections, as these are visually less dominant. The framing is highlighted against the dark night sky, making its joinery more visible at night than during the day.

## *THE IDEA BEHIND FRAMING*

Steel evolved as an elemental system of construction derived from early industrialized practices that were developed for cast- and wrought-iron buildings. Discrete members are either bolted or welded together. Buildings are typically created from a series of prefabricated pieces that are sub-assembled in the fabrication shop, with final assembly and erection taking place on site. Maximized shop fabrication is preferred, as it is more expedient to cut, shape, weld and finish elements in controlled conditions. Lifting is simply done by an overhead crane. Quality is improved. Economies are possible through modularity and the production of larger quantities of identical elements.

Transportation from the shop to the site limits the sizes of members that can be shipped. Elements must be designed to fit on the flatbed of a truck. Larger pieces may require a police escort or pose difficulties navigating narrow streets. Sub-assembly of smaller elements into larger ones on site will be limited by the lifting capacity of the crane as well as the size of the staging area.

Framing simplifies fabrication, erection and structural analysis. Basic steel framing is based upon a rectilinear arrangement of straight members that are connected at framed joints. Regular geometry and even grid-based arrangements of columns work to minimize eccentric loading on the structure. Orthogonal geometry, although good for spatial planning, is inherently unstable. A language of reinforcement and bracing provides lateral stability either by using solid panels, moment-resisting connections or triangulation.

Framing also allows for a simpler method of structural analysis, as most steel systems can be broken down into two-dimensional segments and determinate structures – unlike concrete systems, which use continuous members and monolithic construction methods.

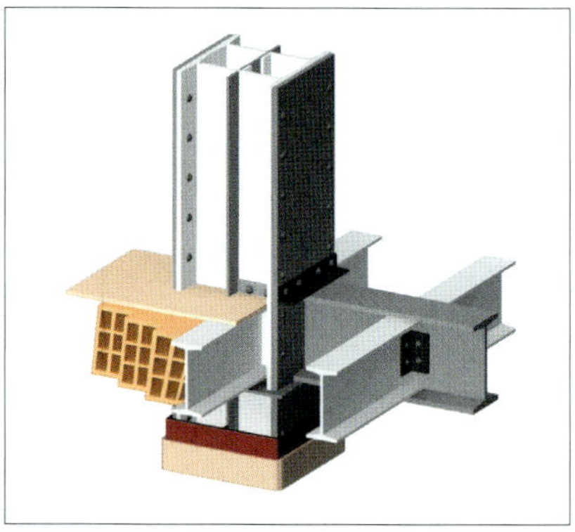

The Fair Store in Chicago, IL, USA, designed by William Le Baron Jenney in 1890, was one of the multi-story buildings which began to generate a language of standardized framing. At the time, structural member types were limited to I-beams, angles and plates. These were connected for the most part using hot rivets. The framing language of today is derived from these early structures.

## *BASIC CONNECTION STRATEGIES*

All steel framing, no matter how complicated, is based upon standard methods of connections and means of satisfying load path requirements. The majority of connections are designed to function as "hinges", transferring vertical and horizontal shear forces. They are not intended to resist moment, bending or torsional forces. This permits simple bolted or welded methods of fastening for the connections. In cases where moment or bending forces are high, connections can be reinforced to become stiff. This may be achieved by adding material in the form of plates or angles to the connection by additional welding or bolting in order to resist moment forces. Lateral loads can be resisted through the addition of bracing systems that introduce triangles into the frame, triangular forms being inherently rigid. The additional requirement of seismic stability builds upon the same connection strategies and methods of jointing of the frame.

Connections between steel pieces are either bolted or welded. Bolts can vary in terms of their strength and head type. If the steel is concealed then the choice of bolt type is purely a structural consideration, ensuring that the bolts are adequate in number to resist the shear forces and that there is sufficient plate area to accommodate the bolting pattern. The design of the framing systems and connections feeds directly into practical considerations of construction methods. It is faster to erect using bolted connections, but this does not preclude welding if this is a design requirement, be it for aesthetic or structural reasons.

The two types of bolts typically used are Hex Head and Tension Control (TC) bolts. Both types of bolts are fabricated from high-strength steel and both serve the same purpose. The Hex Head bolts need access from both sides for tightening, but no special equipment. The TC bolts need a special type of equipment to install and snap off the end, but only one side needs access for tightening.

The "turn of nut" method is visible in this bolted connection on the Canadian Museum for Human Rights in Winnipeg, MB, Canada by Antoine Predock.

Most bolts can be simply installed to a snug-tight condition, i.e. to the maximum of a worker's strength. They do not have to be pre-tensioned. Bolts only need pretensioning under special conditions: when slippage cannot be tolerated, for seismically stable connections, when subjected to impact or cyclic loading, when they are in pure tension or when oversized holes are used. Otherwise, the snug-tight condition is adequate for the normal end connections of beams. Deciding to pretension a bolt is a question of the application rather than how large a load it needs to transfer.

If bolts do have to be pretensioned, "turn-of-nut" is the preferred method. After the bolts are snug-tightened, an additional fraction of a turn is applied to the nut to achieve the desired tension in the bolt. Usually, a worker will draw a chalk mark across the diameter of the bolt before applying the extra turn. Hence, an inspector can check if the fraction of turn was observed. In many conditions, only an additional third of a turn is needed to achieve the desirable pretension in the bolt.

TC bolts are another way of achieving the desired tension in the bolt, but many feel that the conventional "turn-of-nut" method is the most reliable. It is actually very difficult to determine the tension in a bolt based on a torque value because friction plays an important role. For calculating the tension in the bolt it has to be derived from the torque value. Once converted, the value is often not representative of the real tension in the bolt. This is especially true for galvanized bolts.

Left: The head of the Tension Control bolt is quite distinct from the regular Hex Head bolt. The washer and nut for tightening are on the backside of the connection, so connection design must provide access to the rear for tightening. TC bolts are used where slip prevention is important. On the Bow Encana erection they are being used to secure the temporary column to column connections prior to finish welding.

Right: This beam is ready to ship, its splice plates attached with high-strength Hex Head bolts. Structural bolts like these will normally place the nut side where access is easiest.

In Architecturally Exposed Structural Steel design (see Chapter 6: AESS: Design and Detailing) the choice of bolt head, pattern of attachment and preference for the side of the connection on which the bolt heads are located will be important to the visual architectural appearance. Much of the required construction tolerance for erection will be a function of the degree of precision in the alignment and drilling of the holes for the bolts. It is a common misconception that bolt holes are routinely oversized to make it easier to align members during erection. Imprecision will result in accumulated errors that actually make erection more difficult. Bolt holes within a steel framing system have tight tolerances – tighter even in AESS design where "fit" is important. Slotted holes are only used where secondary systems, such as curtain wall, are attached to the steel framing, in order to adjust for deviations between the alignments of the systems used.

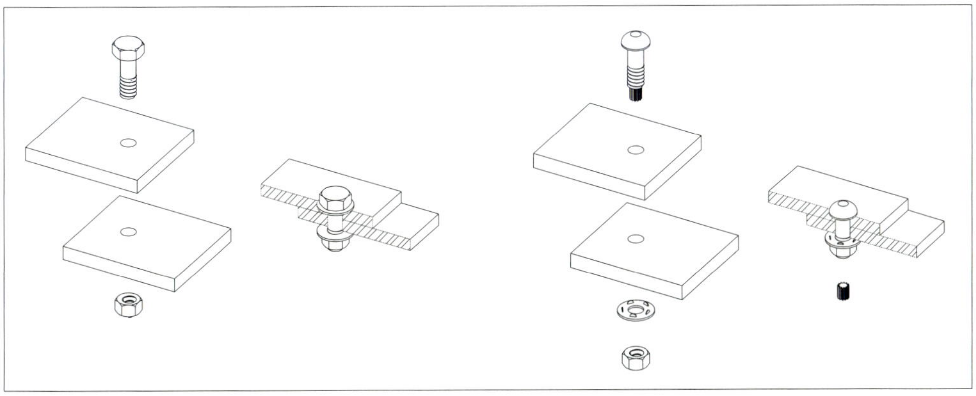

Hex Head versus Tension Control Bolts

Left: Assembly of a Hex Head bolt. A standard washer, sitting on either side of the connection between the steel and the head/nut, assists in distributing the load. These types of bolts are usually installed to a snug-tight condition and they normally do not need to be pretensioned.

Right: Assembly of a Tension Control bolt. The special compressible washer is placed only at the rear side of the connection. There are some proprietary types of washers that contain small pockets of brightly colored material that will squeeze out when the desired tension is achieved.

The steel pieces that are being joined may be attached either by lapping the primary-load-carrying portion of the member or by placing the elements "in line".

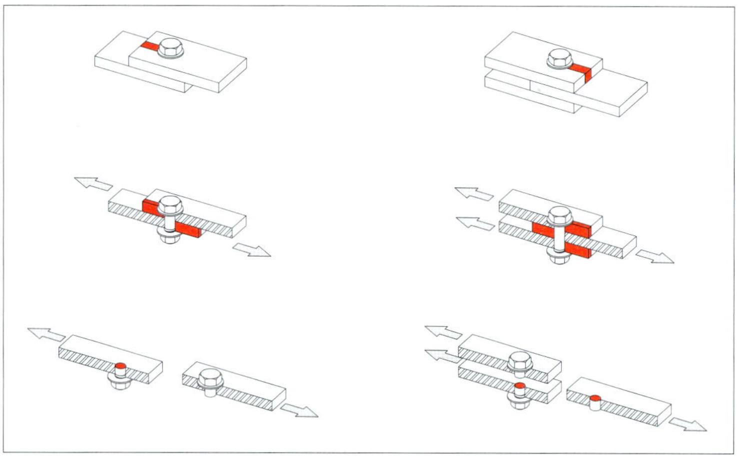

Lap joints: A lap joint is typically used as a tension splice. It is suited to connections that do not need to be symmetrical. In the left hand diagrams, the two plate elements change their alignment on either side of the connection. When force is applied to the connection, it can fail either by the stretching the hole to the point of pull through (middle) or by shearing through the bolt (bottom). The higher the load on the connection, the larger or more numerous are the bolts required. Plate thickness is also important to resist the tension loads. There must be adequate space between the bolt holes and the edge of the plate to distribute the load. In the right hand diagrams the steel on either side of the connection is unequal. The area shown in red is the plate that will be pulled out if the connection fails (middle). The bolt will be sheared in two planes in this instance (bottom).

Left: The bracing connections at the Bow Encana Tower all use simple lapped connections. The array of bolts in the connection keeps the members in a precise geometrical arrangement and provides adequate cross section in the bolts to transfer the load.

Right: Where extra resistance is required, the number of lapping plates at the Guelph Science Building is increased. Also visible in this connection are two different bolt types. The connection of the X-shaped plate to the underside of the flange is being done with TC bolts, while there is a Hex Head high-strength steel bolt through the pin connection. The single bolt in this pin connection is designed to allow rotation so as to make erection alignment simpler.

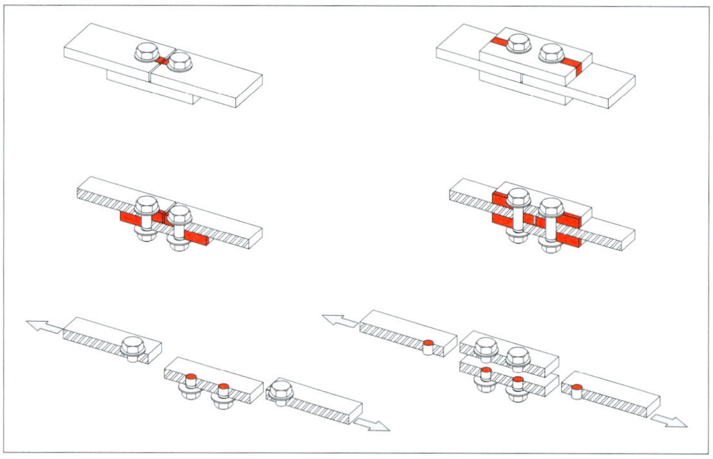

Butt joints: This connection is used where it is important that the primary line of geometry of the steel plate and the forces are "in line". The connection is completed by the addition of steel plates on one or both sides of the splice. The number of bolts in the connection will be determined by the area required to resist the shear forces. In the left hand diagrams there is only a splice plate on one side of the connection. This results in a single shear plane through the bolts (bottom). The right hand diagrams illustrate a connection that doubles the shear area in the bolts by using plates on either side of the primary member (bottom). If the splice is in tension, there also needs to be enough steel between the bolt hole and the end of the plate to resist pull-through (middle).

Left: The splices between the wide-flange members of the diagrid structure for the Seattle Public Library, WA, USA by Rem Koolhaas use butt joints, as it is necessary for the web members to stay aligned. Plates are set on either side of the splice. Additional reinforcing plates can be seen on the top and bottom of the connection flanges. These have been welded to appear more discrete as well as to eliminate interference between the structure and the curtain wall cladding.

Right: A butt joint is used to splice the beams. A pointed slug wrench is inserted to align it during erection. Partial bolting allows for the detachment of the crane.

Welded connections will normally be used when fabricating large primary elements like a large plate girder or composite sections in the shop. Quality welding is best done under controlled conditions. Welded connections are also preferred when fabricating complex trusses from HSS members, as common methods of attachment such as plates and angles are more suited to connecting members with webs and flanges. Welded connections present different issues for concealed versus exposed structures. Chapter 6 on Architecturally Exposed Structural Steel will address issues of aesthetics and cost implications for welded joints.

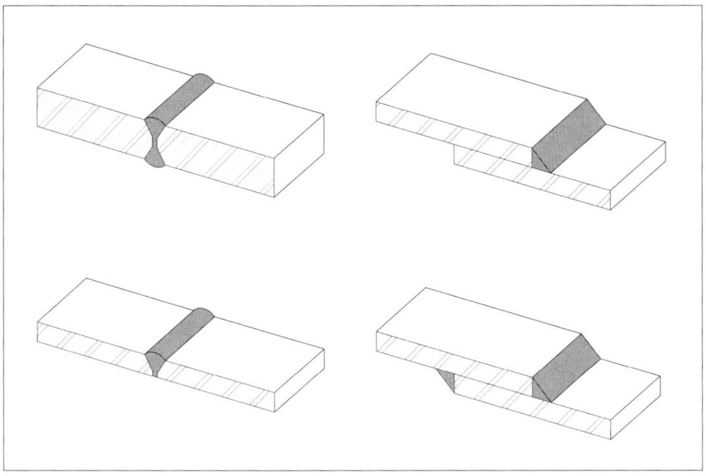

Welded connections: Plates can be spliced together using two basic types of welded connections. Groove welds (left) are used where the two plates must be maintained in line. Thicker plates will use a double Vee weld, (top left), whereas thinner plates will use a single Vee weld. If it is not important to align the plates, then lap welds can be used (right). If the load on the lap joint is small, a single fillet or edge weld can be used (top right). For higher loads it will be necessary to use a double fillet weld (bottom right). For plate elements that are to be joined in line, groove welding can produce a clean-looking connection if side plates are not desired. Depending on the finish requirements the welds can be left "as is" or ground smooth. Grinding should be reserved for special high-profile applications as it is expensive and time consuming. Grinding also weakens the weld by removing weld material.

## *FRAMED CONNECTIONS*

Steel structures are assembled using a basic suite of connection types. All other connections are variations of these to one extent or another. The basic framed connections were developed with an assumption of the use of flange type sections. Flange-type sections allow for access for bolting from both sides of the member. If hollow sections are used the connections must be adapted, as the simple use of through bolting is not possible.

### BEAM-TO-GIRDER CONNECTIONS

There are three basic ways to frame a beam into a girder. The choice will depend upon the bearing requirements of the flooring system, floor-to-floor height limitations and providing space for service runs. Services can be run below the assembly although in some cases holes may be cut in the beam or girder web to provide passage.

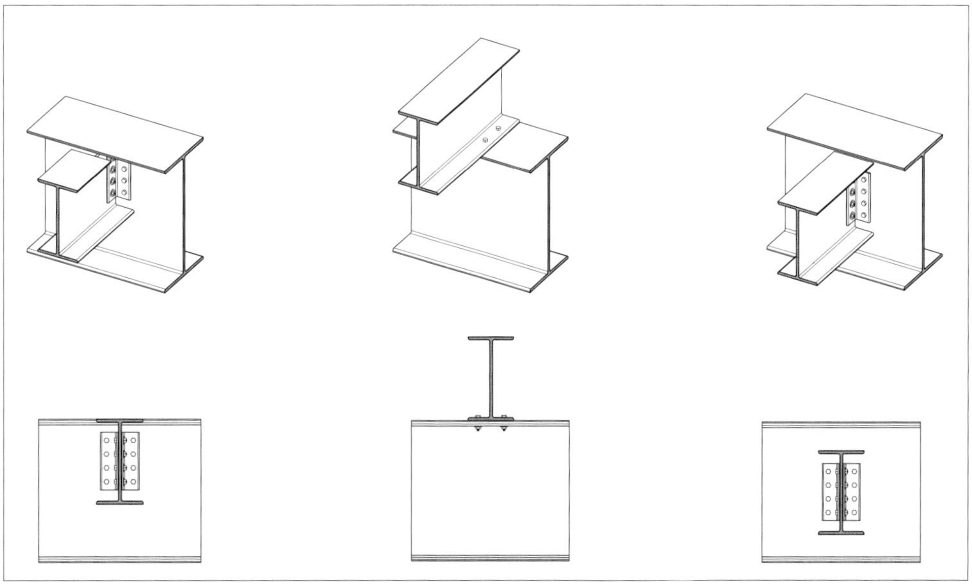

Left: Coped connection: In this connection the top flange of the beam is cut away so that the top edges can remain level in order to provide a flat surface for the flooring system. The web is normally attached to the girder web with a pair of angles that are bolted to each member.

Middle: Bearing connection: The beam bears on the girder. The flanges are simply bolted together. This method is used where floor height is not an issue or where it is desired to create passage for services above the girder.

Right: Simple framed connection: The beam connects into the web of the girder without coping, where there is no floor element to be supported.

Left: At the Leslie Dan Faculty of Pharmacy in Toronto, ON, Canada, a coped connection provides a level surface for the installation of the floor deck in spite of the difference in size of the beams that are framing into the girder. The variation in the number of bolts in the connections is a clear indication of the differences in shear forces to be transferred.

Right: Framing infers a clear hierarchy for the transfer of loads through the building. The addition to the Art Gallery of Ontario in Toronto, ON, Canada by Frank Gehry, uses steel framing for the extension to the gallery. The very deep beam is a transfer beam that is permitting a large clear-span exhibit and gathering space. Holes are cut into the beam to permit the passage of services. Additional steel is welded around the cutouts for reinforcement of the web of the beam. Major steel floor beams frame into the transfer beam using coped connections. Smaller beams carry the future floor loads into these. This type of framing makes it possible to apply simple structural analysis in spite of its complexity.

Framed connections using standard wide-flange sections are commonly used in structural steel that is not intended to be architecturally exposed. Architecturally exposing the steel will add extra detailing requirements for alignment as well as precision. Aesthetics might require that both the top and bottom chords align or that the range of steel sections be standardized, to create a more uniform appearance – even if this means that the sections might be larger or heavier than required for loading purposes.

Left: The large brise soleil at the Las Vegas Courthouse, NV, USA, designed by Cannon Design uses deep wide-flange sections to create the structure for the grid. Smaller steel sections are used as infill to provide shading. Exposing the steel places the priority on a uniform appearance.

Right: The grid requires that the deep beams be given coped connections for both the top and bottom chord to achieve the appearance of a uniform, non-directional grid.

## GIRDER- OR BEAM-TO-COLUMN CONNECTIONS

Girders and beams transfer the loads that they have received from the floor to the columns. The connection can be made either to the flange of the column or to the web, depending on the orientation of the column, which is a function of the structural layout. Columns are generally oriented so that the dominant wind load strikes perpendicular to the flange of the column. Connecting to the flange provides easier access for the ironworkers to tighten bolts.

Beams and girders will be lifted into position by a crane, the matching holes in the angle connectors are aligned with a slug wrench, and the bolts inserted. For some projects temporary angle "seats" will be attached to the column to provide a ledge upon which to sit the beam, allowing the crane to detach earlier and to speed up erection. These seats can be removed after the connection is complete, or remain in place to stiffen the connection.

**If the beam is connected to the web of the column, adequate space must be provided for access by the ironworkers.**

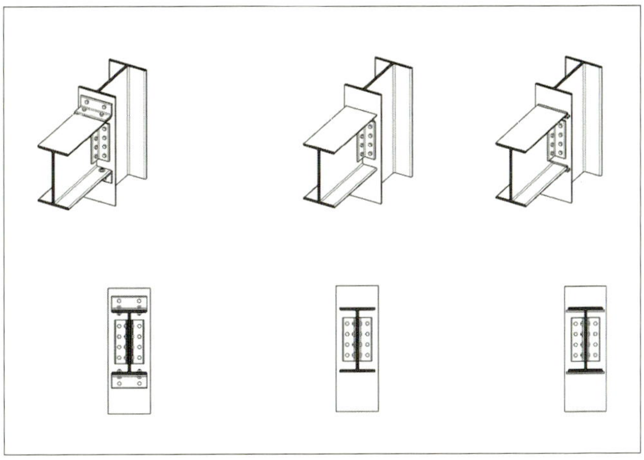

Left: Seated connection. Angles are bolted to the column to provide a ledge for the beam during erection. The angles may remain to provide additional support if required, or they can be removed if structurally unnecessary.

Middle: In this standard framed connection the angles are bolted to the web of the beam at the shop and then bolted to the column flange on site. The connection acts as a hinge in that it is only designed to resist shear.

Right: This connection has been reinforced to resist moment. Plates have been welded to the column prior to erection. They are also welded to the flanges of the beam so as to provide resistance to bending at the connection.

The roof of this transit station in Vancouver, BC, Canada uses a variety of standard framing methods to transfer the loads to the column. The direction of span is always perpendicular to the support member. In this instance the girder frames into the side of the wide-flange column, attaching with bolted angles to the web. Note the transfer of loads from the profiled decking through the beams and back to the column.

## COLUMN CONNECTIONS

**Steel columns are generally welded to a base plate that is used to attach the column to the foundation pier or supporting system. The plate is normally larger than the column, drilled with holes, and lowered over threaded rods that have been set into the foundation.**

Left: This simple base connection uses four threaded bolts to anchor the plate. The plate sits slightly above the concrete foundation in order to allow for leveling nuts to sit beneath the plate, thereby permitting alignment. The void below the plate is packed with grout both to assist with load transfer and to fix the position of the nuts. The aesthetic could have been improved if all of the threaded bolts had been trimmed to the same height. The column member is pin-connected to the base.

Middle: A round plate is welded to the base of the round HSS column.

Right: Larger columns that must transfer more load as well as resist potential lateral forces will require a more substantial base design. Here the threaded rods penetrate a double-plate system that is reinforced with the addition of steel fins welded around the perimeter. The geometry is carefully designed for access to tighten the bolts. Leveling bolts sit below the bottom plate – hence the gap prior to finishing.

**As vertical loads are carried down the structure the loads accumulate and increase on the columns on lower floor levels. Columns for higher floors are smaller in their strength requirements than for lower floors. The columns in multi-story buildings must be spliced, as the longest lengths possible are a function of shipping. There needs to be a full transfer of load from one column to the next. In simple connections, without eccentric loads, and where columns do not change in size at the splice, the meeting surfaces are machined smooth in order to maintain the load path and side plates can be bolted to the flanges and web in order to maintain the connection. Where the lower column is only slightly larger, so that the flanges essentially align, fill plates will be used on either side of the flanges of the upper column. Where the upper column is substantially smaller, so that the flanges do not align at all, base plates are attached to both columns to complete the load path and prevent pressure points in the connection. Column splices can either be welded or bolted.**

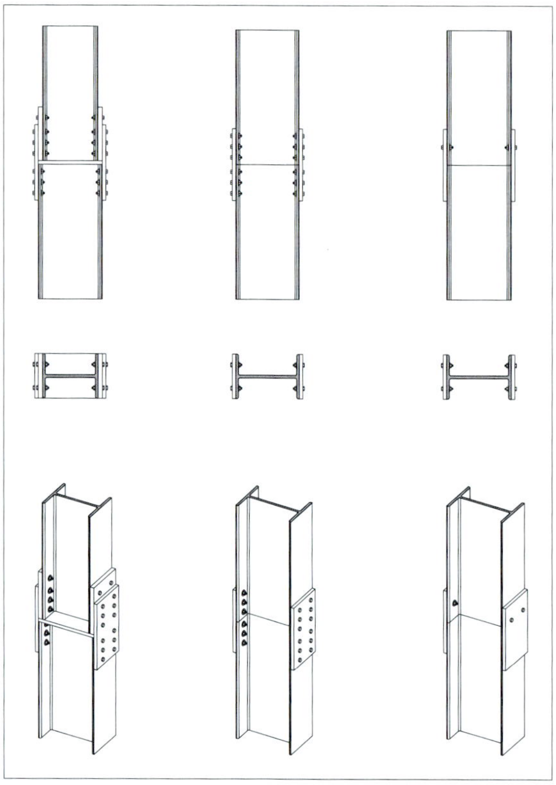

The diagrams illustrate the standard ways to make column splices for concealed structural steel. The splice is normally placed around 600mm/24in above the floor level.

Left: Where the top column is smaller than the lower column, filler plates are required to keep the flanges in line and allow for bolting of the outside plate connectors. A horizontal plate between the columns prevents concentration points and assists in load transfer.

Middle: The size of the columns is identical and the connecting plates are bolted. This is essentially a butt joint.

Right: The outside plates are welded to the lower column. The upper column will be lowered into place and secured with bolts. The size of the columns is identical so that no filler plates are required.

Left: At the Bow Encana Building in Calgary, AB, Canada by Foster + Partners and Zeidler Partnership, this square steel column has been erected and is being prepped for Groove welding. The bolted tabs on either side of the columns are temporary and will be removed once the finish welding is complete. The edges of the upper column have been machined away to leave room for the weld. This is to increase the exposed area of steel to engage the weld. These two column sections are identical in size, so no other accommodation is required.

Right: These two wide-flange columns have been welded at their splice. As the upper column is slightly smaller than the lower one, an additional plate has been welded to ensure proper load transfer through the connection. The long "bumps" on the edges of the meeting flanges indicate where the temporary steel connecting plates have been removed.

Left: This column splice employs matching plates that are bolted. The size of a plate must be adequate to accommodate the bolt holes and provide access to tighten the bolts.

Right: This column splice shows the use of side plates to connect the two identically sized column pieces. The holes at the top of the side tabs are used by the crane to lift the column into place.

## PIN CONNECTIONS

Most connections are designed to act as hinges in that they transfer horizontal and vertical shear loads and are not intended to resist moment. Some hinge connections are even designed to look like hinges, making their function more apparent. Connections whose structural intention is to actually permit rotation are characterized by their use of a single bolt or other attachment mechanism and are referred to as pin connections. Framed connections that are transferring vertical and horizontal loads and are not intended to rotate will have as many bolts as are required to resist the shear forces at the point.

Left: This structure at Heathrow Terminal 5 in London, UK, designed by Richard Rogers, uses a variety of pin connections to join the members.

Right: In this connection at Heathrow Terminal 5 different colors of finish are used to accentuate the intersection of different structural systems. The language of a single point of attachment, a pin connection, is extrapolated to keep the same appearance but increase the rigidity and hence the resistance to shear between the blue beam and grey connector – providing four points of attachment.

Left: The base connection for the primary steel ribs of the Dubai Metro stations, UAE sits on a pin connection. The slight, V-shaped void on either side of the connection not only permits some variation in alignment during erection, but also accentuates the function of the joint.

Right: The base of the tapered steel column for the Theme Pavilion of the Expo in Shanghai, China is resolved by a custom pin connection.

**Even the most unusual steel connections are variations of the basic methods covered in this chapter. The appearance of some is due more to an aesthetic drive than to functional requirements.**

This connection at Brookfield Place in Toronto, ON, Canada, designed by Santiago Calatrava, uses a combination of welding and bolting. The fabrication of the elements is quite precise and the actual bolted connection is fairly simple.

## *FLOOR SYSTEMS*

**The distribution of gravity loads in a steel-framed building follows a logical path. The sizing and spacing of members will be a function of the type of flooring system that is to be used – most particularly of the type and spacing of members to support the floor itself. This will be different for a standard concealed structural application and Architecturally Exposed Structural Steel – as well as a function of the type of AESS application.**

The floor deck can consist of:

- → profiled steel decking with a concrete topping (deck depth varies from 38 to 91mm)
- → hollow-core precast concrete slabs

The support system for the floor can consist of:

- → beams (normally wide-flange sections or Universal sections)
- → Open Web Steel Joists (OWSJ)
- → cellular beams
- → trusses

The spacing of the floor support members is a function of:

- → the spanning capabilities of the floor system itself
- → the span length
- → the member depth (this is likely limited by floor-to-floor height specifications)
- → the loading (dead load of the building and live load as a function of the building use)

For lightweight profiled decking (38mm/1.5in deep with a concrete topping), the support members may need to be as close as 1.8m/6ft on center. This spacing would usually suggest the use of OWSJ members. If the profile of the decking is deeper (76 to 91mm/3 to 3.5in) and the concrete topping more substantially reinforced, the support members may be several meters apart, and heavier beams used.

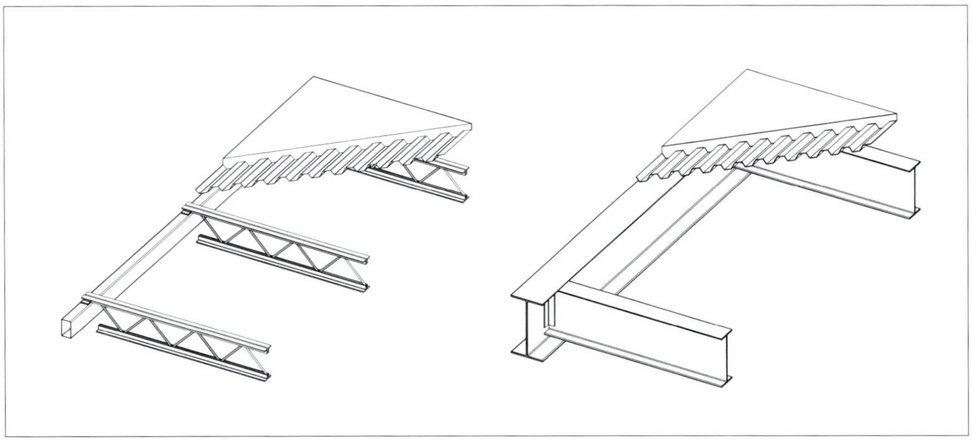

For steel flooring assemblies the direction of the decking will run perpendicular to the beam or joist span. The distance between the beams or joists will be a function of the span capabilities of the floor deck as well as the strength of the beams or joists related to their span. The lighter and shallower the members, the tighter the spacing. Left, OWSJ are spaced more closely, whereas right, beams with deeper deck are further apart.

Left: One of the advantages of steel framing is that construction can proceed year round, even in very cold weather conditions. The steel framing for the Bay Adelaide Center in Toronto, ON, Canada uses OWSJ members to support the deck.

Right: Prior to pouring the concrete floor slab, the decking is prepared by the addition of studs, reinforcing bars and welded wire mesh, to assist in strengthening the concrete and prevent it from cracking and also to reinforce the structural connection between the floor and the steel framing.

Where non-rectilinear geometries occur, modifications in the layout of the framing members must follow. Shorter spanning lengths result in the ability to use lighter members. Column and beam grid layouts should try to maximize the use of regular geometry to increase efficiency and reduce cost. Specialized, non-rectilinear situations can usually be isolated. These will normally occur at the perimeter wall of the building or around larger openings in the floor. At the exterior edge there are usually accommodations for the attachment of the curtain wall or cladding system.

Although many practices of steel framing are relatively standard around the globe, different members are used as lightweight floor support members. Where North American buildings tend to use Open Web Steel Joists, projects in the United Kingdom and the European Union tend to prefer cellular beams. While the double angles that form the top chord of an OWSJ must be seated on top of the beam into which the joist is framing, cellular beams use standard angle-type connectors. Cellular beams are the modern evolution of the castellated beam, created from wide-flange or Universal beams that are cut along the web using a patented "ribbon cutting" process. The upper and lower sections are welded together, forming round holes in the web of the beam. The beams are 40 – 60% deeper than the parent beam and up to 2.5 times stronger. It is possible to camber the beams during the rewelding process. Cambering induces an upward curvature of the member to offset a future deflection due to load. The holes are used for service runs.

This building in London, England is using cellular beams cut with round holes in lieu of OWSJ framing that is more common in North America. The holes in the web member allow for the passage of services and lighten the dead load of the member. The edge of this building creates a sawtooth structure to accept the curtain wall. The sawtooth structure is created using standard wide-flange or Universal beams that form a cantilevered extension of the floor plate beyond the column line.

Left: The sawtooth extension on this floor edge is not large so does not require as extensive an alteration to the general framing system to accommodate.

Right: A view to the underside of the floor framing for this London office building shows how the framing is modified to accommodate a rounded corner condition.

## *BRACED SYSTEMS*

Framed and pin connections are inherently unstable. Buildings must have additional means to provide lateral stability to the frame. The floor system will provide a degree of stability, particularly for heavier concrete and steel composite decks where there is sufficient reinforcing in the concrete, provided that the reinforcement is tied into the steel structure. Concrete structures to house the elevator and stair core are commonly used to provide stability as the monolithic nature of cast construction is inherently rigid.

Three other methods to add stability are:

→ reinforcement of the framed connections themselves to provide moment resistance
→ addition of bracing to the frame
→ use of shear walls (either in concrete or steel plate)

The Seattle Space Needle, WA, USA is located in an active seismic zone. X bracing is used to reinforce the frame of the all-steel tower. The plates also serve to reinforce the framed connections.

When the connections themselves are reinforced to resist bending moments, this is called portal frame construction. It can be used for taller buildings or in seismic zones.

In lieu of connection reinforcement, diagonal or K bracing can be used in the frame to triangulate the system, thereby adding rigidity. Diagonal bracing is not always desired, as it can interfere with the use of the space. Although all buildings require bracing to achieve stability, those located in seismic zones require additional or heavier bracing. This is a specialized field of engineering and will not be addressed in this text, but there should be an awareness of the nature of the measures required by seismic design for steel-framed buildings.

# *TRUSS SYSTEMS*

A truss is a structure comprising one or more triangular units constructed with straight members, whose ends are connected at joints referred to as nodes. External forces and reactions to those forces are considered to act only at the nodes and result in axial forces in the members that are either purely tensile or compressive. Moments (torques) are explicitly excluded because all the joints in a truss are treated as hinges or theoretical pin connections. Trusses are capable of spanning much further than solid beams or girder members, with less material.

Trusses can be planar, box or space type. A planar truss is two-dimensional, with all of the members lying in essentially a single plane, the loads of the truss being picked up from their end connections. Box-type trusses also span only in one direction but have a three-dimensionality to them that is usually rectangular or triangular. Space trusses are also called spaceframes. These systems can span in multiple directions, with their loads transferred from any node in the system (see Chapter 11: Tension Systems and Spaceframes).

## PLANAR TRUSSES

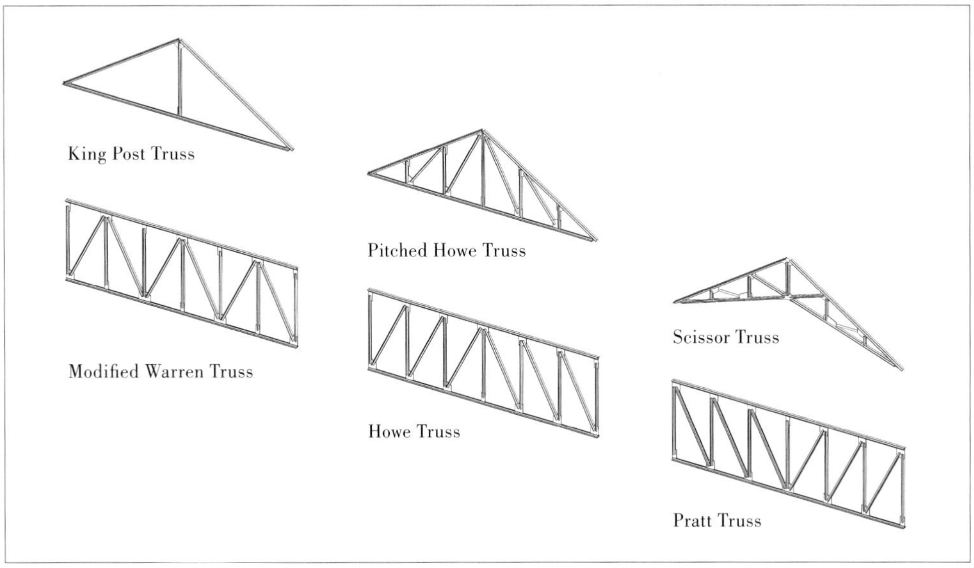


Planar Truss Types: Although there are countless variations of planar truss types, these diagrams outline some of the most common ones. Fabricated from common steel angles and plates, they represent the least expensive options for fabrication. The top and bottom members of the trusses are referred to as "chords" and the intermediate steel as "web members". Under typical loading the top chord will act in compression and the bottom chord in tension.

Beams and joists are intended to accept loads continually along their length ("distributed loads"). As a result, these members are designed to resist flexural or bending stresses. Trusses are designed as pin- or hinge-connected structures, with the intention to transfer loads axially along each member. Hence the members are designed to resist either pure compression or pure tension, but not bending. Therefore, loads must only be transferred to the truss at its node, panel points or joints.

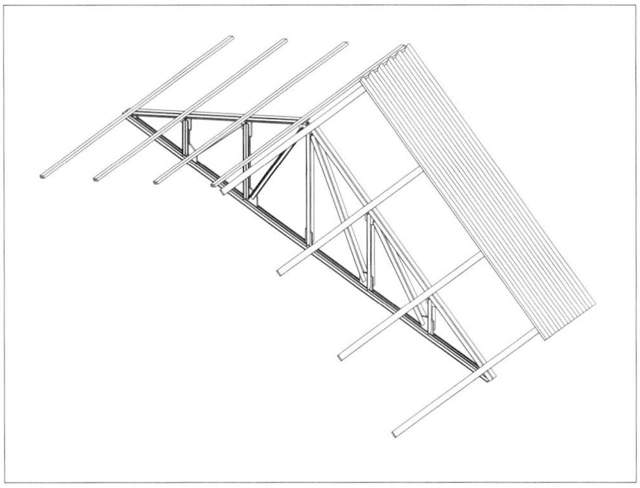

The steel decking for this roof sits on purlins. Purlins are used to span between trusses and transfer the loads to the truss at its panel points. If the geometry of the connection is precise, the load should be transferred through the centroid of the connection, resulting in only compressive or tensile axial loading in the chord and web members. The further apart the trusses are spaced, the more substantial the purlins will need to be. The dimensioning of the truss itself will be a function of the spanning capabilities of the decking, as the spacing of the purlins will be directly impacted.

From an architectural perspective, trusses present an enormous design potential for a building. Where common steel trusses are fabricated from standard sections, the fact that there is only pure tensile or compressive axial loading implies that the member selection can be finetuned so as to reflect the nature of the loading. Rods or cables can be used for tensile members, creating a contrast with the use of sections for compression members. This presents unique opportunities for designing the connections between the members in a way to develop an individual architectural detailing language for the project. (For more information on innovative truss design see Chapter 11: Tension Systems and Spaceframes)

Left: This Paris rail bridge is a modified Pratt truss. To allow for the steel to expand and contract, one end of the bridge is designed as a hinge connection, and the opposite as a roller connection.

Right: The importance of the geometry of the node can be seen in the alignment of the incoming members of this node. An attempt is made to ensure that the centers of gravity of all members coincide at one point.

Left: The long-span Warren trusses at the Canadian War Museum in Ottawa, ON, Canada, designed by Raymond Moriyama, are fabricated from square HSS members. The web members are slightly smaller in section than the top and bottom chords, making it simpler to fabricate the welded joints. Wide-flange sections carry the load of the steel decking to the trusses. Cross bracing is introduced in the plane of the roof.

Right: The trusses in the Design Studio at the University of New Mexico School of Architecture, Albuquerque, NM, USA, designed by Antoine Predock, are fabricated from wide-flange sections. The incoming beams that support the steel deck frame into the panel points of the truss. The members are all designed to be uniform, regardless of their tensile or compressive capacity, as a deliberate design intention.

The skylight support system for the Edmonton City Hall, AB, Canada, designed by Dub Architects, uses a two-way Vierendeel truss system created from welded square HSS members. A Vierendeel truss is a special form of truss that does not use triangulated geometry, preferring to create fixed, moment-resisting joints. The choice to use this truss type for the City Hall roof resulted in a simplified geometry for welding the joints. The choice of square HSS simplified some of the welding of the individual units, but made some of the intersections difficult to resolve.

## THREE-DIMENSIONAL TRUSSES

Three-dimensional truss systems are used as a means to limit the span requirements of the structural members that carry the roof or floor loads to the trusses. The added third dimension of the truss also provides additional lateral stability in situations of long span. Box-type trusses have a linear span direction. This is very different from a space frame, which can span freely in multiple directions. As with other truss types, loads must be transferred at the nodes to ensure that there is only axial loading of the members.

Three-dimensional trusses are typically custom-fabricated for each project. They are often used in architecturally exposed conditions, so member selection and connection design are important. As their connections are often geometrically challenging, round HSS sections are normally used, as it has been found to be simpler to resolve welded connections for this member type.

Left: The canopy support system at the Baltimore Convention Center in Baltimore, MD, USA uses triangular trusses that are braced between with lighter round HSS members, giving the structure a space frame-like appearance. The primary trusses have much larger structural members.

Right: The connections for the truss are all welded. The plates between the members are not intended for stiffening but to conceal the light fixture behind. Smaller round HSS members are welded to join the bottom chords of the triangular trusses to provide lateral stability.

**There is no limit to the forms that can be created using trusses. In instances of curved geometry, the trusses can be fabricated to incorporate the curved structure into their span. These trusses can use curved members for the top and bottom chords, and straight segments for the web members.**

The form of this Dubai Metro station, UAE is created through the use of curved triangular trusses.

The curved triangular trusses that span across the Dubai Metro stations have single round HSS top chords and a pair of round HSS bottom chords that are separated by smaller round HSS web members. The welded joints combined with the curved steel help to keep the truss stiff in spite of a lack of diagonal web members in the plane of the arch/truss.

Left: The fabric roof of The Bank of America Pavilion in Boston, MA, USA by A-Form Architecture, is supported by a single three-dimensional trussed arch. The truss can make use of ground access to assist erection, so it was possible to fabricate the truss as a series of smaller elements.

Right: As it was not possible to fabricate and transport the truss in one piece, it was divided into sections. High-strength moment-resisting connections were then used to create continuity in the chords. Joints were fabricated by welding plates to the ends of the round HSS members. The connection between the tube and the plate is stiffened by the addition of triangular plates between each bolt hole.

**Trusses are one of the more versatile framing systems in that they can be used both as spanning members and as inhabitable spaces. If the depth of the truss is sufficient, it is possible to plan around the web members to create usable space.**

Left: Warren trusses are used on alternate floors of The University Hospital in Edmonton, AB, Canada to house the vast mechanical systems, thereby leaving the patient floor areas free from mechanical interference.

Right: The Phoenix Convention Center in Phoenix, AZ, USA uses a cantilevered truss to extend out over the street, thereby providing a shade canopy. These truss elements are tied back into the primary structure of the building to allow them to make such a significant cantilever extension.

**The unusual shape of the addition to the Ontario College of Art and Design in Toronto, designed by Will Alsop, uses deep trusses to create a cantilevered two-story classroom structure that sits atop 27m/90ft-long hollow steel legs.**

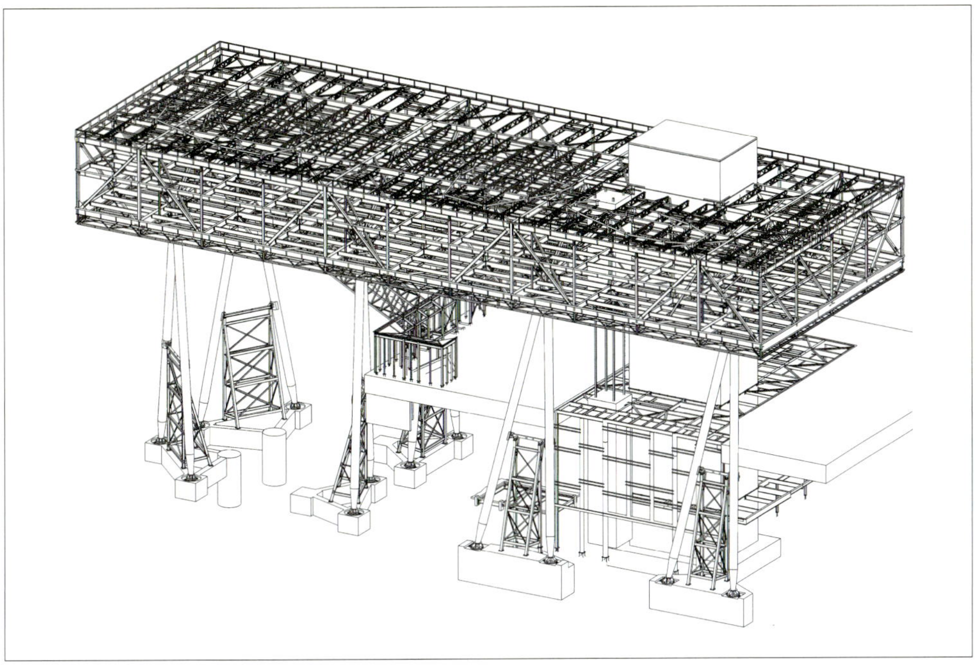

This structural isometric of the addition to the Ontario College of Art and Design in Toronto, ON Canada, designed by Will Alsop, was used by the steel fabricator and erector, Walters Inc., to visualize the construction of the steel frame. The ability of the large two-story-deep steel trusses to cantilever from the concrete core facilitated the erection of the structure. The trusses were incrementally extended over the legs.

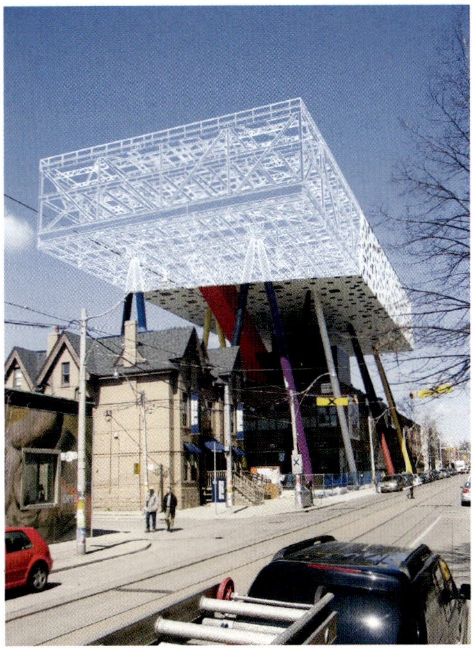

Top left: The inherent tensile strength of the steel allows the deep trusses to cantilever from the support legs and the reinforced concrete core. Steel decking is being installed for the floors and roof. The two-story classroom building that is supported on the legs is housed within these large trusses. The floor plan/program is arranged around the structure.

Bottom left: The diagonals of the trusses cut through the interior of the studio space of OCAD. The presence of the structure is not difficult to work around and brings a tectonic reality to the finish of the space. The majority of the structure is buried in the walls of the smaller rooms. Much of the steel is left exposed on the interior and treated with a combination of intumescent fire-retarding coatings and a suppression system.

Right: Working with steel structures requires a high degree of visualization by the members of the team. This illustration, created by the steel fabricator, Walters Inc., shows an understanding of the relationship between the structural capacity of the steel and the architecture.

**If the basics of connection design strategies and the intentions of framing are well understood, then it is possible to build upon simple solutions to create an innovative architectural language of connections in steel.**

*CHAPTER 4*

---

# *FABRICATION, ERECTION AND THE IMPLICATIONS ON DESIGN*

---



Steel erection is about teamwork. A large number of personnel are on site to oversee the lift of the "pod" at the Leslie Dan Faculty of Pharmacy in Toronto, ON, Canada, designed by Foster + Partners. This is the first installation of its kind for the architect as well as the fabricator, Walters Inc. The bright orange dots on the chains allow the sighting of levels during erection and to check the lift for alignment.

PCL

# *TRANSFORMING ARCHITECTURAL DESIGN INTO FABRICATED ELEMENTS*

There is significant work involved in transforming the architectural idea of a steel-framed building into a series of (pre-)fabricated elements that can be readily erected on the building site. Even into the 21st century, and in spite of advances in technology, the design, fabrication and erection of steel buildings is a hand-crafted process. There is human interaction, workmanship and decision-making during every step. With the exception of steel framing for standard big-box stores or the like, each project is unique, and aspects of the design, fabrication and construction must be customized to suit the project. This might seem to run counter to the idea behind the early development of iron and steel as being suited to mass fabrication and assemblage construction. However, the industry still relies on these precepts as the basis for achievements in economy and speed of erection. Aspects of pure craft and pride in workmanship remain core to steel design.

In instances where the architect's proposal begins to stretch the limits of the use of successful precedents in detailing, fabrication and erection, fabricators are often brought into the discussion, ahead of the finalization and tendering/bid phase of the project, to inform the detailing. This runs counter to the procedure in less complex projects where the steel fabricator will simply bid the project after it has been put out to tender. In straightforward projects the fabricator might suggest only minor modifications to the structural set as outlined by the engineer, to improve efficiency.

The ironworkers that erect a project are critical to its proper completion. In all projects, but particularly with challenging ones, there is usually a lead ironworker whose problem-solving skills can make or break the pace, speed of erection and timely completion of the work. The ironworkers will have a sense or feel of the fit of pieces. They will be responsible for ensuring the proper alignment during erection and the quality of finish of any site welding and finishing operations. This is also a dangerous job. Even if tied off and wearing proper fall protection much of the work is done at a great height, during all sorts of weather and around moving elements that may weigh thousands of tonnes.

This chapter will use two detailed project profiles to describe this process. The Addition to the Royal Ontario Museum by Studio Daniel Libeskind and the Leslie Dan Faculty of Pharmacy by Foster + Partners, both in Toronto, are extraordinarily complicated projects that required specialized detailing, fabrication and erection. Nevertheless, an understanding of the methods used in these projects will assist in the understanding of processes used in a wider range of more basic projects.

The ironworkers pose for the press at the lift of the final piece of steel for the Royal Ontario Museum by Studio Libeskind in Toronto, ON, Canada. There is significant pride in workmanship and the achievement of an accident-free project. The truss element is covered with signatures of everyone involved.

# *PROCESS PROFILE: ADDITION TO THE ROYAL ONTARIO MUSEUM (ROM) - MICHAEL LEE-CHIN CRYSTAL / STUDIO DANIEL LIBESKIND*

Design Architect: Studio Daniel Libeskind
Local Architects: Bregman and Hamann
Engineers: ARUP London/Halsall Associates
General Contractor: Vanbots Construction Corporation
Steel Fabrication and Erection: Walters Inc.

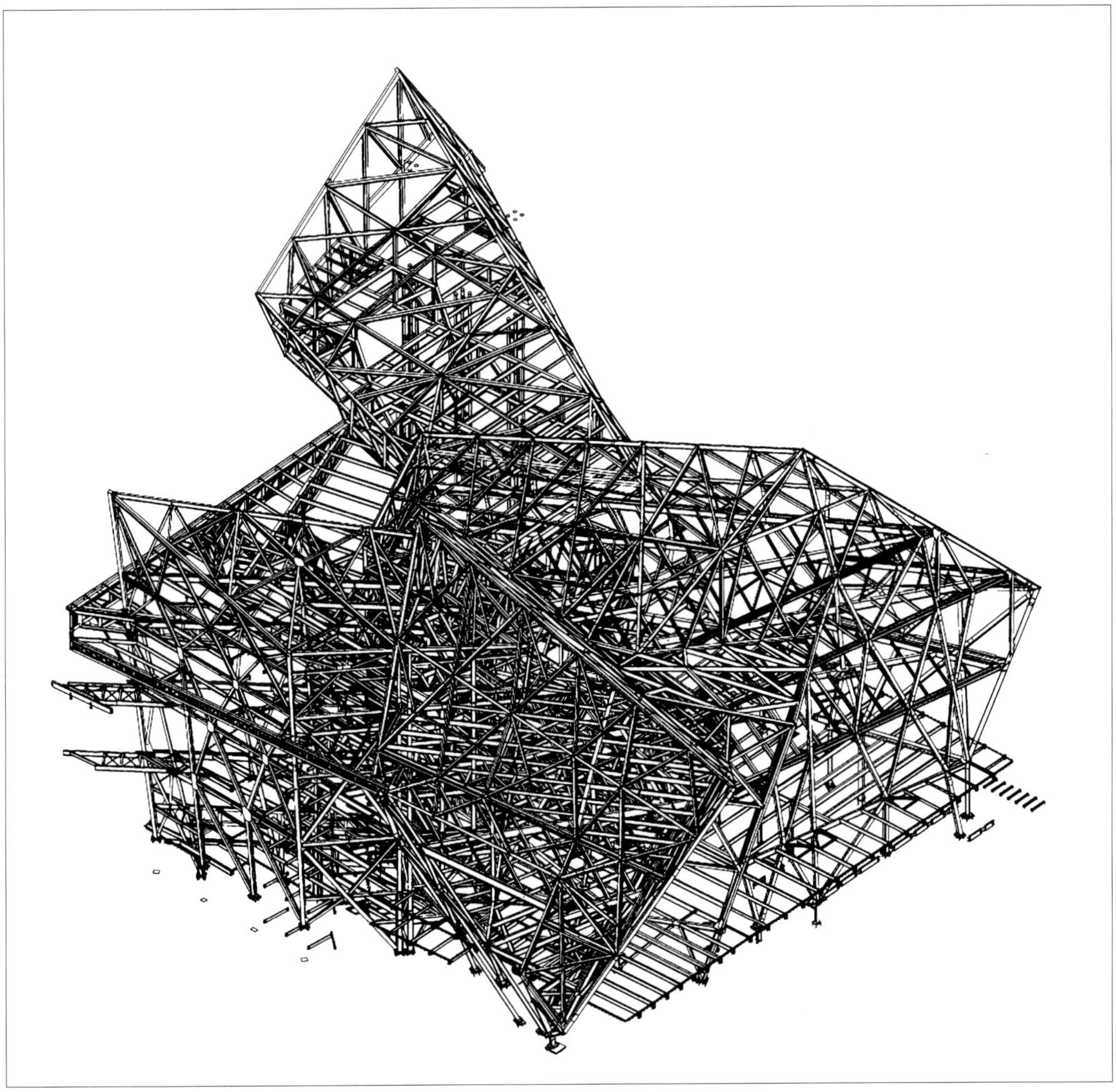

Overall structural isometric of the ROM as drawn by the fabricator and erector, Walters Inc. of Hamilton, ON, Canada. This drawing served as an overall reference for the entire project. It shows every single piece of steel.

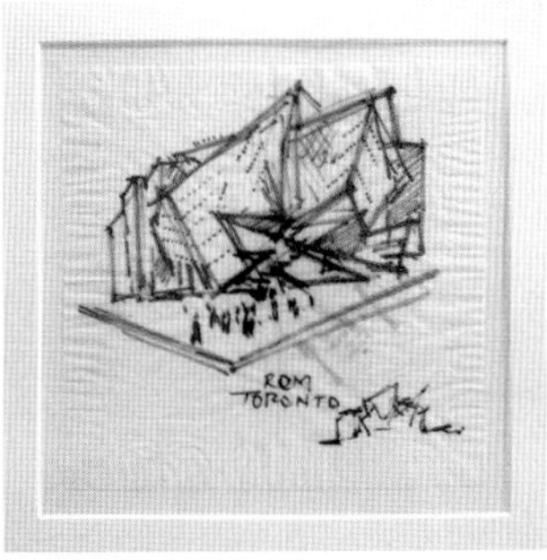

The ROM addition began its life as a classic napkin sketch.

Complex buildings, particularly those with irregular geometries, require the use of multifaceted drawings and models, both digital and physical, as the means of communication among team members. Simple orthographic drawing convention was not useful in defining the volumes or details of this project at virtually any stage of design, fabrication or construction. 3D architectural modeling provided the basis for the eventual generation of the more technical structural steel models created by the fabricator. Standard architectural plans, sections and elevations were developed for bids and permissions, but these drawings required significant supplementation to make them serve as communication tools. The varied angled planes of the walls generated a plethora of unique steel diagrid components and connections. Material take-offs and dimensioning needed to be done via drawings taken in plane with the angled surfaces. While methodologies for constructing and assembling the planar areas of the skin of the building may be straightforward or repetitive, each face, peak and valley required distinct detailing to account for the technical challenges presented by unceasing anomalies.

In most "standard" architectural projects the architect and engineer define and prepare contract documents for bidding, often in concert with the project management team. In this instance it was the steel fabricator, detailer and erector in concert with the engineers who had the facility and expertise to transform the three-dimensional crystalline aspirations into actual steel members and realizable connections.

## THE ROLE OF PHYSICAL AND DIGITAL MODELS

As in most architectural projects, physical models were used in addition to digital models. There were models of the traditional finely crafted type complete with interior lights, people and cars used for client-related display purposes. Additional models were created specifically to comprehend and then work through the geometry of the project and create the structural details.

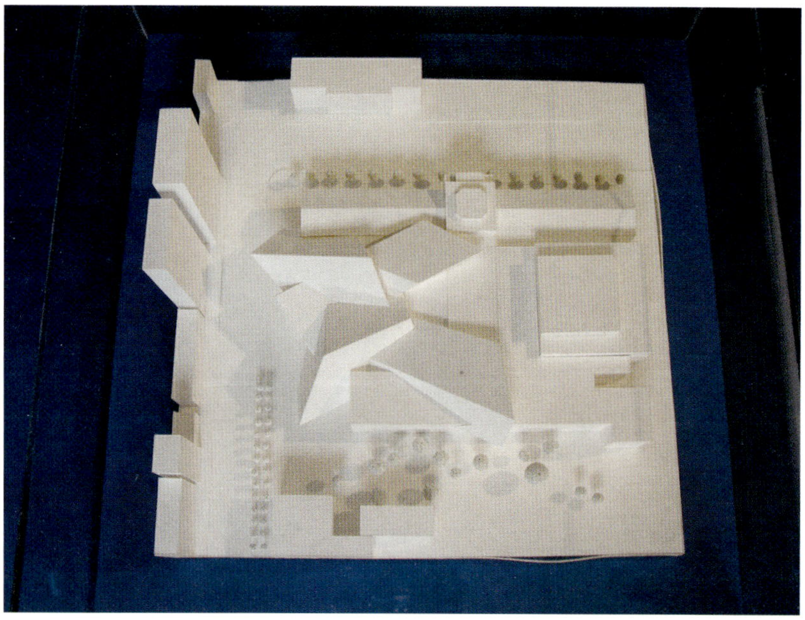

One of the massing study models created by the architects to look at the intricacies of the crystalline form as it overlays the rectangular base of the original historic building. Many models were created before the final form was settled. This physical model has little linkage to any sort of digital model used to actually construct such a complicated building. It is a tool to convince the client and compare massing options.

Three-dimensional physical models were also used to visualize the steel structure, showing the floor framing layers or the steel diagrids of the crystal faces overlaid on the building volumes. The set of fabrication drawings used in the shop comprises one drawing for each unique piece of the frame.

Although the triangulation in the diagrid form itself gives stability to many of the inclined planes, moment connection systems are also used throughout the structure to reinforce and increase lateral stability, particularly where large truss members or skylight enclosures were left hanging or cantilevering during construction but also in the final design.

Left: A model used by the fabricator to examine the steel on the faces of the crystals.

Right: This paper model uses the drawings for the steel floor framing to create a sense of the "floating" floor plates themselves, as independent of the sloped diagrid walls. There are numerous cutouts in the floors and not much aligns vertically. The floor plates of the model are held apart by thin wires.

Walters Inc. used proprietary 3D modeling software to work out the myriad of connection details. Such programs allow the detailer to generate a three-dimensional model of all steel components that incorporates loading and is able to be rotated and pulled apart to look at the distinct sections, member sizes, plate thicknesses or bolting and welding requirements. As virtually none of the steel in this building was intended to be exposed, the choice of member shape and size was left to the detailer's discretion in response to issues of strength, connectability and economy. Were AESS the end wish, the detailer would likely have seen a significant increase in input from the architectural team.

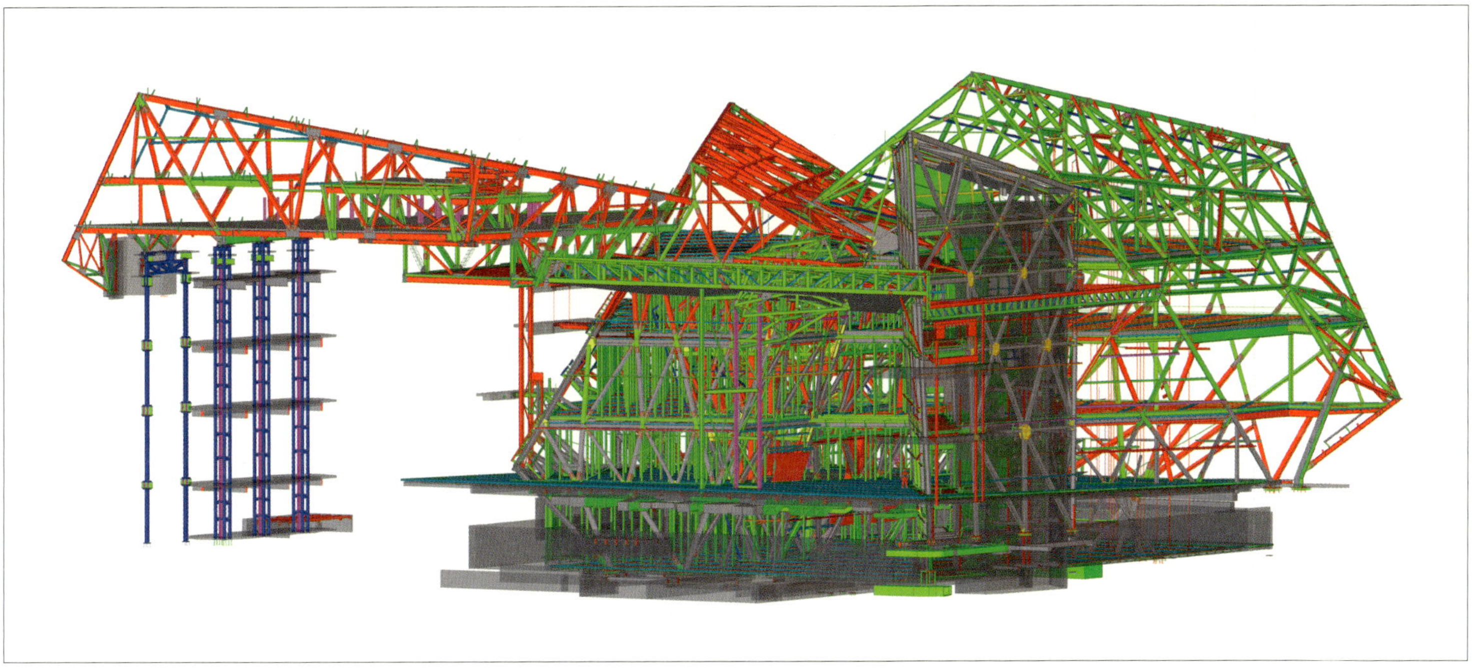

The 3D model generated by the fabricators was created with specialized steel detailing software. The model of the whole building is required to connect all of the separate joints into a structurally cohesive whole.

The structural design of the steel is initiated by the structural engineers and completed by the fabricator and detailer. The engineering data are fed into specialized industry-standard software that is used by the fabricator to design and detail each connection. This detailing must acknowledge the load transfers that occur in the joints, include the dimensions of all steel elements that are resolved at a given joint, and account for bolting and welding.

The detailed design of each node in the larger model will correspond to a set of actual fabricated pieces in the project. The digital model must also take into account limits on member sizes for shipping and erection. From this information a separate drawing sheet is created that will be used to fabricate each unique element.

Left: Digital model showing the detailing of a face of the crystal.

Right: Photograph taken at the same angle as the digital model, showing how precisely the two images align: the built case exactly replicates what is set out on the drawing.

In a standard project based upon rectangular bays, the reference to elements is normally based on their column-and-grid intersection and floor level. For a project like the ROM, alternate means were developed to reference placement. Each piece of steel was assigned to one of five major crystals. Within these, vertices refined the location. In addition, many of the elements had such unusual shapes as to warrant nicknames which, given the complexity of the project, proved more useful than locating a piece by its column-and-grid number.

The element illustrated here first as a digital model, then during fabrication and finally in the fabrication shop was affectionately dubbed "The Owl".

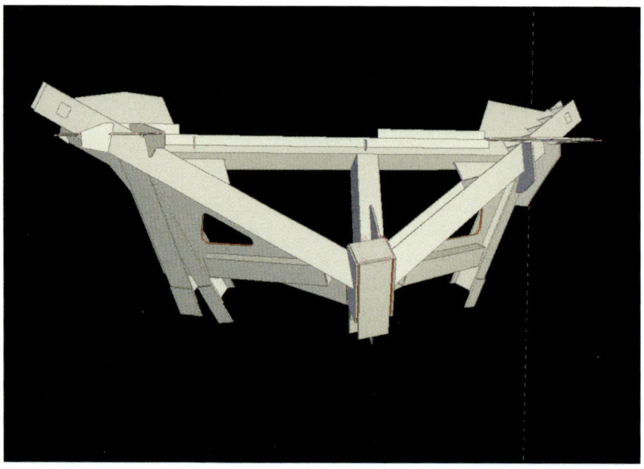

Drawing of the element as extracted from the digital model. It was to be shop-fabricated so that the most complex pieces that required welding could be completed in the shop. The element was sized to fit on a flatbed truck for transport. As the joints of site connection were to be bolted, all bolt holes were drilled in the shop and any plate attachments required to be movable were precut and in some instances loosely fit so as to be erection-ready.

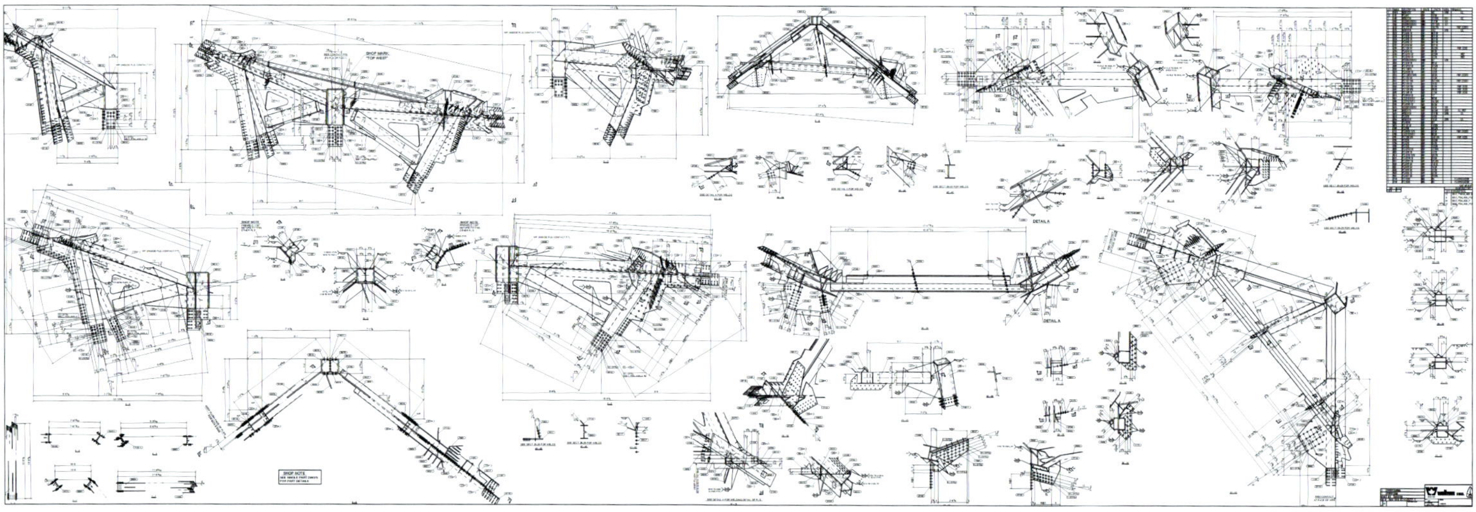

Top: The digital image was then transformed into a single sheet of drawings to be used in the shop to fabricate the element.

Left: "The Owl" nearing completion. All of the smaller steel pieces have been cut based on the drawing sheet. The steel element required significant lifting and turning in the shop during fabrication to ensure access to do the work.

Right: "The Owl" is in place in the structure on site.

The level of detail provided by the digital detailing model allows the designers to get a real feel of the way that the piece will work in the field. As the digital model created by the fabricator is used to generate a very precise set of drawings from which the elements are fabricated, there should ideally be no difference in the final erected piece. Any adjustments to force-fit one element on a project like this would result in a disastrous ripple effect of non-fit for all subsequent pieces. If a project has odd angles or uses AESS the fit tolerances are normally reduced to one half of standard dimensional tolerance that would be used for standard structural steel. There are no slotted holes or shim plates permitted to ease the fit of members.

Top: Two men in the fabrication shop reference a drawing to transfer markings onto a piece of ROM steel.

Bottom: Seeing the ironworkers in relation to the steel elements gives a better understanding of the scale.

Even though digital technologies are used to detail the connections, it is very important to remember that the elements are hand-crafted. The pieces of steel required for the elements are measured, cut and assembled via welding, using rudiments such as the carpenter's square and a pencil. Not all pieces are cut using CAD / CAM.

Tack welds are used in the shop to stabilize the position of the individual elements. This allows either the overhead bay crane or temporary supports to be removed and full welding done later.

## APPRECIATING SCALE

One of the more difficult aspects when conceiving and detailing a steel structure is to appreciate the scale or size of the pieces. Much of the steel that we may have experienced is situated far overhead, removing any sense of comparison. This is less of an issue in the design of concealed structural steel than it is for AESS, which is often situated near the viewer for closer examination and scrutiny of the details. This also impacts the selection of fabrication methods and style.

## TRANSPORTATION AND SITE ISSUES AND THE IMPACT ON DESIGN

Individual pieces of steel cannot be any larger than can be transported to the site. This limit in size will determine the placement of the connections between pieces: the more connections that can be shop-fabricated, the more economical the pieces, and the quicker the erection. It is preferable to weld in the shop and bolt on the site. If the project aesthetic is for all-welded connections, then further thought has to be given to how the site welding will be accomplished during the erection process.

For almost every project there is a distance to be traveled between the fabrication shop and the construction site. The necessary route of travel must inform the design and detailing of the connections. The fabricator must know the overhead clearance of every overpass as well as critical turning radii for the carrier. Access to the site may be further constricted as the widths of local streets may be significantly smaller.

Preference is given to making the pieces fit on a standard trailer, as most fabricators will own a fleet of these. Custom trailers or sets of wheels can be fabricated for the project. Ensuring that the steel pieces fit within the width of the trailer is also helpful, as any oversized elements will also require a police escort, or in extreme cases, road closure, to assist in shipping to the site. Timing to avoid peak traffic hours can alleviate some congestion.

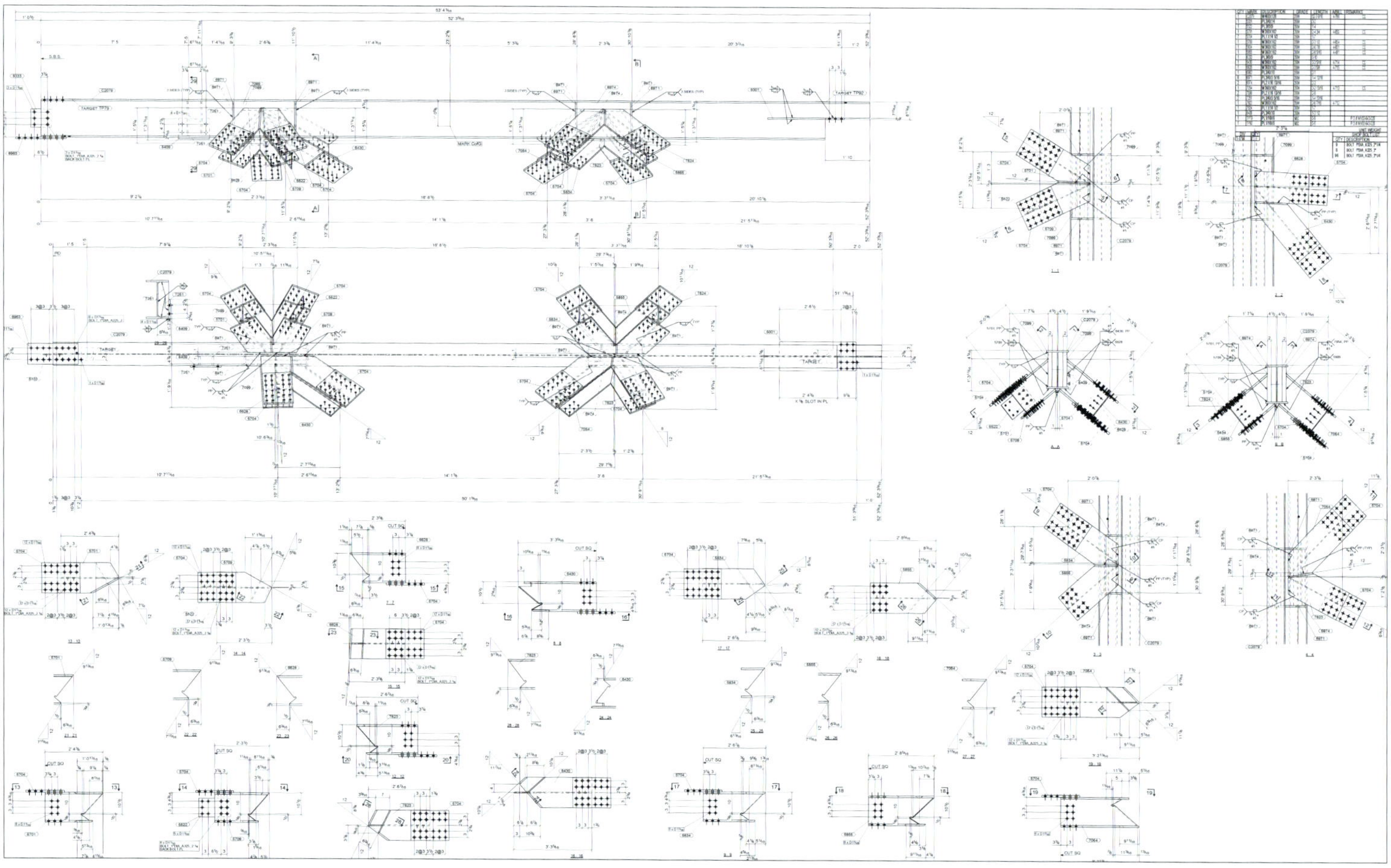

The permitted member size will also be impacted by the amount of staging area for the project. Even if the member size is limited due to transportation, some controlled sub-assembly can take place in the staging area for the project prior to lifting. This can speed erection time and make the connections easier to access. The site crane can be used to lift and rotate the members in the staging area in order to allow the ironworkers ground access to complete the connections.

At 17.18 m / 53 ft – 4 1/16 in this element was at the upper end of the size of steel that could fit on a flatbed. The nodes into which the other elements of the diagrid would fit were shop-welded to ensure the maximum degree of accuracy of the piece.

Left: The staging area on the north edge of the site was extremely tight so the steel was offloaded and laid very compactly in a sequence that reflected the order of erection. Many of the larger angled pieces of the diagrid were shipped essentially as straight members with their palm-like heads attached in the shop, and assembled into larger configurations in the staging area prior to erection. As the erection proceeded, the staging area steadily shrunk as building displaced the free area of the site. This made sequencing and placement of deliveries even more critical.

Right: Ironworkers are assembling a number of smaller pieces to create a larger entity to erect. They are using the limited staging area in front of the project. This requires that the erector carefully sequences the deliveries to ensure that only the pieces to be erected on any one or two days are at the site.

## ERECTING THE STEEL

The location and reach of the crane impacts the design of the structure. 99% of the erection of the ROM was achieved with the use of a single-tower crane located at the center of the project. The positioning and reach of this crane was critically calculated to be able to access all of the lifts. Cranes add expense to the project so reduction in number is helpful. Again, the restrictive site area and location played a role in this project, as the nearness of the street and the tight staging area negated the use of larger boom cranes to routinely assist with the erection sequence. The selection of the crane type or types will impact the design of the steel as well. Cranes are sized according to the weight that they can lift.

The location of the single-tower crane was chosen to provide the maximum reach for the crane arm. The steel framing had to be worked around the crane to ensure that no major structural runs of the diagrid were interrupted. This would not be as much of an issue in locating a crane in a conventional building.

As the structure is being designed, a specific erection sequence for the pieces is devised. In a project based on orthogonal geometry this is quite straightforward. For the ROM this had to be carefully planned, due to the complexity of the steel and the limited access for erection, as the addition was bounded by an existing structure on three sides. The larger digital model that was used to design the connections was repurposed to divide the structure into lift sequences. The erection of the steel proceeded first around the concrete core for initial stability. Other sections were systematically filled in.

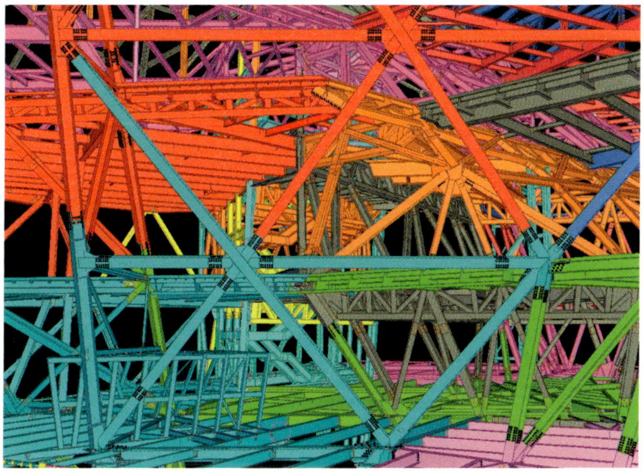

The color coding on this illustration reveals the groups of members that comprise a particular part of the erection sequence.

Lifting points are calculated on the members so that when the crane lifts them they are at the correct angle to approach the connection for bolting or welding. For normal steel erection gravity assists in pulling the pieces into their final position. Columns will have an attaching point onto which to hook the crane. Symmetrical beams can be lifted from one central point for short members or via a sling for longer or slightly asymmetrical members.

Gravity was the enemy of much of the erection at the ROM. Lifting points and chain lengths for the complex angled pieces had to be carefully calculated by the erectors to reflect the gravitational centers of the odd-shaped assemblages. Precision was critical to obtain the correct lifting angle or position so that the piece could be slid into its receiving connection. This sometimes required that the staged pieces be turned over or rotated within the tight staging area prior to their final hoist.

Left: The crane attachment for this truss element is at the gravitational center of the top of the piece. The ropes attached to the sides are for the ironworkers to grab in order to assist the crane operator in maneuvering the piece into its final position.

Right: The ironworkers grab hold of the incoming diagrid element by handling the steel and using the ropes to guide it in. As the bolt holes come into alignment the ironworker inserts a spud wrench (recognized by its long pointed end) into the holes. The wrench is left there while bolts are inserted into the other holes and hand-tightened to initially secure the connection.

Left: Ironworkers simultaneously handle both ends of a large steel beam with angled ends to guide it into position. Beams are fitted with supports and ropes along their length while still on the ground to provide an attaching point for the fall protection that the ironworkers must wear when walking the beams.

Right: The lead ironworker troubleshoots a connection. This is an instance of the "last piece" being inserted into the diagrid in this section. The piece must enter from below and slide up into the connection. The lower connecting plate is rotated out of the way to allow the element to enter. The plate will then be swiveled into position and the bolting completed.

All of the steel on this project was sized as required for economy in the structure. It may appear heavy and oversized at first sight, yet the large eccentric forces on all of the non-vertical members put enormous deflecting loads on the unbraced system. The angled members had to be sized much larger than standard vertical columns to prevent increasing sag in the structure, which had to be virtually self-supporting until the permanent concrete floor systems were in place, and also to avoid the need for large numbers of temporary shoring members or systems. A system of diagonal tension cables was used to brace the structure during erection and left in place until completion of the deep concrete floors, whose diaphragm action was essential to locking in the shape of the frame.

In order to use the crane efficiently, not all of the bolts are inserted as the piece is erected, just sufficient to hold it in place. The lead ironworkers are given the task of handling the erection. A second, following crew of ironworkers fill in the remaining bolts and tighten them snug-tight to specification. These men are using a small lift to access the connection. The bright orange paint on the frame is to allow the surveyor to verify the position of the steel.

Work proceeds on the ROM during the winter months. Snow must be cleared from the elements as they are being worked on. Diagonal tension braces are used to assist with temporary support of the structure.

## THE EFFECTS OF WEATHER AND CLIMATE ON ERECTION

Climate and temperature impact steel erection. Although severely cold or hot temperatures are not as problematic as for a concrete structure, where the curing of the concrete may be negatively affected, steel does expand and contract significantly, which can make fitting the pieces difficult. One of the benefits of structural steel over reinforced concrete is that it can be installed year round, which is an advantage in climates with snow and extremely cold temperatures.

One of the critical aspects of the differential change of the steel due to temperature rests in the fluctuation that may occur during the installation of the cladding system. The steel structure will eventually rest at a consistent interior temperature if the insulated envelope is placed on its exterior. When the cladding is being installed, the temperature may swing from sub-zero to extremely high values. This requires that there be provision in the design of the cladding system to shrink or expand until such time as the structure has reached its final size.

Left: It took more than a year to install the cladding on this building. The structural steel was completed during the heat of summer, so that the cladding installers had to accommodate significant changes in size as the temperatures plummeted for winter construction.

Right: Attachment of the sub-frame system for the custom titanium cladding. Around 10,000 small posts were welded to the frame to provide support. As the steel in this project is largely concealed, spray fireproofing was applied.

## PROVIDING PERMANENT STABILITY FOR THE FRAME

There are various ways to provide lateral stability to a steel-framed building. Often concrete stair and elevator cores are used as well as concrete floor systems. The temporary bracing for the steel cannot be removed until the permanent stability system is functional. Often a concrete floor system is incorporated into a steel building for this reason. Steel buildings will normally use profiled steel decking as the permanent formwork for the concrete floors. Although this will still require temporary shoring until the concrete has reached its 7- and 28-day strengths, it is still far less formwork than would be required for an exposed concrete underside of the floor structure.

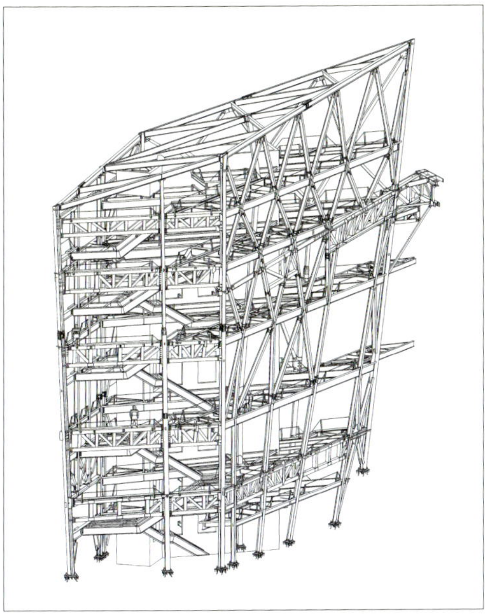

Left: This isometric drawing by the fabricator shows the steel of the first ROM crystal as it surrounds the concrete core for the primary stairs. This provided inherent stability for the start of the construction process. These sorts of isometric drawings are created in part to help the team visualize the steel in the project.

Right: The early phase of construction began by erecting the steel of the first ROM crystal around the concrete core for the stairs and elevator. At this point in the project much of the site was available to be used as a staging area.

The installation of the steel decking continues as access is no longer required to various areas of the project for erection. On most traditional jobs this would proceed floor by floor. As some of the ROM steel needed to be threaded through the structure and there was limited access to do so, installation was less regular.

Left: The installation of the steel decking transformed the work site, as access was improved to complete work on the structure.

Right: Temporary shoring stayed in place until the concrete had reached its full strength at 28 days.

## COORDINATION WITH OTHER SYSTEMS

The design and detail of the structural steel for the building must also be coordinated with the mechanical and electrical systems. In traditional buildings these systems are often concealed in a suspended ceiling. Normally enough clearance is given between the underside of the steel and the top of the suspended ceiling to accommodate duct runs and lighting.

Buildings with unusual layouts, angled planes or those with large atriums or voids in the plan will have more difficulty in working the runs for the HVAC system. Building Information Modeling (BIM) systems allow the various members of the team to more easily troubleshoot a conflict-free situation. Even the use of CAD drawings allows for good prevention of conflicts.

Left: Some of the duct runs in the ROM project are massive. Even with a coordinated set of 3D drawings, this was a difficult job.

Middle: The vertical distribution risers for the air handling system in the ROM had to be worked into the planning of the steel structure.

Right: Even the installation of the great expanses of gypsum wallboard over the infill light steel framing provided a challenge.

From an architectural perspective, even though this project makes almost exclusive use of concealed structural steel, there remains a sense in the experience of the spaces that it is "not a concrete building". The translation of the angularity of the planes as well as the nature of the window penetrations hint at some of the essence of the structural steel diagrid. This goes back to the reasons behind the selection of structural steel for this unusual diagrid building. There are some building types that can be done equally well with either a reinforced concrete or structural steel frame. The selection of materials for those projects can be left to the local preference of trades and economic or sustainability factors affecting the availability of materials.

Left: A preview of the finished building prior to installation of the exhibits. The angular nature of the steel diagrid has been highlighted through the placement of windows. Fragmentary views of the steel frame can be seen through the slices, maintaining the feel of the steel structure although it is concealed.

Right: Exterior view of the completed museum. Traces of the structure are visible through the windows.

# *PROCESS PROFILE: LESLIE DAN FACULTY OF PHARMACY / FOSTER + PARTNERS*

Architect: Foster + Partners
Local Architect: Cannon Design (formerly Moffat and Kinoshita)
Structural Engineers: Yolles Halcrow, Toronto
Contractors: PCL Constructors Canada
Steel Fabrication and Erection: Walters Inc.

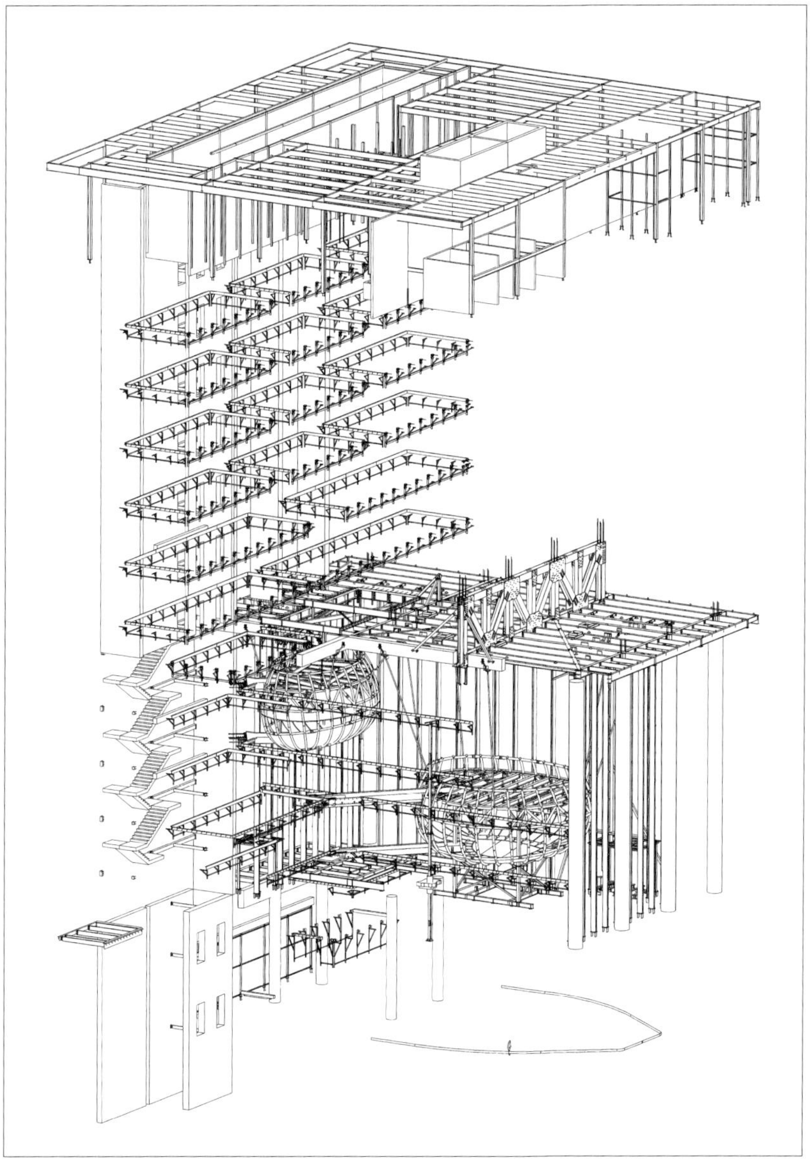

Overall structural isometric of the Leslie Dan Faculty of Pharmacy at the University of Toronto, ON, Canada, as drawn by the fabricator and erector, Walters Inc. of Hamilton, ON, Canada. This drawing serves as an overall reference piece for the entire project. It shows every single element of steel for the building (note the absence of the concrete frame). As the main part of the building is constructed from reinforced concrete, the drawing truly highlights the aspects which are structural steel.

Different structural materials are chosen for different buildings for varying reasons. The predominant material used in this building was reinforced concrete. The main tower of classroom and lab spaces was conceived in monolithic cast concrete. The design also called for the construction of a large five-story atrium space at the front of the building with multiple floors of classroom space above. Additionally, two large "classroom pods" were designed to be hung from the ceiling of the atrium. It was felt that to construct the ceiling of the atrium out of concrete was not practical, as it would require significant formwork and this would delay the project as well as obstruct access to a large portion of the site. Steel was chosen instead for the ceiling of the atrium, as it was more quickly erected, required no scaffolding, and once complete would provide the base for the construction of the remaining floors in concrete. A 50-tonne steel truss was designed that would serve to support one of the suspended pods and also provide interstitial support to shorten the span lengths of the steel beams.

This project required some innovative input from the fabricator for the detailing of the suspended pods. The pods are constructed from a series of prefabricated panels made from curved and welded HSS tubes. The logistics of suspending the pods was the overriding factor for most of the decisions surrounding the design of the steel.

This drawing is taken from the specialized 3D modeling program used to design and detail the steel. This view highlights the primary steel elements of the pods and shows clearly the thin suspension system for the pods. The single steel column on the right is used to provide the end support for the 50-tonne steel truss. It is ultimately enclosed in concrete so that its appearance matches the balance of the columns. The concrete columns are absent from this drawing. Only the steel is shown highlighted in green.

## SHOP FABRICATION

The pods were designed to be constructed from a series of prefabricated panels for ease of site assembly. It was physically impossible to prefabricate and ship the entire pod as a function of size. The fabricator chose to fabricate the pods from round HSS elements that were prefabricated into panel segments. Where the panels were to be joined, steel plates were set into the tubes that would lap and provide a simple bolted connection. As the pods were intended to be clad, aesthetic considerations were not part of the decision-making process. The pods needed to be as light as possible to reduce the load on the hangers, yet sturdy. HSS is structurally better when compared to W sections by weight. For this geometry the joints were also easier to fabricate using round members.

Whereas the vertical ribs of the pod have been specially curved at a steel bender (see Chapter 8: Curved Steel), the members that run laterally are fabricated from straight sections. The spheroid form will be created when applying the support members for the cladding. This reduces the cost and complexity of the pods. Note the curved end cuts on the tubes to allow welding to the vertical ribs, as well as the "slices" that will accommodate the insertion of the plate connectors.

The pieces are welded together in the shop to provide better control of the processes. The panels have been prefabricated to an optimal size for transportation and handling. A plate has been let into the HSS tube to provide for a bolted connection. Additional reinforcement has been added to the welded connections between the tubes in the form of linear plates. Small clips are welded to the tubes to provide attaching points for the final drywall finish.

A special socket has been designed to seat the ball of the slender hanger. This and the hanging rod are the only parts of the project that are classed as Architecturally Exposed Structural Steel. The machining of both the ball and the socket is extremely important as there must be a perfect fit for the penetrating welding that will serve to transfer the load of the pod to the hanger.

The steel ball that forms the end of the hanging rod. This element requires precision machining to achieve full contact. It is attached to a solid rod of steel.

The termination points of the hangers that will attach to the ceiling. Although these appear to have sockets that can rotate, the pieces are welded in place. The idea behind the ball and socket was to accommodate changing geometry for the hangers and give consistency in appearance for the hangers.

Structural steel that is designed to be concealed with fire-protective coverings does not necessarily need to be primed. There are arguments for and against the use of primers in this instance. Primed steel tends to have a better appearance during construction and if the site is subject to rain and weathering prevents oxidation of the steel. However, a moderate amount of surface rust during construction will not harm steel and deciding not to prime can save money. Where the steel is to be welded it cannot be primed. Primer will need to be removed prior to welding. As this project made predominant use of bolting and was exposed to weather for a considerable time it was decided to use primer. The priming was done in the fabrication shop prior to shipping.

The base section for one of the pods clearly shows the geometry of the major connection that resolved eight round HSS sections. Plates were used along the long direction to provide additional stability and allow for sub-assembly of the groups of three tubular members.

## ASSEMBLING THE PODS

Although the project had a generous amount of staging area for the steel, there were logistical issues as a result of the need to complete the fabrication of the two pods on the ground, close below their final location in the building. The assembly of the pods preceded the erection of the floor from which they were to be suspended, as the crane required overhead access to lift the panels. The pod panels were shipped to the site and offloaded "curve up" to minimize contact with the ground and prevent damage to the shape. It was necessary for the pieces to be lifted and turned to ready the pieces for the correct lifting position. Complex pieces will typically need to be repositioned by the crane after delivery to allow for the proper attachment of the crane hooks.

The fabricator's isometric drawing of the small pod shows the panel connections and placement of the plate steel bridges that secure it to the building.

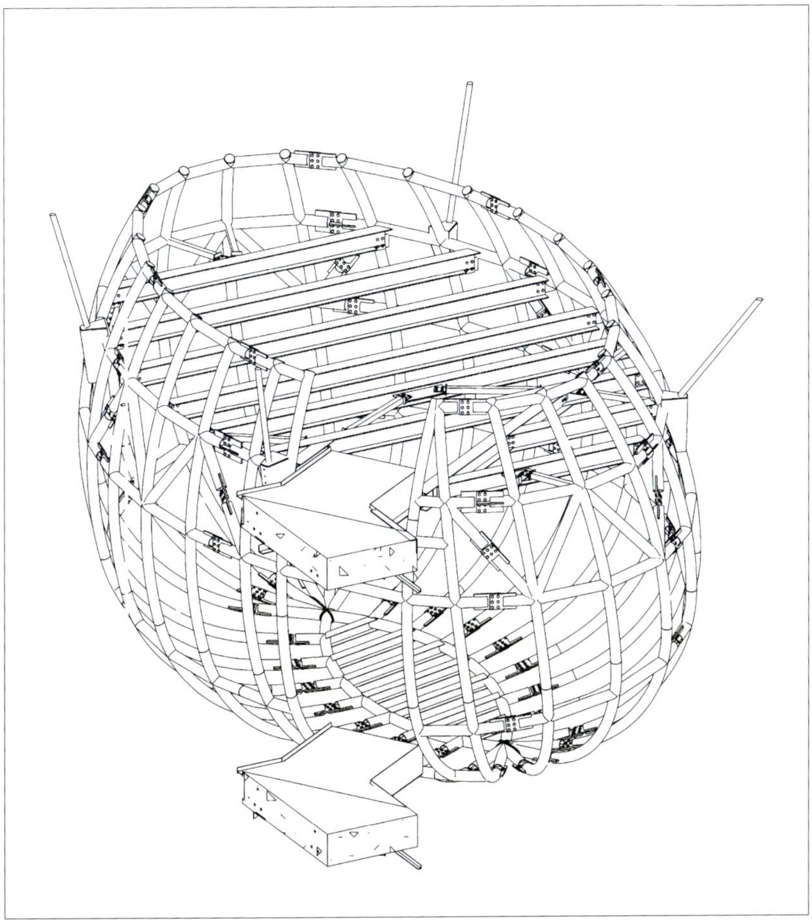

An ironworker works with the crane operator to reposition the pod section. The lifting hooks will be removed from their current position and moved to the wide end of the section for proper lifting alignment.

The ironworker and crane operator work through the arrival of the pod section to the pod, using a combination of hand signals and a walkie-talkie (if visibility is restricted). The ironworker guides the panel with ropes to make sure that the bolt holes align perfectly so that the first bolts can be inserted and the piece becomes secure enough to release the crane.

Once the piece is in place, the ironworkers complete the bolting and ready the pod for the next panel. This takes a high degree of teamwork and coordination. The object is to keep the crane operating at an even pace, as this is a very expensive piece of equipment and it should not sit idle.

## ERECTING A BEAM

The concrete structure for the building was complete to the sixth floor before steel arrived at the site. The six-story-tall architecturally exposed concrete columns that sit in the atrium and support the upper floors of the building were in place. Great care had to be taken throughout the lifting of the steel to prevent damage to the columns. The tops of the columns were fitted with small steel column stubs, which provided the attachment points for the steel framing that comprised the sixth floor.

The steel beams are prepared on the ground prior to lifting. The rope system that will provide anchorage for the fall-arrest gear worn by the ironworkers is attached. The crane chains are hooked to predetermined lifting points that will ensure that the steel beam arrives level.

The ironworkers are in place to receive the beam. This particular beam will join to the stub and sit in a temporary cantilever position as it will next be bolted to the major 50-tonne truss. The angled support attached to the beam is a temporary support. The rectangular holes in the web of the beam are precut to provide passage for HVAC.

The ironworkers work together to pull the flanges of the steel beam into the connection. Once aligned, a slug-wrench or two will be inserted to hold the beam while bolts are inserted.

## ERECTING THE COLUMNS

It was necessary to bear the load of the 50-tonne steel transfer truss that would span across the atrium on a steel column. The five-story unbraced reinforced concrete columns were not sufficiently strong and it was desired to at least give the appearance that all of the columns in the atrium were the same. As the transfer truss was to be concealed in the floor above, there was also no point in expressing the increased load that the column would be carrying. Making the core of the column in steel allowed for the column to be encased in concrete and leave the exterior appearance identical. The column itself was custom-fabricated from heavy steel plates that were welded together to form a square. Temporary braces were required to ensure its verticality.

The column is made up of welded plates. Temporary braces were used to keep it plumb during the erection process. It has not been primed, as it will be encased in concrete and the primer would inhibit bond between the materials.

The 50-tonne steel truss will sit on the column and allow the cantilevered beam to frame into its side.

A steel column stub is also required for the support of the far end of the truss where it connects to the reinforced concrete frame. The rebar surround indicates that it will be encased in concrete for both appearance and fire protection.

## LIFTING THE 50-TONNE TRUSS

The large transfer truss that spans across the atrium and supports the upper stories of the building arrived at the site more or less in one piece. The truss itself was not symmetrical, which complicated the placement of the lifting chains. When a truss is symmetrical, the lifting points are simple to determine. Any eccentricity in the shape of a member will require extra calculations and experience in determining the lifting points. This lift was also more difficult as the truss had to clear some trees on site that were in the way, slide down into the support at the building bearing end, sit squarely on top of the steel column and allow the beam to match its angle connectors at the side. As this was the largest element to be lifted for the project, it determined the crane capacity.

The truss is fabricated from W (Universal) sections. Surface-mounted gusset plates are used to reinforce the panel points of the truss. The truss is raised and checked for its degree of level prior to proceeding with the lift.

Ironworkers simultaneously work at all three connection points to ease the truss into its final position. On simple jobs this can be done fairly quickly. For this lift it took a couple of hours until everyone was satisfied with the position of the truss.

An ironworker assists in guiding the rear of the truss into alignment.

Once the truss is secured in place, the installation of the remaining steel beams that comprise the sixth floor proceeded quickly. Steel decking was installed on the floor framing. Small steel angles were welded to the truss to support the edge of the decking.

## LIFTING THE PODS

The one architectural aspect of this project that required the most innovation on the part of the fabricator and erector was the hanging of the pods. There were two pods: a small one that was suspended from four hangers as well as being attached by plate-steel bridges to the fourth and fifth floors, and a larger one that was hung from six rods and that was attached by bridges to the second and third floors. The lift was accomplished using chainfalls that were secured to the top of the sixth floor, which was fitted with reinforced openings for the chains. The erection of the suspension rods was quite difficult, as their geometry had to be resolved three-dimensionally in the atrium space with little physical reference. The digital model was used to determine the correct angle for the weld of the ball in socket of the ceiling mounts. The balls on the bottom of the rods needed to come into precise alignment with the sockets on the pods to allow for proper welding. The rods could not be forced, as any bending would be an obvious defect.

Each hydraulic chainfall-lifting mechanism required an ironworker to manually control its lift. Lifting had to be coordinated so as not to put the pods out of level. Although the pods could have been erected in place as an alternate to lifting, this would have required that substantial scaffolding be used. The reason for framing with steel in the first instance was to avoid the use of scaffolding and formwork that would have obstructed the atrium space.

The steel hangers are installed at the correct angle. Each hanger was unique. The points in the structure to which they are attached, whether in the concrete or the steel frame, required reinforcing.

The lift proceeds with all of the hydraulic chains pulling evenly to avoid putting the pod out of plumb. The smaller pod also traveled horizontally along a set of crane rails to its final position. Great care was taken not to damage the adjacent concrete columns. The larger pod was simply lifted vertically.

Both the ball and socket have been polished and all rust and scale removed so that they are ready for welding once the position is correct. The socket is protected with tape to keep its machined surface rust-free.

The plate steel bridges that attach and stabilize the pods are clad. Access panels are visible on the underside. The bridges have been used to run all services to the pods and access will be required from time to time.

The exterior of the completed pods has been finished in curved gypsum board.

Not all detailing, fabrication and erection is as challenging as the two projects addressed in this chapter. These projects do address a fairly complete range of issues that can be encountered when designing a steel building. Basic steel-framed buildings are often priced "by the tonne" of steel. For specialized construction, this does not hold and the increase in cost will completely depend upon the level of difficulty and the number of additional hours required to detail, fabricate and erect the steel.

The completed project. The presence of the pods is only barely evident from the exterior. Elaborate night lighting is employed to highlight the pods.

The completed bridges provide access to the top and mid level classroom inside. The lightness of the hangers is quite evident in the completed project.

A view down to the larger pod showing the lounge and light nature of the suspension system.

CHAPTER 5

---

# ARCHITECTURALLY EXPOSED STRUCTURAL STEEL (AESS): ITS HISTORY AND DEVELOPMENT

---



The Centre Georges Pompidou in Paris, France was constructed between 1972 and 1977. It was designed by the team of Renzo Piano and Richard Rogers and clearly exemplifies the early High Tech use of expressed and exposed steel systems.

## *THE INVENTION OF HOLLOW STRUCTURAL SECTIONS (HSS)*

Steel detailing and connection design is intrinsically connected to the types of shapes that are being connected. Early steel manufacturing processes in the 1800s were only able to fabricate angles, plates and later I-beam sections. The invention of processes that could hot-roll larger wide-flange or universal-column types generated the type of connection detailing typical in Early Modern structures, like those designed by Mies van der Rohe. Although round pipe had been technically available for use since the early part of the 20th century, the material was cast in nature and predominantly intended for use in plumbing and services, i.e. it was not weldable nor particularly friendly to work with in structural applications.

Modern hollow structural steel sections were not invented until the 1970s. HSS were first used in England. Experimental and theoretical studies were done on welded connections with square and round members at Sheffield University in 1970. In 1971 Stelco in Canada published the first HSS connection manual. Patents were subsequently applied for by numerous steel mills, including U.S. Steel of Pittsburgh in 1972, which was seeking to expand to the use to polygonal sections.

Left: A view of a truss-to-diagonal support connection on the Eiffel Tower in Paris, France. Angles, plates and rivets form large members from a multitude of smaller, lighter, and easier-to-manage parts.

Right: The New National Gallery in Berlin, Germany uses an exposed steel frame in a very symmetrical manner. (The sculpture in the foreground is by Alexander Calder, 1965.) This is considered to be Mies' last built work and one of the purest examples of his ideas. The black finish, use of wide-flange or modified wide-flange sections, as well as avoidance of trusses and suspension systems to create his large spans and cantilevers were considered the state of the art in exposed steel architecture prior to the High Tech Movement. There are only two cruciform column supports on each side of the square pavilion, creating significant cantilevers to the corners. Substantial cantilevers are also trademarks of Modern steel structures and reflect the tensile qualities of steel.

The invention of HSS marks a major stylistic break in exposed steel expression. The range of available sizes increased slowly and had eventual impact on the design of exposed steel structures. Very large diameters and elliptical sections only became available around 2005. The availability of the new range of section types was closely followed by technical advancements in CAD and structural calculation programs, which resulted in an explosion of possibilities in the application of the materials to buildings with increasingly complex geometries.

## *THE EVOLUTION OF AESS THROUGH THE HIGH TECH MOVEMENT*

The basic understanding of High Tech design lies in its roots as an "assembled" and largely prefabricated methodology. It is about taking "rationalized industrial technology into building construction" (Peter Buchanan). The 1970s marked a distinct paradigm shift in the way that steel was used and expressed in architecture. The High Tech Movement in England had grown out of experimental work by designers like Archigram and instead incorporated this energy into architectural manifestation through a transformed reinvention of earlier Structural Rationalist methodology. Also influential were the works of Buckminster Fuller with geodesic domes and prefabricated housing design, and Ezra Ehrenkrantz with the SCSD prefabricated school system in California. High Tech is similar to Structural Rationalism in its exposure of the structural framework and embellishment of the connection details. It differs in that it begins to more clearly differentiate the members by their tensile or compressive load capabilities as well as to include the exposure of mechanical services and systems.

Common to most High Tech buildings is an expanding use of lightweight tension systems, combined with increased use of expansive glazing and much more inventive ways of supporting glazing than could be provided by standard curtain wall systems. Many of these projects are about "doing more with more" and create elaborate structural systems to solve problems that could arguably have been constructed more simply. Yet the buildings do serve to explore the architectural potential of steel and connections as expressive devices and thus bear revisiting as precedents for contemporary detailing in AESS structures.

## *THE TYPOLOGY OF EARLY HIGH TECH ARCHITECTURE*

The industrialization manifested in early High Tech was limited by the state of engineering and detailing of the time. This was an age reliant on the slide rule for calculation. The three-dimensionality of these structures stretched engineering to new limits. The regularity of the systems and ease of repetition made up for the difficulty in the design of the primary elements. The typology of early High Tech "assembled" architecture can be differentiated as:

Buildings based on a structural portal-type frame that result in an extruded plan

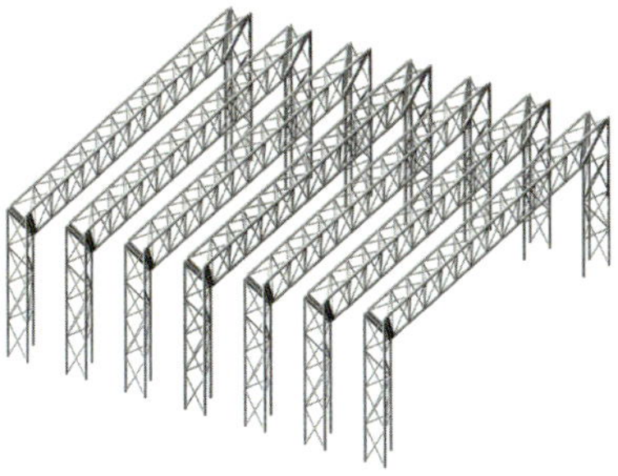

Buildings based on an expandable grid/bay system that can be extended uniformly in any direction

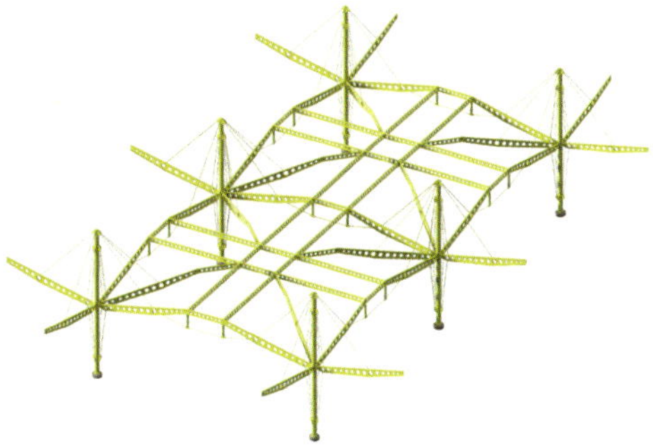

Linear buildings that rely on towers and tensile systems to suspend many structural elements (including roof planes) that would normally have their load path follow columns

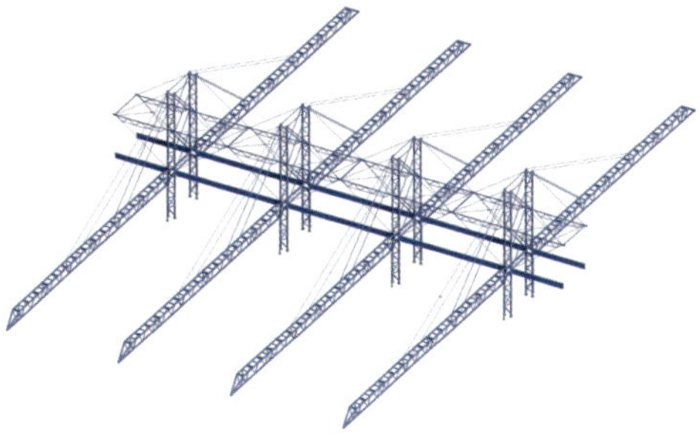

Further to this we see buildings that

- make fairly exclusive use of purpose-fabricated components
- make predominant use of standard, off-the-shelf components
- use an even mix of specialty and off-the-shelf components

Lastly, early High Tech buildings can be differentiated by those that

- make use of vibrant color to bring emphasis to the exposed steel
- use white or more muted shades to help the tactile nature of the exposed system recede into the background

Early High Tech buildings created a clear distinction between the fabrication processes that were best handled in the shop - involving welding - and the erection processes that were most efficient on the site - involving bolting. Pin-type connections as well as framed connections were used for their speed of erection.

If overly elaborate in their steel detailing, the early High Tech buildings tended to be formulaic in their adherence to the basic typology of extruded, grid or tensile. This proves useful to inform contemporary design and systematic detailing of AESS structures. High Tech architecture introduced intense collaboration between architects, engineers and those fabricating and erecting, a tradition continued in AESS.

## THE "EXTRUDED" TYPOLOGY

The idea of the extruded form was to establish a limited set of components that constituted an articulated frame from which a building of variable length could be created. Ideally a later addition would be accommodated by simply adding to the length of the building. The modularity provided by the rhythm of the intervals of the frame could further define limits and module sizes for cladding systems. Many early High Tech buildings also experimented with new types of metal and glass-cladding systems that benefited from mass production and whose speed of erection matched the idea of "assemblage" of the structural components.

### Sainsbury Centre for Visual Arts, Norwich, England | Norman Foster

The "extruded" type can be characterized by the Sainsbury Centre designed by Norman Foster in 1977. The building uses a triangular truss whose width and center-to-center spacing fit with a custom-designed modular lightweight cladding system that allowed for the interchangeability of solid, glazed and vented components, consistently along both the length of the building as well as across the roof. In this case, the mechanical services are run within the steel truss, allowing for the inner surface to be comprised of a louver system capable of modifying the amount of natural light that enters the space.

The design makes predominant use of round hollow structural sections, which necessitated new approaches to the design of the connections within the 3D truss as well as between elements, as there was little precedent for their architectural use.

This end view of the Sainsbury Centre for Visual Arts, Norwich, England clearly shows its extruded profile and the modular cladding system. The end wall uses structural mullionless glazing. Although the concept behind the extruded form was to allow for an addition, in fact the bollards are there to prevent traffic over the lawn, as the addition that was constructed in 2000 sits below the grass lawn.

A close view of the main connector shows the detail of the connection as well as the quality of the welds. The design of the connection is innovative in that it provides a "seat" so that the long truss can bear on the connection pad for ease of bolting. The close view of the truss illustrates a differentiation between the larger member sizes used for the exterior limits of the triangular truss and smaller diameters for the interior members. This alleviates some issues where multiple members must be joined at the same panel point in the truss. The trusses were prefabricated so that they could be simply joined on site at their end points. This level of off-site fabrication allowed for increased quality control and precision in creating the welds.

The spacing of the vertical members of adjacent trusses has been kept consistent to create a modular framework. An infill network of smaller round HSS members connects the trusses to each other and is also used along the wall to increase stability within the truss. Tabs have been welded onto the main truss to allow for a bolted connection of the X bracing members on site. Rectangular HSS members are also used within the truss itself.

The ultimate benefit of the construction type is the creation of a large column-free space. The 3m / 9.84ft-deep truss system satisfies the span requirements without requiring any supports mid-span. Services are run through the trusses.

## Centre Georges Pompidou, Paris, France | Renzo Piano and Richard Rogers

The international competition held in 1972 for the design of the Centre Georges Pompidou in Paris, France brought the High Tech Movement to the architectural forefront. Prior to this time, High Tech buildings tended to be smaller in scale and complexity, British in locale, and rare. The Pompidou Center follows the "extruded" typology, maintaining a column-free interior space with structural supports and services relegated to the exterior side walls. The nature of the design of the truss system used to support the floors was to create a multi-story building that provided a column-free space beneath the truss to house the exhibits and a space above and within the truss to run any internal services. The column-free space allowed for maximum flexibility in planning changing exhibits.

Where early High Tech architecture derived its expression from exposing highly articulated steel structural systems and revealed servicing on the interior of the building, the Pompidou Center designers chose to run the major mechanical services and ducts on the outside of the structure, leaving the interior freer for modifications to exhibit designs. The steel structure was the only part of the building designed with permanency in mind. The floors and transportation systems were created to be able to be moved if required, allowing for the building to change over time. This concept ran counter to the design of almost all buildings constructed to date, for which permanency and durability would have been a given – particularly for museums prior to this point.

Where Sainsbury made predominant use of standard steel shapes that were fabricated into repetitive custom trusses, the Pompidou Center designers created a comprehensive suite of custom components. Both buildings place the entrance on the side of the building, making minimal inflection into the rhythm and presence of the structural grid.

The "extruded" type can be characterized by the Centre Georges Pompidou in Paris, France, designed by Renzo Piano and Richard Rogers. The multi-storey variant of the clear-spanning truss is easily read in this end view of the building. The public side of the building is to the left and the service side to the right.

The façade of the building that addresses the public square is structurally light and transparent-looking, in contrast to the traditional stone façades in the neighborhood.

The extruded layout of the structural framing system has no inherent stability along the length of the building. Steel-rod X bracing is added in every bay to provide this stability. You can see a layered language of connection details that, although not identical to each other, begin to form a coherent approach. The detail at the "hub" must allow the intersection of numerous elements. The ring connector has a round cover plate to hide the access to the interior to complete the bolted connections.

The outrigger elements by which the walkway and mechanical service systems are suspended from the main frame are called "*gerberettes*". These specialty cast pieces were fabricated in Germany and shipped to the site. They are 11 tonnes apiece. The larger elements in this project brought the issue of scale to the forefront of the design and logistical issues for both fabrication and erection of the building.

The suspension system from which hang the transportation tubes uses a series of connectors. These are created from circular plate sections in order to resolve the juncture of multiple elements with varying angles of entry to a point. This type of bolted pin connection would also ease erection issues.

The interior of the building leaves the truss structure exposed and provides for unobstructed space for program.

## THE "GRID/BAY" TYPOLOGY

The main idea of the grid typology was to develop a prefabricated kit of parts that could be deployed to create a very regular framework, allowing the building plan to extend in any direction. This breaks from the restricted character of the extruded type that would only allow linear plans. Although much extra expense was involved in the design and production of the new unique elements, certain savings were to be had through mass production and the creation of a fairly regular plan. Although the grid was uniform and potentially non-directional, the spanning members that supported the roof deck adhered to a direction that could be used to assist in lateral stability; e.g., if the bay sizes were not square, then the beams would span over the shorter distance.

### Renault Centre, Swindon, England | Norman Foster

The expandable grid can be characterized by the Renault Centre in Swindon, designed by Norman Foster in 1980–82. Ove Arup contributed to the execution of the project, this engineering practice taking an international leading role in the development of many high-profile technologically advanced projects. Renault was based upon a regular grid and a true "kit of parts", each bay identical to the next. The selection of members included round HSS for the column supports and modified wide-flange sections for the horizontal beams. Material was removed from the neutral axis of the beams, the circular holes adding to the texture of the exposed frame. The circular motif was continued in the shape of the plate tabs that were welded to a collar around the column to which the beams were attached. This type of development of a consistent language that could be applied to all connections, without actually forcing them to be identical, is a concept that continues to inform current exposed steel design.

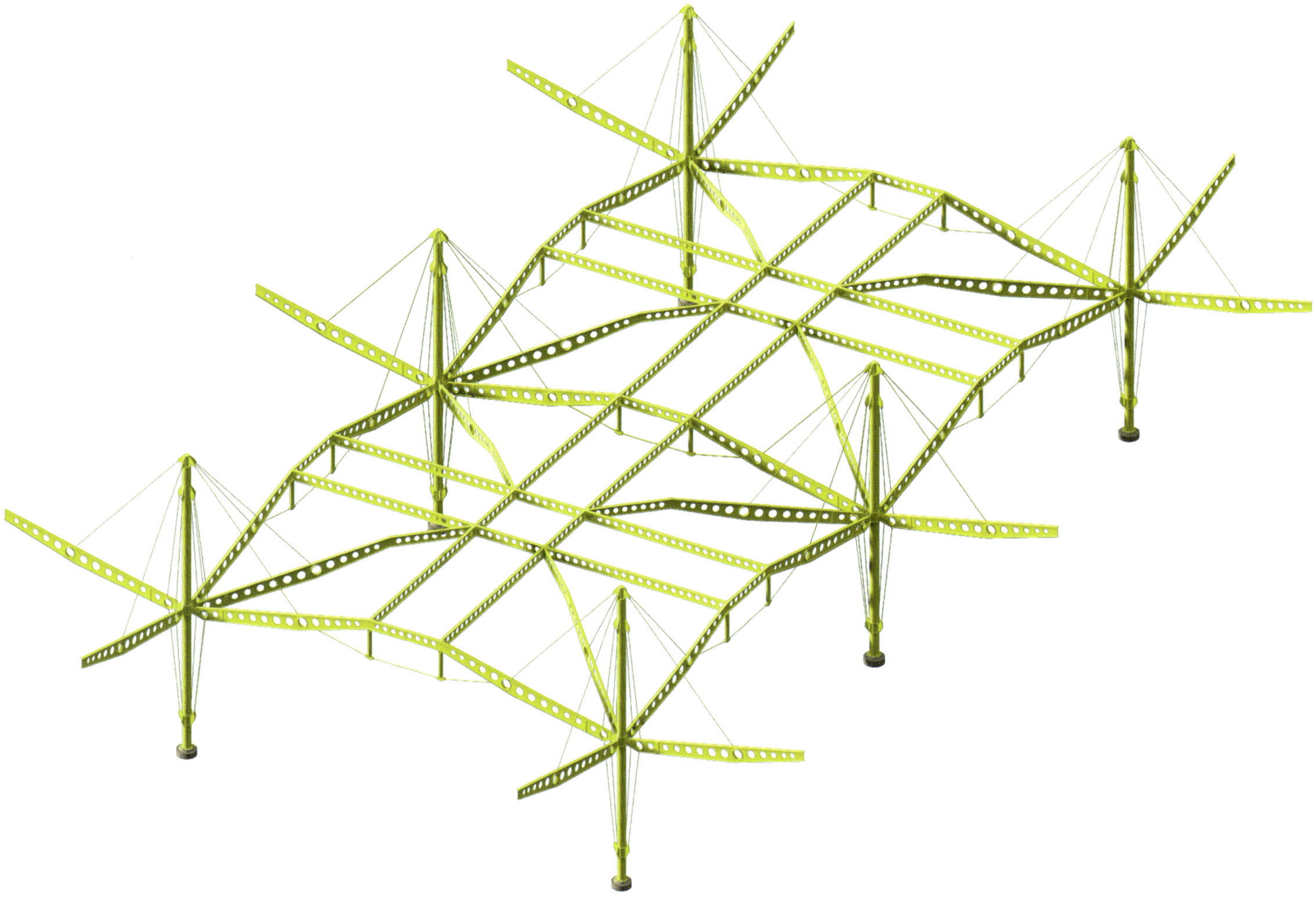

An isometric view of the typical column for the Renault Centre. The modularity of the building is based upon the repetition of this element in an extending grid. Although each detail is quite articulated, there is economy to be gained in the industrialization of the fabrication due to repetition.

This detail at the top of the tower has served as a precedent for many subsequent mast designs. The round tubular column is set with a "capital". Radiating triangulated sections of plate steel have been welded to the top as the means to disperse the loads and create a detail that is adequate to facilitate the connection of the incoming tensile members.

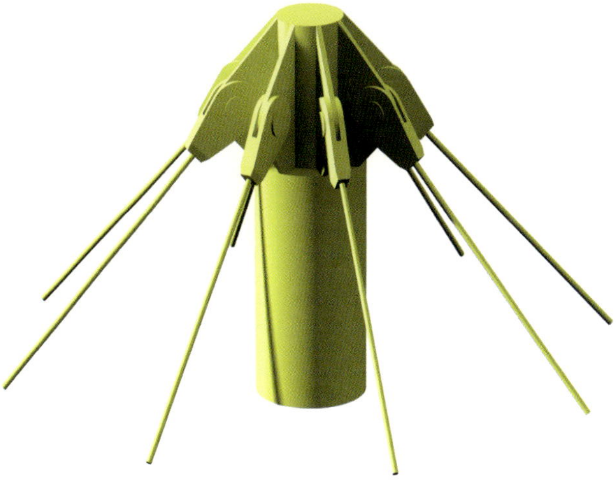

Detail of the collar illustrating the design of the collar and use of reinforcing around the cut-outs to facilitate the connection of the tension rods. This additional material is necessary to avoid punching shear. The connection sets a precedent for the division between shop welding and site bolting.

This view of the upper collar shows how the connection language is subtly modified to suit the reduced complexity of the intersection, yet keeps to the same motif. The rotation permitted in the pin connections both acknowledges that they are "hinges" and allows for some adjustment during erection.

## The Menil Collection, Houston, TX, USA | Renzo Piano

The expandable grid typology as used in the Menil Collection varies from the non-directional system as used in Foster's Renault Centre and instead chooses to use directional spanning members as its means of daylight control. Although the plan of the building is rectangular, the style of the plan and design of the members would theoretically allow for expansion of the bay system in any direction. Piano's approach to High Tech was different from that of many of his contemporaries in terms of his use of alternate materials as well as a softer language in the detailing.

Exterior view of The Menil Collection, Houston, TX, USA, constructed 1982–86, showing the external steel frame and trellis that surrounds the building. Much attention was paid in the design of the gallery to the management of the harsh Houston sunlight.

Left: This view of the structure shows the connection between the wide-flange columns and the articulated truss support system. The detail for the "capital" of the column is created by adding wide-flange sections to the main support. These hollow boxes provide for the bolted connection between the cast truss and the vertical load path.

Right: Detailed view of the junction between the truss that runs the width of the building and the triangulated cast frames from which are hung the ferro-concrete light scoops. Although each of the vertical supports for the nearly flat custom-glazed roof system is highly specialized and articulated, some economy was possible through mass production and bolting instead of site welding.

The flexibility of the grid/bay planning of the building is evident as the exterior walls of the building step back, leaving the canopy intact, to create a courtyard at the entrance to the building. The setback creates a relatively informal side entry to the museum.

This interior view shows the way the repetitive roof structure continues over the exterior courtyard, allowing for flexibility in the creation of the gallery volume, even with regard to the placement of the environmental enclosure.

## THE "TOWER-AND-TENSILE" TYPOLOGY

The development of the expression of the tensile capabilities of steel in early High Tech buildings is perhaps the most flamboyant aspect of their design. From a purely structural perspective none of this is necessary. The use of towers and tension cables or rods to support roofs and canopies could more economically have been accomplished with some simple columns. This is, however, an element of design that has provided huge potential for the development of connections and assemblies that showcase the tensile capabilities of this material – an attribute that is not shared by any other common construction material. This will be further discussed in Chapter 11: Tension Structures and Spaceframes. These early examples initiated experimentation with connection design that has influenced exposed steel detailing to the present. It is an aspect of design that has found widespread use in mainstream buildings, with particular reference to the construction of canopies and "cable assisted cantilevers".

### Oxford Ice Rink, Oxford, England | Nicholas Grimshaw

The "tower-and-tensile" system model can be characterized by the Oxford Ice Rink designed by Nicholas Grimshaw in 1984. The portal-framed column-and-beam sections spanning across the rink are supported at their mid-span by a pair of rectangular hollow structural steel sections that in turn are supported at four tensile support points that connect back to two towers, one at each end of the building. The towers are stabilized at each side by tension tiedowns and ballasted at each end by massive concrete piers.

The suite of details illustrated for the tower and associated tensile system demonstrates the interconnectivity that must be recognized between all of the pieces during the design of the connections. The diameter of the tower had to accommodate the attachment of the tension members at its top. The diameter of the column also fits between the pair of HSS beams that hold up the roof. Had the tower not been designed as a tension/truss member (when it would normally be a compression member), and had it a larger diameter, then it would have altered the dimensions and methods of connection of all other joints in the system. The steel system on the Ice Rink has been treated as a clear industrial design problem that must also satisfy engineering load-path requirements.

The roadside view of the Oxford Ice Rink, Oxford, England. The glazed end wall permits natural lighting of the interior space.

**Although the materiality of the structure is indeed durable, the selection of finishes was not. The Oxford Ice Rink suffered substantial neglect leading to the need for significant repair to the skin. Fortunately for the facility, a contract was let in 2010 to a facilities management team that has promised to undertake the refurbishment of the rink.**

A view of the underside of the parallel HSS beams that run the full length of the building. The beams are separated by a same-sized HSS bridge that permits the attachment details to the tiedowns to be neatly integrated.

The detail of the pass-through of the diagonal tension members past the pair of HSS beams was the determining reference for some critical design dimensions. The size of the "hollows" at the box supports where the tension rods terminate had to be large enough to allow for the bolts to be tightened. In turn, the spacing between the HSS beams was based upon their ability to sit on either side of the vertical column.

This cylindrical concrete pier serves as the foundation and tiedown for the major tensile members as the load of the roof is balanced. Access is provided at the hollows of the box attachments for tightening the tension rods.

Detail of the tension connections to the top of the tower. The angled box sections that are welded to the round HSS column are dispersed to allow for the multiple connections to the single loading point as well as access to the interior of the boxes to attach the rods.

## Inmos Microprocessor Factory, Newport, Wales | Richard Rogers

The Inmos Microprocessor Factory, designed by Richard Rogers in 1982, uses a central spine of towers from which the roof structure is suspended. This provides for column-free spaces on either side of the organizational spine. The exterior steel elements that might appear to be columns are in fact tiedowns to prevent uplift of the roof due to wind forces. In a similar fashion to the "extruded" typology, this structure restricts the natural expansion of the building to a linear one. The dimension and nature of the central spine provides a place of entry to the building that is different from the informality of the side-entry models of the other early High Tech buildings discussed.

Overall view of the main stayed-tower module of the Inmos Microprocessor Factory in Wales by Richard Rogers. The long triangular trusses are supported by the cables that tension back to the central towers. To prevent wind uplift, they are tied down at the perimeter of the building.

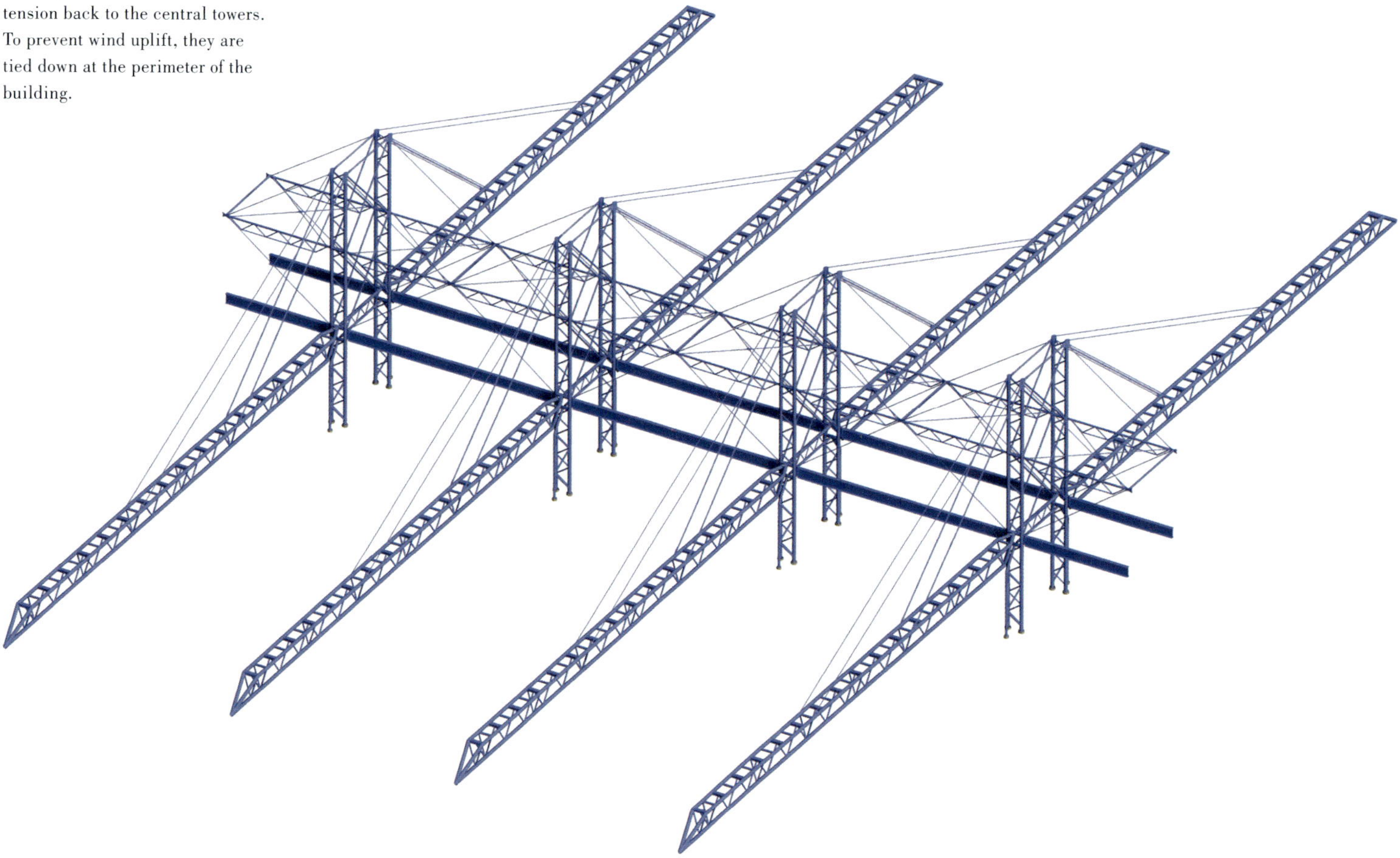

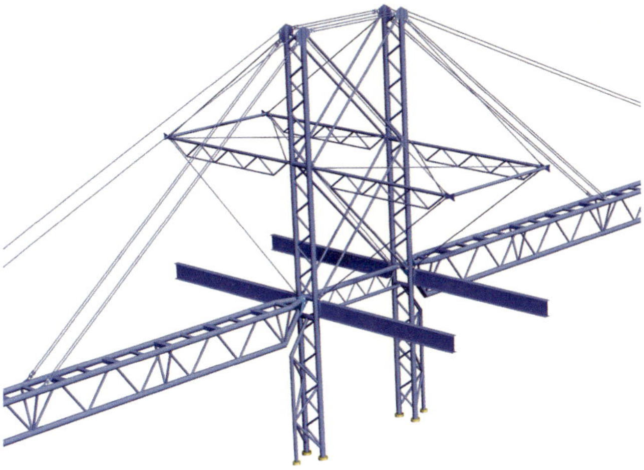

The legs of the central tower element are developed as triangular trusses. They transform into planar trusses at the roof level in order to resolve the simultaneous connection of the wide-flange beams, long triangular truss and planar trusses that connect the two vertical compression masts of the towers. Pin-type connections are employed to facilitate quick assembly of the building.

A detailed view of one of the central connections showing the use of fairly standard techniques involving lapped plates of steel. Although extensive welding was required to fabricate the trusses, almost none was required on site due to the method of assembling this structure.

Architecturally Exposed Structural Steel appeared as a specific typology in North America in the late 1980s. The International Terminal at Chicago O'Hare Airport, IL, USA by Murphy/Jahn Architects has been recognized as a turning point in its popularization of exposed steel. The project retains much of the energy and detailing of early High Tech projects, but with subtle changes that allow it to break from the more rigid formality of the types first established in Britain in the 1970s.

## *HIGH TECH BECOMES ARCHITECTURALLY EXPOSED STRUCTURAL STEEL (AESS)*

Early High Tech buildings stood distinctly apart from the balance of mainstream architecture of the same period, most of which employed reinforced concrete and concealed steel construction. It did assist in transporting exposed steel into more regular use, as architects and engineers became more comfortable with its appearance and more confident in its design, detailing and application. The buildings discussed in this chapter experimented with different member shapes and connection types and created a legacy and language of connection detailing that continues to be referenced, built upon and adapted for contemporary architecture.

One of the key aspects of High Tech architecture of the 1970s and 1980s that has been carried through to contemporary Architecturally Exposed Steel Construction is the differential application of member types to suit their loading requirements. Compressive members are stout, and tensile members are slender.

As consistently demonstrated through Structural Rationalist and High Tech design, steel construction is "elemental" in nature, and its artistry reliant on not only the appropriate choice of members (e.g. shapes versus tubes), but also heavily on the method of attachment. AESS steel design, like these earlier methods, requires detailing that can approach industrial design standards when creating joints between members. The structural requirements of shear and moment resistance must be accommodated, along with tighter dimensional tolerances, as well as larger design and aesthetic considerations such as balance, form, symmetry and economy.

Economy is an important design consideration. Many of the early High Tech projects were created for unusual clients with a desire to showcase innovation, even at an expense. Budgets are not always this generous. If the creation of connections requires an excessive degree of unique fabrication detailing, and the remediation and finishing of welds and natural steel surfaces, the designer can price the project out of existence. The method of preparation and finishing of the connections can also radically increase costs. A more thoughtful examination of the actual technical requirements for the creation of effective AESS projects will be taken up in detail in the following chapter.

## *RESULTANT BUILDING SCIENCE PROBLEMS*

Invention and experimentation with materials brings risks as well as rewards. Lightweight structures and materials have increased susceptibility to problems associated with weathering and corrosion over more historic heavy-mass materials.

Much of the early High Tech building took place in temperate climates. In many projects, the steel structure was either predominantly situated on the exterior of the building, or the structure penetrated the building in many locations. This poses some building science and thermal bridging issues. Adapting this style of building to an extreme climate with large diurnal and seasonal temperature swings creates sometimes insurmountable issues of thermal expansion and thermal bridging. If the steel penetrates the skin uninterrupted there can not only be excessive heat loss at the point of penetration but also condensation that can lead to corrosion. It is critical to address the local climate type and then detail the interface of the structural and cladding systems accordingly.

The choice of finish system and color also begins to become increasingly of issue. The early work of Mies van der Rohe, with its predominant choice of black as the finish color, might have exacerbated issues of thermal expansion, but not of weathering and wear. White paint tends to both show environmental grime and also necessitate more frequent maintenance to repair peeling paint. Regardless of these issues, it continues to be the most popular choice for finish and color. For detailed discussion of finish systems refer to Chapter 7: Coatings, Finishes and Fire Protection.

The elaborate steel canopy system that covers the passenger loading area at the Denver International Airport, CO, USA by Fentress Bradburn Architects presents ongoing maintenance issues due to the color of finish and outdoor exposure of the steel. Problems persist with the build-up of dirt and presence of pigeons. Transportation applications that are open to the environment often deal with these types of problems.

CHAPTER 6

---

# ARCHITECTURALLY EXPOSED STRUCTURAL STEEL (AESS): DESIGN AND DETAILING REQUIREMENTS

---



Architecturally Exposed Structural Steel, such as that used in the Reichstag Building of the German Bundestag in Berlin, Germany designed by Foster + Partners, has significantly higher requirements for fabrication, erection and finishing than regular structural steel. These requirements must inform the design from the outset of the project and form the central element of communication between the architect, engineer and fabricator.

*Significant credit is given to the members of the National and Regional AESS Committees of the Canadian Institute of Steel Construction for the development of these standards.*

## *STANDARD STRUCTURAL STEEL VERSUS AESS*

Structural steel framing can be employed in both hidden and exposed systems. The choice to expose or hide the steel is based on decisions surrounding the desired architectural expression, type or character of finish desired, type of building use, and fire protection requirements. The level of fire protection required is a function of building size and use as relates to the level of hazard. Where high-hazard conditions prevail, the steel is normally protected by concrete, gypsum and coatings that obscure any exposure of the steel. If the level of hazard is low, the steel systems can be left relatively exposed, fire protection being provided by intumescent coatings and fire suppression systems. *It is necessary to consult local building and fire codes to ascertain these limitations prior to selecting AESS.*

Standard framing systems, as discussed in Chapter 3, form the basis for further elaboration and the development of steel systems with a level of exposure that creates the architectural character of the building.

The concealed standard structural steel for the Bay Adelaide Tower in Toronto, ON, Canada is designed to be covered with spray fireproofing and gypsum board. Therefore, it must respond only to structural load path requirements for its detailing.

Left: Although the massive steel truss at the Baltimore Convention Center in Baltimore, MD, USA is clad in gypsum board for fire protection, its overall design and proportion is a powerful part of the design of the space. While it is not architecturally exposed, it still requires exceptional coordination among the architect, engineer and fabricator.

Right: The triangular HSS trusses that provide the bracing for the glazed wall of the Beijing International Airport, China, must respond not only to load-path issues but achieve a high level of workmanship in terms of design, fabrication, erection and finish, as this AESS can be viewed at very close range and constitutes the architectural expression of the space.

# *WHAT IS AESS?*

Architecturally Exposed Structural Steel (AESS) is steel that must be designed to be both structurally sufficient to support the primary needs of the structure of the building, canopies or ancillary structures, while at the same time be exposed to view, hence constituting a significant part of the architectural language of the building. The design, detailing and finish requirements of AESS will typically exceed those of standard structural steel, which is normally concealed by other finishes. This naturally increases the cost to design, detail, fabricate, erect and finish AESS systems.

Whereas designers tend not to be involved in connection issues for concealed structural systems, exposed systems become the architectural trademark of the building, hence requiring much involvement. Unfortunately, not all designers are adequately informed either to choose appropriate methods of attachment or to the cost implications of their choices.

The surge in the use of AESS has created a paradigm shift in the sequential communication that usually takes place in a more conventional building where the steel structure is hidden. The paradigm shift centers on the simple fact that a "nice-looking connection" or a "smooth surface" has very different meanings, depending on whether you are talking to an architect, an engineer or a fabricator. Such a situation can create a misalignment of expectations in terms of what can be accomplished within specific budget limitations.

# *PRIMARY FACTORS THAT DEFINE AESS*

AESS has significantly different design criteria than standard steel framing. Early High Tech use of exposed steel and early AESS applications tended toward a very high-end product that was typically constructed using predominantly custom-fabricated pieces with high-quality detailing and finish throughout. It must be recognized that some projects can be priced out of possibility as the expectations of finish outstrip the project budget. In order to design and detail AESS appropriate to a specific project, a differentiated approach must recognize the following conditions.

→ Distance and Visibility: if you cannot see the steel up close or touch it, the finish requirements can be softened.
→ Bolted versus welded connections: different connection types result in different aesthetics, requiring differing levels of finish.
→ Tolerances required at fabrication and erection: different tolerances are needed as a function of the scope and complexity of the project, but typically tighter tolerances are needed for AESS than for standard structural steel framing.
→ Access to detail to perform required finish: the greater concern for workmanship may mean altering the detail or its location in order to allow access for different types of tools. Highly articulated connections or details need to be constructible and maintainable.
→ Degree of expression: the complexity of structure and connections will impact the detailing and cost.
→ Size and shape of structural elements: W (Universal) and HSS shapes have different connection requirements, and their use infers a different approach to detailing and finish.
→ Interior or exterior setting: this includes weathering issues, cleaning and maintenance access, the need to fire protect, and the potential for impact damage.
→ Paint finish, corrosion resistance, fire-protection: depending on the relative thickness of the finish material, more or less care may be required when preparing the surface, edges and welding of the steel.

The primary factors of influence can be further summarized as "Form, Fit and Finish" (Walter Koppelaar, Walters Inc. Steel Fabricators, Hamilton, ON, Canada). A large amount of emphasis is placed on the Form of the steel in the design. The overall form may vary greatly from regular framing and include curves, unusual angles or three-dimensional elements. Bolted or welded connections may sometimes be chosen less for their structural capabilities or ease of erection than for their appearance as relating to the overall intention and the form of the design.

"Two Different Trees" – the remarkable contrast in the requirements of AESS can be seen in the tree structures of the Reagan International Airport in Washington, D.C., USA by Cesar Pelli Architect (left) and the University of Guelph Science Building in Guelph, ON, Canada by Young + Wright Architects (right). The airport trees are fabricated to appear very faceted, while the Guelph trees are free from any evidence of connections and finished in unforgiving high-gloss paint.

Highly articulated steel structures are by their nature more difficult to Fit. There is significantly less play in the connections, and accumulated errors can result in overall misalignment. This need to ensure accuracy, ease of fabrication, as well as bottom-line constructability, puts greater pressure on the details and requires narrower tolerances throughout the entire project. Tighter tolerances will carry through when the exposed steel framing must coordinate with other trades, in particular, areas of significant glazing and curtain wall. The use of stainless-steel spider connections for structural glass systems puts additional pressure on allowable tolerances. If exposed steel is used with heavy timber or glue-laminated systems, then the fit must also take into account the differential movements and erection idiosyncrasies of these other materials.

While the Finish might be the last phase of construction, the selection of the finish must take place at the beginning of the AESS design process. Finishes will vary in exposed steel both as a function of the design intention as well as issues relating to weathering, interior or exterior exposure and fire protection. A high-gloss finish will reveal every imperfection and will require more fastidious fabrication. A thicker intumescent coating will conceal many surface imperfections. Galvanizing itself has issues with consistency of finish, and its selection may accompany a less polished selection of details. The bottom line for the contract is that both time and money will be wasted if the level of fabrication care greatly exceeds the nature of the finish.

This connection at the Bloomberg Headquarters in New York, NY, USA, designed by Cesar Pelli Architects, uses a thicker intumescent coating. The coating masks some of the detail and texture of the welds used on the truss, obviating the need for grinding to make them smooth. Had the truss required a high-gloss finish, different treatment of the welded connections might have been called for, resulting in increased costs for the structure.

Three primary physical conditions feed into the detailing of the structure.

Viewing Distance: 6m / 20ft is chosen as a critical dimension to differentiate whether an occupant is able to scrutinize the finish from close range and even touch the product. 6m represents a normal height of a high ceiling. The ability to see the structure from close range can impact the required level of workmanship of the finished product. It makes little sense to grind welds on a structure many meters out of eyeshot. When designing atrium spaces, it is important to also use this measurement in the horizontal and downward direction, as view across or down a space is as critical as view upward. Where steel is viewed from above, care must also be taken to detail the steel to avoid the build-up of grime and trash, as well as contemplate access for regular cleaning and maintenance. Viewing distance can also impact the requirements of the surface finish on the steel members. Some natural blemishes in the steel from the manufacturing, fabrication or mill processes will not be noticeable at a distance.

Type or Function of the Building: The exposed steel over an ice rink and the exposed steel in an airport are likely to have different aesthetic and finish requirements. The program of a building and the range of spaces within a project should be examined to assess whether a range of types of AESS needs to be specified. The exposed roof trusses may use a lower-end AESS and the columns or base details a higher-end AESS product. If this is clearly marked on the contract drawings, the fabricator can adjust the bid according to the appropriate level of finish.

Range of Potential Cost Increase: There is a range of increase in the cost to fabricate and erect the AESS over the cost to fabricate and erect standard structural steel. Additional time is involved in fabrication. The erection costs will also increase as a function of the complexity of the steel, the degree to which complex connections can be fabricated in the shop, transportation, access and staging area concerns and increased tolerance requirements to fit the steel. This increases the time to erect the steel and the cost as the labor portion associated with the material grows.

## *CATEGORIES OF AESS*

*Although this section refers specifically to the Canadian system, the idea of differentiated categories is applicable world-wide as they directly incorporate changes in finish and detailing that respect viewing distance, function and cost. For more information and specifications visit:* www.cisc.ca/aess. *For more information on the SSPC rating system, see Chapter 7: Coatings, Finishes and Fire Protection.*

### AESS 1 – BASIC ELEMENTS

AESS 1 – Basic Elements is the first step above standard structural steel. This type of application would be suitable for basic elements which require enhanced workmanship. This type of exposed structure could be found for instance in roof trusses for arenas, warehouses, big-box stores and canopies and should only require a low-cost premium in the range of 20% to 60%, due to relatively large viewing distance as well as the lower-profile nature of the architectural spaces in which it is used.

Left: The Ricoh Center Arena in Toronto, ON, Canada uses trusses for its roof. Less precision in fabrication would be required, given its use.

Right: The skylight framing at Les Ailes Shopping Center in Montreal, QC, Canada is located far from view. The truss connections are less finely detailed, saving fabrication cost, although the overall appearance and design of the truss itself is handsomely done. Skylights are often backlit by the sky so that their detail is masked. This is reversed at night if uplighting is used, which tends to accentuate the steel framing against a black background.

AESS 1 applications will see the use of fairly straightforward section types such as W, HSS and often Open Web Steel Joist (OWSJ) and exposed profiled decking. Generally, this type of framing might appear similar to basic structural steel applications except that it is left exposed to view. Therefore, more care is required to ensure that the standard structural members are aligned in a uniform way, spacing is kept consistent and the surfaces of the members are properly prepared to accept uniform finishes and coatings. A greater level of consistency in the use of connections, bolts and welds is also required.

AESS 1 characteristics include:

- The surface preparation of the steel must meet the standard of the Society for Protective Coatings, SSPC-SP 6. Prior to blast-cleaning, any deposits of grease or oil are to be removed by solvent cleaning, SSPC-SP 1. All sharp edges are to be ground smooth. Rough surfaces are to be deburred and ground smooth. Sharp edges resulting from flame-cutting, grinding and especially shearing are to be softened.
- There should be a continuous weld appearance for all welds, with an emphasis on "appearance". Intermittent welds can be made to look continuous either with additional welding, caulking or body filler. For corrosive environments all joints should be seal-welded. The seams of hollow structural sections would be acceptable as produced.
- It is assumed that bolted connections will use standard structural bolts (including tension control (TC) bolts. When bolting, the heads should all be located on one side of the connection but need not be fastidiously aligned. There should also be consistency among connections.
- Weld splatters, slivers and surface discontinuities are to be removed, as these will mar the surface and are liable to show through the final coating. Weld projection up to 2mm/.08in is acceptable for butt- and plug-welded joints.
- These types of applications may or may not require special fire protective design. This is determined as a function of the use of the space. In some situations the steel may be left completely unprotected or sprinklered and will need to receive only a paint finish. Intumescent coatings could be used where the rating would be one hour or greater. The detailing on AESS 1 elements should not be greatly impacted by the relative thickness or finish of the intumescent coating, as much of this type of steel will be located well above eye level and out of range of touch.

As it is anticipated that many AESS projects will specify more than one category of steel, it will be common to specify AESS 1 for the ceiling elements of a design where the distance to view is in the 6m or greater range, and specify a different class of AESS for those elements, like columns, that are located at a closer proximity.

## AESS 2 – FEATURE ELEMENTS

AESS 2 – Feature Elements includes structure that is intended to be viewed at a distance of > 6m/20ft. The process requires basically good fabrication practices with enhanced treatment of weld, connection and fabrication detail, tolerances for gaps and copes. This type of AESS might be found in retail and architectural applications where a low to moderate cost premium in the range of 40% to 100% over the cost of standard structural steel would be expected.

The galvanized steel framework that supports the canopy at the Stata Center at MIT in Cambridge, MA, USA by Frank Gehry Architect can be designed as AESS 2, due both to its distance from the viewer as well as the choice of galvanization.

In the case of the National Works Yard in Vancouver, BC, Canada by Omicron Engineering, the use of exposed steel has reduced finishes and helped in achieving a LEED™ Gold rating. The predominant section choice is a W shape and the detailing has been kept fairly standard. The specialty details that support the roof structure and the Parallam® wood beams remove the details from close scrutiny. The primary connection choice to join major sections is bolting; however, the elements themselves have been shop-welded prior to shipping. Although the steel is able to be viewed more closely from the upper-floor level, a decision was made to keep the tectonic of the W sections and bolted connections consistently, with regard to the use of the building as a Works Yard office. Some specialty details have been added to the repertoire in the support of the PV skylights and the wood structure.

**AESS 2 will generally be found in buildings where the expressed structure forms an important, integral part of the architectural design intent. The defining parameter of viewing distance greater than 6m infers to use this sort of steel in high-level roof or ceiling applications. For this reason, AESS 2 steel might be specified for the distant components of a structure, and higher-quality AESS for the low-level elements of the structure. These should be clearly marked on the drawing sets so that the treatments can be differentiated and the respective cost premiums separated out.**

AESS 2 characteristics include all of the characteristics of AESS 1 and also:

→ Visual Samples may or may not be required, depending on the scope of the project.
→ One-half-standard fabrication tolerances as compared to standard structural steel are required, recognizing the increased importance of "Fit" when assembling these more complex components.
→ Fabrication marks (number markings put on the members during the fabrication and erection process) should not be apparent, as the final finish appearance is more critical on these feature elements.
→ The welds should be uniform and smooth, calling for a higher level of quality control in the welding process as the viewing proximity is closer.

It will be more common to see W or HSS members specified for this category rather than more industrial-looking members such as OWSJ. This type of application may use a combination of bolted or welded connections. As the viewing distance is great, there is normally less concern about concealing the connection aspects of larger pieces to each other, hence no hidden connections are called for.

The welded connections of the fabricated sections on this truss at the Sony Center in Berlin, Germany by Helmut Jahn have not been ground as smooth as if the truss were situated closer to viewing level.

The cost premium for AESS 2 ranges from 40% to 100%. There may be lower costs associated with the clean use of standard structural shapes with bolted or simple welded connections and higher costs associated with the use of HSS shapes, complex geometries and a predominance of welded connections. As one of the common applications of AESS 2 will be for roof, skylight or ceiling support systems, the fire protection method must be known from the outset of the project. If intumescent coatings are used, these can help to conceal any inconsistencies in surface conditions.

## AESS 3 – FEATURE ELEMENTS

AESS 3 – Feature Elements includes structures that will be viewed at a distance of ≤ 6m/20ft. This would be suitable for elements where the designer is comfortable allowing the viewer to see the art of metalworking. The welds should be generally smooth but visible and some grind marks would be acceptable. Tolerances must be tighter than normal standards. As this structure is normally viewed closer than 6m, it might also frequently be subject to touch by the public, therefore warranting a smoother, more uniform and more durable finish and appearance. This type of structure could be found in airports, shopping centers, hospitals or lobbies and could be expected to incur a moderate cost premium that could range from 60% to 150% over standard structural steel as a function of the complexity and level of final finish desired.

AESS 3 characteristics include all of the characteristics of AESS 1 and 2 and also:

→ The mill marks are to be removed so as not to be visible in the finished product. Removal of these marks would typically be accomplished by grinding.
→ Butt and plug welds are to be ground smooth and filled to create a smooth surface finish. Caulking or body filler is acceptable.
→ The normal weld seam that is the product of creating HSS shapes is to be oriented for reduced visibility. In general, the seams are to be oriented away from view in a consistent manner.
→ Cross-sectional abutting surfaces are to be aligned. The matching of abutting cross-sections shall be required. Offsets in alignment are considered to be unsightly.
→ Joint gap tolerances are to be minimized. A clear distance between abutting members of 3mm / 1/8in is required.
→ AESS 3 feature elements may or may not require all-welded connections, acknowledging that a particular aesthetic might purposefully choose bolted connections.

When AESS structural elements are brought into close range for view as well as potentially for touch, it is necessary for the project team to come to a clear understanding about the level of finish that is both required and expected of the steel. The natural look of welds that would be out of view in AESS 2 steel will now be visible to the user in the space. Simple bolted connections may need to be designed to look more artful if they are to become part of the language of the architecture. Connections will come under closer scrutiny, hence their design, tolerances and uniform appearance will become more important and the workmanship required to improve these beyond both standard structural steel and AESS 1 and 2 could have a significant impact on the cost of the overall structure. If the required attributes or characteristics of the steel are not thoughtfully considered, the AESS for the project can easily be priced out of viability.

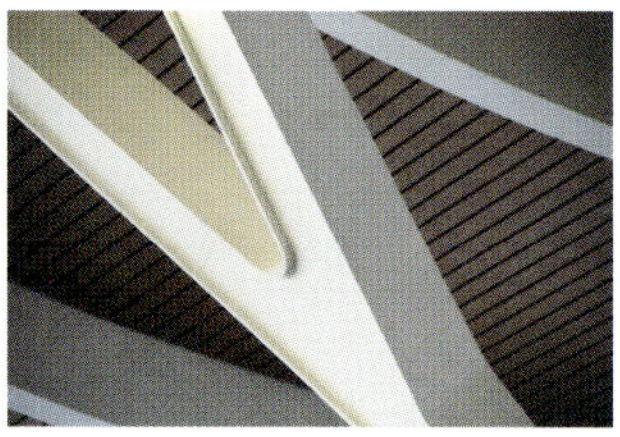

Left: Airport architecture makes predominant use of AESS 3 for all but the highest-profile projects. Pudong International Airport in Shanghai, China by Paul Andreu has steel that is both near to view and distant, and whose workmanship is highlighted by both the contrast in the color of the steel to the ceiling plane beyond, as well as by the lighting.

Right: Not all seams in the plate elements that make up the forked supports need be ground completely smooth, depending on the distance from view, but overall the fabrication quality is very good. These shop welds are the result of the specialty fabrication of these pieces from plate steel.

The cost premium to be found in AESS 3 steel will depend greatly upon the types of members chosen, the nature of the connections and the desire of the designer to either conceal or express the materiality of the steel itself. Effort will be put into further preparation of the surface to increase its smoothness to ensure that some of the natural finish on the steel and millmarks do not show through the paint.

When welds cannot be done in the shop, where conditions are more controlled and jigs can be used for precise alignment of the components, a large amount of site welding of complex elements will result in cost premiums. Some site welds may not be of the same quality as can be expected of shop welds. It would be expected that the welds would be of a higher quality than those for AESS 2 structures. AESS 3 welds will be expected to have a very uniform appearance. Although some touch-up grinding of the welds may be required to ensure uniformity, complete grinding of all welds would not be included in this category of steel. It is assumed that good-quality uniform welds would be left exposed.

Where bolted connections are employed, more care will be taken to ensure that there is an aesthetically based uniformity in the connections. This will likely require more fabrication time and potentially more material. Simple approaches such as ensuring that all bolt heads are located on uniform sides of the connections can greatly enhance the details with little extra cost. If bolted connections are required for erection ease but are visually unacceptable, concealed connections can be employed to give the appearance of a seamless or welded connection without the associated price tag. For these types of connections the attaching plates are kept within the general line of the members so that cover plates can be attached over the bolted elements. For exterior application, concealed connections must be made weatherproof to prevent hidden rust.

Left: This close view of the bolted connections of the War Museum shows a combined use of welding and exposed bolts that have been purposefully chosen to create the aesthetic of the structure.

Right: The Canadian War Museum in Ottawa, ON, Canada designed by Raymond Moriyama uses HSS sections with custom connections to create the rugged look of Regeneration Hall in emulation of a tortured landscape. Not all close view AESS need be fabricated from entirely custom materials. A combination of standard structural shapes and specialty connections will work.

Underlying AESS 3 steel is the idea that it is possible to change the appearance of the final product to make it smoother to the eye without always necessarily using more expensive fabrication techniques.

### AESS 4 – SHOWCASE ELEMENTS

AESS 4 – Showcase Elements or "dominant" elements should be used where the designer intends that the form is the prevalent feature showing in an element. All welds are ground and filled; edges are ground square and true. All surfaces are sanded and filled. Tolerances of these fabricated forms are more stringent, generally to half of standard tolerance for standard structural steel. All surfaces would be glove-smooth. The cost premium of these elements would be high and could range from 100% to 250% over the cost of standard structural steel – completely as a function of the nature of the details, complexity of construction and selected finishes.

AESS 4 represents the highest standard quality expectations of AESS product, and the applications are diverse. There is a wide variety of member types employed, each for their specific purpose within the structure or connection. Many of the column or spanning members are custom-fabricated. In some cases this may be due to the very large size and structural capacity required of the member. In other cases it is due to the particular architectural style desired in the exposed structure. Many of the members tend to employ steel plate that has been custom-cut to idiosyncratic geometries. Unless based on a combination of simple "circular holes" and straight cuts, such geometries will increase the fabrication costs of the project.

Brookfield Place in Toronto, ON, Canada, designed by Santiago Calatrava, has glove-smooth finish steel at the pedestrian level that shows no signs of fabrication. This fully welded AESS 4-type material is topped by steel canoes that, due to their relatively large distance from view, use bolted connections and could be classed as AESS 3.

Left: A closer view of the connections at Brookfield Place shows the transition from welded to bolted connections as a function of viewing distance. These sit high in the atrium.

Right: The Newseum in Washington, D.C., USA by Ennead Architects creates its AESS through fairly exclusive use of specialty plate steel to fabricate the vertical trusses. The sharp edges and clean lines are characteristic of high-end AESS installations. Crisp edges require more care in the application of coatings to ensure good multi-coat coverage at the corners. This truss is located away from danger of chipping due to pedestrian traffic.

Left: The connection to the main arches that span the departures level at Pearson International Airport in Toronto, ON, Canada by SOM Architects is formed by a specialty piece called a "wishbone". The wishbones were shipped in one piece from the fabrication shop. Pin connections at the base connection to the reinforced concrete abutments and at the top to the roof arches simplified erection. It is interesting to note that one of these members was used as the visual sample for the architect's approval and was incorporated into the building in spite of minor modifications made to the balance of the pieces.

Right: A view of the "crotch" of the "wishbone" as it connects to the roof arch, showing the multiple layering of plate steel that has been skillfully designed to reinforce the member. The piece also distributes the load from the major arch, so that the thrust forces from the arch are partially balanced at each concrete abutment, making for a stronger end connection.

On many of these projects the edges of the steel have been finished to be very crisp and precise. The straightness of the line of these members is a critical aspect of their fabrication.

The characteristics for AESS 4 include all previous and:

→ The normal weld seam in an HSS member should not be apparent. This may require grinding of the weld seam.
→ Welds are to be contoured and blended. In addition to a contoured and blended appearance, welded transitions between members are also required to be contoured and blended.
→ Steel surfaces are to be filled and sanded. Filling and sanding is intended to remove or cover any steel surface imperfections. This particular point can incur a high cost premium and is a particular case in point that all AESS need not be created equal.
→ Weld show-through must be minimized. The imperfect back face of the welded element created by the welding process can be minimized by hand-grinding the backside of the weld. The degree of weld show-through is a function of weld size and material.

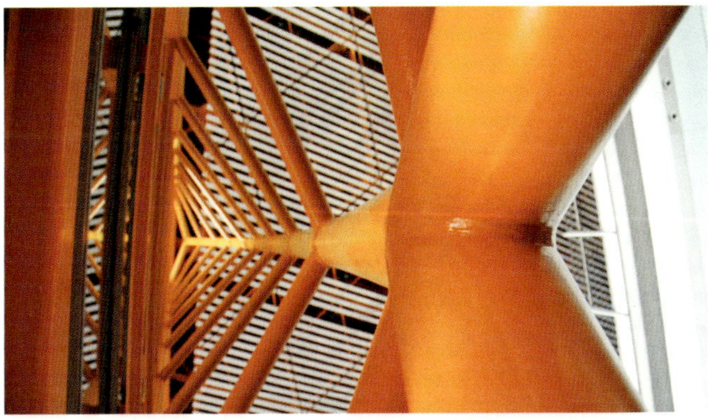

Some AESS 4 is characterized by extreme smoothness and no sharp edges, as can be seen in the trusses at the Beijing International Airport, China.

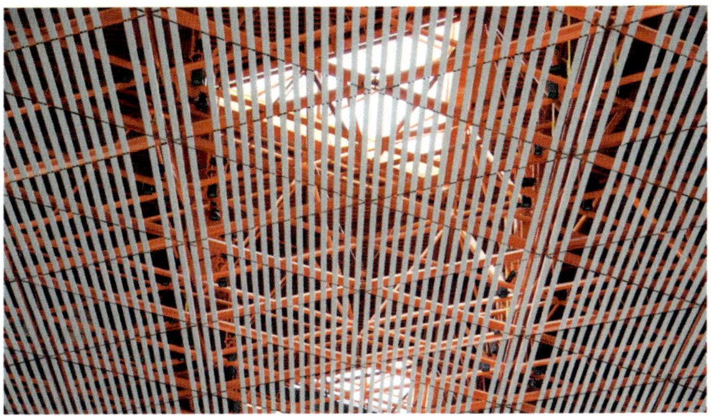

The roof of the Beijing International Airport is comprised of a space frame located above a linear suspended ceiling to permit daylight to filter through but to obscure any direct view to the detail of the steel. Therefore, the steel in this portion of the building can be constructed to lower-quality specifications. Color has been used to provide visual continuity.

This type of AESS is often also painted in the fabrication shop to achieve the best quality finish. Protection of these members during transportation and erection is critical in order to prevent undue damage to the finish.

CUSTOM ELEMENTS

There are certain applications of AESS that will require a customized approach to design and specification. With increases in the reuse of steel for sustainably-minded projects, a unique set of criteria will come into play. Requirements will address the presence of existing finishes, corrosion, inconsistencies between members and whether the project desires to showcase the reuse or blend the material with new material. As some historic steel is fastened with rivets, different treatment may be required where new connections are mixed with old in order to create coherence (see Chapter 14: Steel and Sustainability).

Custom AESS will also include steel that is more sculptural in nature. In some instances, the nature of the steel is intended to be a highlight of the finished project and in other cases, the nature of the steel is to be concealed and the final product has a more plastic expression. The latter may require a higher degree of finish and workmanship than would be required even for structures in the AESS 4 range.

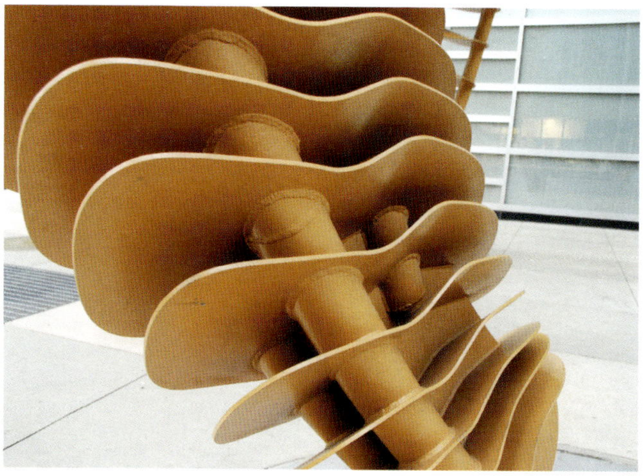

Left: The Ram's Horn, designed by artist John McEwen and fabricated by Walters Inc., is a wind-mitigation device located between highrise towers in downtown Calgary, AB, Canada. An actual ram's horn formed the reference for the steel fabricator to replicate the "feel" and texture in steel. The plates and the evidence of welding to the round HSS section that joins the plates through the center was deliberate in order to add material texture to the piece.

Right: This detail of the Ram's Horn attests to the appreciation of the artist of the art of metal working. Steel is steel, welds are welds and in this custom work the tactile nature of the evidence of the fabrication process is deemed to add to the piece.

## STAINLESS STRUCTURAL STEEL

Stainless Structural Steel has different specifications and particular issues that must be addressed to ensure a high quality of installation. While a painted structure can be retouched after erection damage, increased care must follow with stainless steel, as damage or surface scratching is less easily repaired. Stainless steel also requires the use of dedicated equipment. Any tools used to fabricate, cut or polish regular carbon steel must never be used on stainless steel, as they will embed particles of regular carbon steel in the stainless material and cause rust.

## MIXED CATEGORIES

Mixed Categories are to be expected on almost all projects. It will be very common to specify, based on the distance of view, lower-level categories for roof/ceiling framing elements and higher-level categories for columns and sections that are nearer to view and touch. A maximum of two types is to be expected. It is also possible to mix categories on individual elements, for instance for sections that have one side exposed to view/touch and the other buried or otherwise hidden from view. In this case a high level of finish may be required on the exposed AESS face and a finish as low as standard structural steel for the hidden face. This is of great financial benefit when finishing extremely large members.

The large triangular members that are part of the diagrid system for the Bow Encana Tower in Calgary, AB, Canada, designed by Foster + Partners and Zeidler Partnership, have very sharp edges on the front face that are designed to AESS 4 precision. As the rear face of the member will be embedded it is not designed to AESS specifications.

## DETAILING REQUIREMENTS

By their inherently exposed nature, AESS structures put a greater than normal emphasis on the design of connections. Although the details that are normally used for AESS structures include some fairly standard connection methods, these are mostly modified and enhanced. Connection types can be subdivided by structures that use W, C and L shapes, and those that use hollow sections. These typologies can be further subdivided by the choice to predominantly weld or bolt the connections. Plates can be worked into both types of connections. AESS connections will often incorporate specialty items such as rods and tensile connectors.

It is as a general rule better to maximize the number of connections, particularly welded connections that can be done in the shop, over those that must be done on site. There is more quality control in the shop. Jigs can be set up for repetitive assemblies which will ensure consistency in appearance and finish. It is easier to turn and fix the members into position for welding with crane assist. The application of primer and even finish painting is more efficiently done in the shop, even if it requires more care in subsequent handling.

In the end, the maximum size of member that can be transported to site will often determine the scope of shop-fabricated connections and the number and type that must be done on site. Although it is possible to transport oversized pieces to the site with a police escort, it does increase the cost of the project. Likewise, when the site is constricted and the staging area small, pre-assembling of pieces on site on the ground might also not be possible. Most urban sites will require just-in-time delivery of steel pieces and carefully planned erection to make the best use of the staging area as well as preserve area for staging that might be required to the last moment of steel erection.

Left: The detailing of the connections on this curb-side canopy at the Baltimore Washington International Airport, MD, USA combines shop-welded connections with more discrete bolted connections to simplify erection and provide a unified look.

Right: The bolted connections blend into the exposed structure once the painted finish has been applied. Given the location and use, it would have added needless expense to have these site-welded and achieve an appearance identical to the shop-fabricated connections of the other round HSS joints.

Size limitations presented by transportation may require innovation where a fully-welded appearance is desired but not practical. Where pragmatic issues necessitate breaking a structure into separate parts while aesthetics would prefer otherwise, it is possible to create "hidden connections" to conceal this reality.

### CONNECTION MOCK-UPS

The issue of mock-ups plays heavily into the design issues related to connections. Most designers would ideally like to see and feel specialty connections before they commit to their mass fabrication. This is not always possible or practical. Physical mock-ups can create delays, not only for their fabrication but also to have all parties present for approvals. Viewing distance needs also to be taken into account when looking at a physical mock-up. Normally those present are examining the sample at close range when in fact the in-situ connection may be many meters out of range of view and touch.

The AESS category must be kept in mind when viewing physical samples. It may be possible to verify most of the appearance issues associated with the connections and receive design approval through the use of 3D drawings – a combination of those that are produced by the fabricator's detailing software and others produced with 3D modeling software. If 3D or other sorts of digital models are to be used as the basis of agreement for details, it is important to discuss the finer aspects of welding, bolting and finishing, as these may not be fully represented in the digital model. It may be possible to reference a fabricator's previous work in order to establish a baseline for discussion when using digital references.

Left: The software that the fabricators employ to design the connections can be used as a simple, fast and inexpensive way to look at the aesthetic aspects of connection design.

Right: The constructed view of the connection is very similar, and as it is situated some 27m/90ft away from view, more than satisfactory.

A high-quality 3D rendering can also be used as a point of agreement regarding the connection and finish level. This is cost- and time-effective and can work without constructing a physical sample, provided that previous work by the fabricator and erector is available as a reference.

A combination of smaller physical mock-ups for aspects of detailing and finish might accompany digital representations to achieve a good level of communication.

## CUTTING STEEL

The way that steel is cut will influence the level of detail as well as the amount of remediation required. Most cutting today is performed using CNC control although manual cutting can still be done. Manual cutting requires more clean-up depending on the skill of the operator and the level of AESS expected.

Methods include:

- Plasma cutting: the thickness of steel with this method is typically ¼in to 1-¼in / 6 to 30mm.
- Oxy-fuel cutting: this is the most common method and the thickness of material is unlimited.
- Water-jet cutting: this method is less common and the limits on steel thickness are not known.
- Laser cutting: this method is used on material in the range of 1/16in up to a practical limit of ¾in / 1.5 to 20mm).

For exceptionally thick steel, in the range of 150mm/6in or greater, oxy-fuel would normally be used. Plasma and oxy-fuel require moderate to heavy amounts of grinding if all cutting marks are to be eliminated from the plate edges. Laser and waterjet-cut edges require minimal grinding. Any cut perpendicular to the material can be accomplished using CNC; however, plasma and oxy-fuel have limitations on width-to-thickness ratios of cuts. For example, one cannot practically oxyfuel-cut a hole with a diameter smaller than the thickness, as this would result in too much melting and poor quality.

CNC-driven equipment can cut any shape without additional expense. If manually cut, openings are practically limited to combinations of straight lines cut with an automated torch and drilled round holes.

## *CHOOSING CONNECTION TYPES*

The connection type will be dependent on the structural requirements of the assemblies, the shapes and types of steel members that are to be connected as well as the aesthetic that is desired. The type of connection that is most appropriate for a project might not be clearly evident from the outset. There are many different types of connections and it may be necessary as well as desirable to use as many different types in a project as are suited to the specific range of requirements and AESS categories, recognizing that viewing distances throughout a project may vary. For overall clarity of design, these different connections may use a similar language and form a "family" of typical conditions.

As with any project, the overall structural considerations – loads, clear-spanning requirements and support spacing – will form the starting point for the design. More pragmatic issues such as the type of project, use of the space, exposure to weather and atmospheric grime and choice of fire protection method will begin to influence the choice of AESS category. There is little economic sense investing in highly articulated details if the connections are either out of view or concealed in part by thicker intumescent coatings. If there is significant dirt present in the environment, or if cleaning and maintenance of the structure is difficult, it is best not to create ledges that will collect dirt and surfaces that will highlight lack of maintenance.

Transportation and access to the site will begin to necessitate breaking the structure into smaller elements that may be shipped as well as fit into erection limitations on the site. The majority of site connections tend to be bolted. This does not preclude the use of welded connections on site. Site welding does mean additional costs to put temporary shoring or supporting pieces in place while welding is carried out. These need to be removed when no longer required, and good surfaces be made.

Budget will also directly impact detailing. If the project can be subdivided into different categories of AESS, the more visible areas can be more expensively detailed.

### BOLTED CONNECTIONS

Bolted connections are normally chosen to achieve a more rugged aesthetic for the AESS or to deal with erection issues and constraints. Bolted connections are often chosen when using W, C or L shapes. The more industrial look of these section types seems more aesthetically suited to bolted connections. Often the detailing used on these types of bolted AESS connections is very close to connections that would be used in standard structural steel.

When designing bolted connections, the type of bolt to be used is to be specified, as well as the side on which the bolt heads are to be found with consistency. As the structural requirements of the bolted connection dictate how far bolts need to be tightened, it is not reasonable to expect the rotation of all heads to align.

When bolted connections are used with hollow structural members, there is normally a plate welded to the HSS member that facilitates bolting.

Left: Two types of bolted connections have been employed for the square HSS members of the Canadian War Museum in Ottawa, ON, Canada. One uses a set of overlapping plates (at the X intersection) that are inset into a "slice" in the tube. The other uses a simple connection where the plates are welded to the ends of the HSS members and then bolted. The aesthetic of the space and the desire to mimic a twisted, war-torn landscape inspired these connections.

Right: The Reagan International Airport in Washington, DC, USA by Cesar Pelli uses wide-flange sections with bolted connections. Care is taken to keep the tolerances tight and to ensure that the bolts are carefully spaced and the heads located consistently. Where the railing penetrates the web of the beam, the bolt spacing has been adjusted to suit.

The Seattle Public Library, WA, USA by Rem Koolhaas uses panels created from a diagonal grid of steel whose wide-flange sections have been welded together. The panels are sized for shipping and have been bolted on site quite discreetly. This solution eased the erection issues that would have arisen had welding been desired.

Left: The Lou Ruvo Center for Brain Health in Las Vegas, NV, USA, designed by Frank Gehry, uses bolted connections for a series of prefabricated curved panels to be connected to the steel exoskeleton that provides shelter and shade for the courtyard. The connections themselves are designed to permit some site adjustment during erection.

Right: An interior view of the connection pattern for the steel panels shows that the panels have been fabricated off site, despite their complex geometry, to increase the ease of site work.

Although some bolted-type connections allow for adjustment on site, it is not always desired to have slippage. In complex geometries the steel sections have to be designed to fit – hence half standard tolerance as a minimum requirement, as slight amounts of misalignment can easily accumulate and result in the inability to fit highly complex steel members.

## WELDED CONNECTIONS

Welded connections are used on a high proportion of AESS structures. Welding gives a clean, uncluttered appearance. It is often used on hollow structural shapes and less often for W, C or L shapes.

This all-welded box-truss support at the Home Offices of Waiward Steel in Edmonton, AB, Canada showcases the type of smooth, flowing aesthetic that can be achieved through the combination of welding and round sections.

Welded connections present different problems for the fabricator as a function of the geometry of the connection combined with the choice of member. For complex geometries to be more affordable and for better quality and alignment a maximum of work should be done in the fabricator's plant so that proper jigs, lifting and clamping devices can be used to manipulate the materials. It is necessary to understand transportation restrictions when working through the details of structures that call for all-welded connections. There will be a maximum member size that will be able to clear bridge overpasses and road widths. Where highly articulated assemblies must be broken into smaller elements due to transportation and lifting limitations, the details of the more significant site connections must be discussed with the fabricator if a totally welded "appearance" is the desired end result. It is possible to create site connections that give the appearance of being welded but that are discreetly bolted, the final connection concealed with cover plates.

The majority of the steel in the atrium of the Toronto Eaton Center in Toronto, ON, Canada is fabricated from round members. For a more seamless appearance at the major points, bolted connections are created that are hidden by the discrete plates that blend with the outside faces of the members.

When deciding upon the level of finish of a welded connection, it is extremely important that the viewing distance, AESS category and associated characteristics be respected. One of the major reasons for cost overruns in AESS has historically been the tendency of welded connections to be overworked. Welds are often ground, filled or smoothed out unnecessarily. Welds are structural and overgrinding can diminish their strength. Only in custom or very high-end AESS 4 should grinding be considered as an option for welded connections. Except in the instance of structural necessity, or for seal-welding to prevent moisture entry, welding may not even need to be continuous.

The use of highly specialized fabrication techniques can surpass even the high level of workmanship expected in AESS 4. The custom-casting at the TGV Station at the Charles-de-Gaulle Airport in Paris, France by Paul Andreu and Peter Rice required a high level of workmanship to smoothly connect the tubular columns to the base.

## CAST CONNECTIONS

Cast connections are increasingly used to address complexity in connections while providing a formed and seamless-looking appearance. They are also effective in seismic situations. Economy is found in the mass production of the elements. One-off castings or small runs can be very expensive but are suitable for different projects where specific aesthetics or solutions to complex connections are sought.

Cast members have a characteristic finish. This is due to their manufacturing process and a function of the material that creates the form for the casting. If sand-casting is used, the surface texture of the finished steel will have a rough, sand-like appearance. Special finishing will be required if a seamless final appearance is sought at the transition between the casting and the adjacent tubular member. For higher levels of AESS categories this can call for significant grinding and filling to smooth out the rougher finish of the casting, or remove casting-mill marks. Cast connections are covered in more detail in Chapter 10: Castings.

# *CHOOSING MEMBER TYPES*

## TUBULAR SECTIONS

Tubular steel – either HSS or mechanical pipe – is often chosen when creating AESS projects. In the case of HSS, the section shapes can be square, rectangular, round or elliptical. Mechanical pipe is produced round. The choice of the member shape will have a tremendous impact on the design and appearance of the connections. The geometry of the connection – planar, simple-angle or multi-member intersection – will impact the cost and complexity of resolving multiple HSS shapes. In some instances the joint can be resolved by cutting and welding. In other instances plates may be needed to simplify the intersection.

HSS sections are welded from flat plate and have a weld seam visible also on the exterior of the section. Detailing must acknowledge this and either orient the seam away from view or pay to grind the seam smooth if near to view. The seam may or may not be in a consistent location, varying from supplier to supplier, and will also vary in position as a function of the size of the HSS shape.

In general, HSS tends to be produced using a welding process, whereas pipes tend to be the result of an extrusion process. All HSS sections start out round and are formed to alternate shapes. There will be a welded seam along the HSS, whereas in mechanical pipe the shape will be seamless. The AESS characteristics make the orientation of the HSS weld seam a design issue. A welded seam will tend to be visible even after grinding, depending on the coating process used, as one can only grind perpendicular to a surface. As grinding might not completely conceal the weld seam, even after finish coatings are applied, it is preferable and less expensive to simply orient this natural occurrence consistently or away from the dominant angle of view. Round mechanical pipe is sometimes chosen for complex trusses, as it does not have a seam. Pipe, however, is not permitted in seismic design due to its different structural characteristics.

Modern fabricating equipment permits very efficient junctions of round HSS sections. Jigs are created to make mass production of such complex connections more economical.

The surface of welded HSS tends to resemble that of a rolled shape, whereas pipe may exhibit a light texture akin to an orange peel. This textural difference may be significant if combining hollow section types with other structural shapes in an AESS application where a high level of consistency of finish is desired. The surface texture of the pipe may make it more appropriate for use in combination with cast connections, which also exhibit a more textured surface. It is important to discuss this in detail with the engineer and fabricator. Pipe is not simply a substitute for HSS.

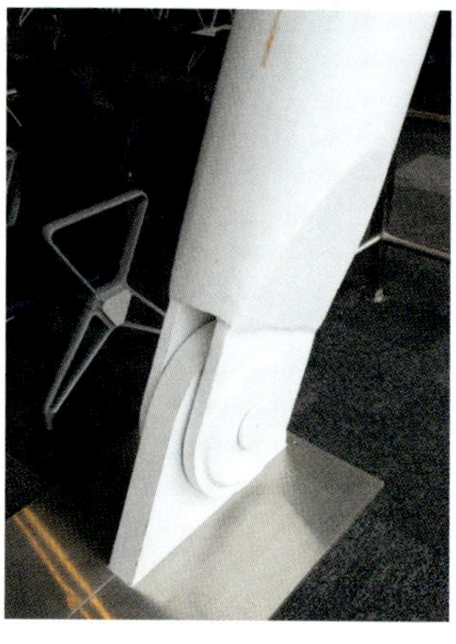

Left: HSS sections can be joined in a variety of ways. Here some plates are being inserted into the cut end of the round member to provide for a pin connection at the end. The inserts are mass-fabricated to ensure uniformity in size and consistency in the welds. The plates are inserted into the cut tubes by hand.

Right: The finished element at Pearson International Airport in Toronto, ON, Canada.

Availability of different section sizes will vary and is not the same for different diameter ranges. For large quantities over 50 to 70 tonnes an order can be placed directly at the structural tubing mill. HSS with a diameter greater than 400mm/16in generally require special ordering. In most cases big tubes will be custom-manufactured and will require a minimum 100-tonne quantity when ordering. As helical welds are sometimes proposed for large HSS sections, it is important to discuss this with the fabricator and explicitly exclude these in the specification documents if they are not acceptable.

Helical welds are visible on the round sections for the Humber River Pedestrian Bridge in Toronto, ON, Canada by Montgomery Sisam Architects.

Tapered tubes are not a regular manufactured product. They must be custom-fabricated from a trapezoidal plate that is rolled to form a tapered pole and the seam must be welded.

### STANDARD STRUCTURAL SHAPES

Standard structural shapes (W, C and L) are used in a wide range of AESS applications. The detailing of these shapes can present greater challenges in the creation of smooth or artful connections. One of the main issues with the use of standard shapes will be the orientation of the members to allow for drainage, if placed outdoors, and also to prevent the accumulation of dirt or debris in the hollows.

## *CONSTRUCTION BEST PRACTICES*

### CARE IN HANDLING

AESS requires more care in handling to avoid damage to the members. Oddly shaped or eccentric members can easily be distorted or bent if improperly handled. Many of the members that come to the site might also be pre-finished with paint, galvanizing or intumescent coatings, in which case padded slings will be required to avoid marking the finish coat when moving or erecting the steel.

Often steel will be shipped with temporary supports, backing or bridging attached to prevent deformation during shipping and erection. These supports are removed after the steel is lifted into place and the weld marks removed (typically by grinding) prior to the application of finishes.

### TRANSPORTATION ISSUES

As quality of finish and precision of installation are paramount with AESS, it is necessary to maximize the amount of fabrication and painting that can be carried out in the fabricator's shop. This may mean that members can become increasingly large and difficult to transport. It will be essential that the fabricator map the clearances from the shop to the site to ensure that the pieces will fit for easy transport, including turning radii for narrow streets. It is obviously better and less expensive to avoid requiring an escort or street closures.

To prevent damage, members may have to be shipped separately rather than maximizing the allowable tonnage per trailer. More delicate members may require the use of temporary steel bracing to prevent distortion from road movement, off-loading and subsequent lifting.

The 27m-long legs for the Addition to the Ontario College of Art and Design (OCAD) in Toronto, ON, Canada designed by Will Alsop Architect, had to be transported from a distance of 100km, via highways and through narrow city streets. The wheel sets on the front and back ends of the legs allowed for maneuvering around corners.

## SEQUENCING OF LIFTS

Just-in-time delivery is needed to ensure proper sequencing and minimize the risk that pieces get damaged while stored on site, as many sites are constricted and have insufficient staging area to provide holding for the steel. The erector will arrange lift sequences to minimize the amount of steel that is on site at any time. Construction sequencing for architecturally exposed steel members places further limitations on detailing and increases the challenge of erection.

The 27m/90ft steel columns that support the upper structure of OCAD were pre-finished at the fabrication shop with a colored fire-resistant intumescent coating. Not only was the street access extremely restrictive, but care had to be taken to preserve the integrity of the intumescent coating during handling and erection. A custom set of supports (blue) was constructed to hold the members in place until such time as proper lateral bracing could be provided. The integrity of the finish had to be touched up intermittently throughout the construction process due to unavoidable nicks and scratches, the result of routine construction processes – processes that would not cause extra expense on a more standard use of structural steel.

## SITE CONSTRAINTS

Constricted sites are common in dense urban areas. Lane closures may be required on fronting streets to provide for staging and erection, particularly when building to the property line. It is not uncommon for sub-assembly to occur on site in the staging area for oversized or geometrically complex members. The size of the staging area will figure into design decisions, thereby affecting the types of connections that are employed in aggregating very large members. While quality welding can be easily carried out in the shop, such will not be as easy in the staging area without benefit of jigs. If an all-welded appearance is desired, the design may need to make use of inventive hidden bolted connections to facilitate erection.

The staging area in front of Frank Gehry's Addition to the Art Gallery of Ontario in Toronto, ON, Canada required that a lane of traffic be closed for more than a year. The staging and erection area was so constricted that the crane operator had no visual of the lifts. Additionally, the crane operator had to avoid hitting the glass or damaging the glue-laminated timber beams. The angled geometry of the members and their support conditions added to the difficulty.

## ERECTION ISSUES

Issues of erecting AESS will vary with the complexity of the project. If the steel members have been accurately constructed with no less than half standard tolerances, fitting issues should be minimized but may not be eliminated. The more precisely fabricated the pieces are, the less force will be required to fit them during erection.

With odd geometries and asymmetry of members, the lifting points will need to be more carefully pre-calculated. Standard structural steel elements with vertical columns and horizontal relatively uniform beams tend to be more regular. The lifting points are predictable and make assembly on site routine and quick. With diagonal or unbalanced members, gravity will not be of assistance, and lifting points may require more calculation than normal. There may be erection delays in projects where each element is unique, as each will present a different challenge to be solved that may have no precedent. It is not unreasonable for some members to require more than one attempt due to alignment issues. An experienced erection crew is an asset.

Where steel is pre-finished, extra care must be taken during erection not to damage the finish. In some cases padded slings will be used in conjunction with regular lifting chains to prevent damage to the finish. This might also be done with primed steel, where a high-gloss finish is anticipated, again to prevent damage to the surface of the steel. Damage to the primer can translate through the final finish.

The back side of the custom-fabricated temporary steel support for the legs is padded to prevent damage to the intumescent fire protection and final finish that was shop-applied to ensure a high-quality coating of consistent thickness.

*CHAPTER 7*

\- - -

# *COATINGS, FINISHES AND FIRE PROTECTION*

\- - -



Much of the structure of the Beijing National Stadium in China by Herzog & de Meuron was finished with metalizing (spray zinc) after welding. Complex joints and surfaces that could not accommodate metallization were finished with a series of coatings of field-applied materials. The surface was first roughened, followed by two spray-applied coats of "Zinga", a spray-applied intermediate layer of Epoxy Micaceous Iron Oxide (MIO), followed by also spray-applied final metallic-grey fluorocarbon finish.

# *THE NEED FOR CORROSION PROTECTION*

There are many different coating and protection systems that can be used on steel structures. It is required to coat the steel if during its service life it will be exposed to moisture in the presence of oxygen; it must have a Fire Resistance Rating; or it is being used as Architecturally Exposed Structural Steel.

These exterior stairs form part of a public walkway system. Salt that is used to de-ice the concrete treads has resulted in a degradation of the steel and the rust is marking the steel, and the walkway below. Care must be taken to ensure that instruction is given regarding limitations on de-icing materials. A simple painted finish was not a durable enough choice for this use.

Regular carbon steel, when exposed to moisture or other corrosive environments, must either be constructed from a type of steel that has inherent resistance to corrosion or be protected with a coating to prevent oxidation or "rust". The chemical reaction of oxidation removes metal and causes weakening and potential failure of the construction element. Rusting can also stain adjacent materials. Corrosion protection is normally a concern for exterior steel that is subjected to weathering, but may also be a consideration when using steel in harsh interior environments such as near chlorinated pools, ice rinks or in industries where chemicals or toxic fumes may damage the steel.

The finish selection for exterior steel structures will need to pay special attention to the prevention of corrosion. Paint will not make up for design deficiencies. Even the most sophisticated epoxy- and vinyl-paint coatings cannot compensate for details that create opportunities for corrosion to occur. The basic selection of member type and connection detailing for exterior structures should ensure that there are no places where water can collect or puddle. With some care and attention, orientation problems can be overcome. Beams and channels should be orientated in such a way that water cannot collect and stand for any period of time. Exposed steel on which moisture can collect should be detailed with a slope to ensure drainage. Drain holes should be added if the section cannot be oriented or sloped to drain.

The W sections used on the Seattle Public Library, WA, USA, designed by Rem Koolhaas, have drainage holes placed uniformly and discreetly at their connections to prevent any build-up of moisture.

When using hollow sections or composite members that create voids on exterior applications, it is also necessary to prevent corrosion on the interior surfaces. Often seal welds are specified to prevent the entrance of moisture or oxygen-laden air into the cavity. For architecturally exposed steel that is to be painted, seal welds may also be specified to prevent unsightly rust bleeding.

Seal welds may be specified on parts to be galvanized, in order to prevent pickling acids and/or liquid zinc from entering into a specific area during the galvanization process. Proper communication is important when deciding on the method of prevention of moisture entry on sealed joints. Seal welds can alter load paths and are prohibited in some structural situations. You never galvanize a closed volume, as it will cause an explosion. It is better to provide a vent space. Galvanizing the interior of hollow sections prevents unexpected rust-out. This will increase costs but may provide a more durable exterior coating.

Exterior applications may require a combination of seal welding and venting. On this railing at the Salt Lake City Library, UT, USA, the curved strut is seal-welded but a drain hole is present at the base of the vertical supports. Galvanizing processes require that gas be vented from interior spaces so vent holes may be a natural part of the design.

The Mandarin Hotel in Beijing, China suffered a catastrophic fire in February 2009 prior to its official opening. As the building was not occupied, the fire suppression system had not been activated. While the level of damage was significant, the structure did not collapse. The many other combustible materials that are used in buildings contributed to the severity of a fire.

## *THE NEED FOR FIRE PROTECTION*

Steel, although not combustible, suffers sudden failure when exposed to heat and must be protected from exposure to fire. The primary concern for fire protection is to allow the safe evacuation of the occupants. The secondary desire is to further maintain the structural integrity of the building so that repair is possible. In many situations, the steel may need to achieve performance levels associated to more than one of the AESS categories at the same time. An AESS structure will require quite different surface preparation in order to ensure a quality finish. Standard structural steel that is not prone to moisture corrosion does not need a Fire Resistance Rating and is also concealed, hence does not require a finish. There are cost and environmental savings possible.

## *PREPARING THE STEEL FOR COATINGS*

The primary reason for the failure of a coating is the inadequate preparation of the surfaces. Steel that comes from the mill will naturally have grease, mill scale and rust. Even if steel is not designated for exposed installation, any steel requiring welding, priming, painting or designated for a fire-protective coating must have its surface cleaned in order for the coating to adhere properly.

The following are the different ways in which the surface is prepared for fabrication processes:

- Degreasing is the most common process and it is used to remove oil, grease and other contaminants. Solvent or degreaser is applied to wash the surface, followed by wiping the surface dry with a clean cloth.
- Scraping and wirebrushing will remove loose rust, mill scale and old paint. This can be removed by hand or with power tools. Power wirebrushes and grinders are more effective than hand tools.
- Sanding is an alternative method for scraping and wirebrushing and is used where the area for treatment is small. Both manual and mechanical (sanders) processes can be used.
- Waterblasting uses a high-speed waterjet for removing rust, loose paint, chemical contaminants and grease. High-pressure waterblasting can also be carried out by using hot water or special cleaning agents.
- Pickling including acid and chemical pickling, can be used to remove rust and mill scale. This is recommended for shop treatment and is not advisable for site work.
- Sandblasting is the most effective method of cleaning steel. It is recommended for removal of mill scale, heavy rust and previous coatings. Prior to sandblasting it is essential to first degrease the steel.
- Steel-shot blasting is similar to sandblasting except that round steel shot is used in an air or wheel blaster. It is recommended for exceptional cleaning, and again degreasing must precede this process.

There is a range of levels of surface preparation that are used with steel construction. North American construction standards refer to these as Surface Preparation (SP) Standards. SP-3 is the designation normally used for standard structural steel. It relies on simple power-tool cleaning and is not adequate for AESS applications. For AESS elements SP-6 should be used. This calls for commercial blastcleaning and is intended to remove all visible oil, grease, dust, mill scale, rust, paint, oxides, corrosion products and other foreign matter, except for spots and discolorations that are part of the natural material.

Surface preparation should be done in accordance with the AESS type if the steel is to be exposed to view. If the steel is to be concealed, significantly less is required to prepare the surface for bolting, welding and erection processes. When different AESS types are used in the project there may also be different surface preparations and different finishes required. It is essential in AESS applications that proper surface preparation takes place. If the surface is not adequately cleaned prior to the application of the coating system, the latter is likely either to fail or to allow the surface deficiencies to show through.

## *FINISH AND COATING SYSTEM SELECTION*

The selection of the paint or coating system should be done at the outset of the project, as both the color and finish will impact detailing decisions and therefore cost. If a high-gloss finish is desired, it will reveal every small imperfection in the steel. Flat finishes are more accommodating. Light-colored paints will quickly reveal corrosion and dirt. Thin finishes will reveal surface imperfections. Thicker coatings, such as intumescent fire protection, can cover or conceal imperfections as well as fine details.

This AESS "tree structure" at the Science Building at the University of Guelph, ON, Canada has a high-gloss finish. This impacted every decision from the need to smoothen the natural finish of the casting to the painstaking grinding and filling of the welds.

### PRIMERS

The selection of the primer is a function of the choice of the finish coating. Not all finish coating systems take the same base primer; therefore, revisions in the final finish type may require remedial correction of primers to ensure compatibility. Care in application of the primer is important, as any drips and runs will translate through both paint and intumescent coating finishes. Not all finish systems require a primer. Steel buildings require no paint if the steel is concealed behind drywall or suspended ceilings, provided that the humidity is below a critical threshold.

## *PAINT SYSTEMS FOR AESS*

Steel exposed to view is generally painted for appearance. A one-coat paint system is sufficient for standard warehouse structures that will not be top-coated. Since the building environment is controlled, no corrosion occurs once the building is enclosed, so that corrosion protection is not an issue. AESS steel that will be top-coated for appearance requires a prime coat for adhesion. A fast-dry primer is sufficient to provide the necessary base. To ensure that this system will perform for longer periods, a greater degree of cleanliness is required by the specification. Hence AESS requires surface preparation to a minimum SP-6 of the rating system of the Society for Protective Coatings. An SP-6 preparation involves commercial blastcleaning so that, when viewed without magnification, the steel will be free of all visible oil, grease, dust, dirt, mill scale, rust, coating, oxides, corrosion products and other foreign matter. Consultants must ensure that the finish coats are compatible with the primer.

The dirty environment of a train station results in severe build-up of black particulates on the upper surface of the white-painted tubular steel framework of the TGV station at Charles-de-Gaulle Airport in Paris, France.

Structural steel that is exposed to view and weathering on the exterior of buildings requires more thorough cleaning and finishing to ensure long-term performance. Higher degrees of cleanliness along with multi-coat paints of better quality should be considered under these circumstances. Epoxy systems over compatible primers are usually the most suitable solution. Urethanes should be used when wear is a consideration. The paint system should be reviewed with the fabricator early in the decision-making process, as it will impact fabrication detailing.

SHORTCOMINGS OF PAINTED FINISHES

Although painted finishes are commonly used due to their economy, great consideration should be given to the long-term impact on maintenance when they are specified on the exterior of a building. White or light colors will very quickly show soil. The dirt collected on the top of the member, when exposed to moisture, will eventually drip and stain the underside of the member. Even on interior applications, a build-up of grime can occur. Darker colors will obscure dirt for a longer period of time. It will be necessary to clean and repaint these surfaces from time to time; therefore, access to carry out these operations should be considered.

Exposure to weather also results in drip marks, as rain or melting snow carries pollutants down the face of the steel to let these drop off of the bottom edge. This situation is worsened by the light color of the finish. This large steel tube at the Beijing Airport is showing deterioration after a couple of seasons of exposure.

The vast exterior exposed structure of the Centre Georges Pompidou in Paris, France has a painted finish (photo taken in 2010 after some 30 years of use). This finish requires almost continuous maintenance and even then still suffers from cracking, peeling and a significant accumulation of paint layers. Although it would appear that the structure is free from corrosion that would compromise its structural safety, an alternate, more durable finish might have been a better choice, initial capital budget notwithstanding.

Painted finishes will degrade more quickly in exterior environments. Even if the paint is properly applied, peeling and cracking will occur over time and require maintenance for the appearance of the building to be preserved. White paints are problematic, as they show wear quickly. Colors such as red can fade due to ultraviolet radiation from the sun. If painted surfaces are to be touched up from time to time, color matching will also be an issue, due both to the availability of the color and that it may have faded over time. This will be the case in instances of repair to impact damage or graffiti degradation.

SHOP VERSUS SITE PAINTING

The painting of an AESS structure can take place in the fabrication shop or on the site. Many fabricators offer shop painting, which can ensure a more consistent, higher-quality finish. Naturally it is expected for the paint finish to be free of drips and runs. Access to the installed structure for paint applications can be a logistical issue, as will the touch-up or repainting of the structure. Shop-applied paint finishes will likely need to be touched up after erection, but this is usually less problematic than the complete painting of the structure on site.

Pre-painted structures will require extra care and protection during transportation, handling and erection. Pre-painted structures will be more in need of just-in-time delivery to the site to prevent site-generated damage. They may also require better staging areas on site to prevent damage to the painted finishes.

The careful preparation of the steel, including the basic removal of sharp edges, will allow for a more even application of the paint and better coverage on the corners. Spray application on sharp corners is difficult and if these are not ground or rounded off can lead to premature wear. For exterior applications this can lead to corrosion.

# CORROSION PROTECTION SYSTEMS

## GALVANIZATION

Galvanized finishes are increasingly seen in AESS applications. It is important to remember that in the view of the steel industry galvanizing was not intended as a finish but as a preventive measure against corrosion. The speckled grey finish will inevitably vary from batch to batch even within the same manufacturer, also as a function of the application technique and the style, size and shape of the member to which it is being applied.

Achieving a high-quality coating requires that the surface be free of grease, dirt and scale of the iron or steel before galvanizing. When the clean steel component is dipped into the molten zinc (approx. 450°C) a series of zinc-iron alloy layers are formed by a metallurgical reaction between the iron and the zinc. When the reaction is complete there is no demarcation between steel and zinc but a gradual transition through the series of alloy layers, which provide the metallurgical bond. This helps to make the galvanized finish highly durable, as it cannot easily be chipped away. The thickness of the coating is determined by the thickness of the steel. This is important to remember when specifying thinner elements in areas of wear. The galvanized coating can be made thicker by roughening the steel, thereby creating more surface area for the metallurgical reaction to take place.

Galvanized coatings protect steel in three ways:

→ The zinc weathers at a very slow rate, giving a long and predictable life.
→ The coating corrodes preferentially, thus providing sacrificial protection to small areas of steel exposed through drilling, cutting or accidental damage.
→ If the damaged area is larger, sacrificial protection prevents sideways creep, which can undermine the adjacent coated area.

The resistance of galvanizing to atmospheric corrosion depends on a protective film which forms on the surface of the zinc. When the steel is lifted from the galvanizing bath, the zinc has a clean, bright, shiny surface. With time this changes to a dull grey patina as the surface reacts with oxygen, water and carbon dioxide in the atmosphere. This forms a tough and stable protective layer that is tightly bonded to the zinc. Contaminants in the atmosphere will affect this protective film. The presence of $SO_2$ greatly affects the atmospheric corrosion of zinc.

Complex shapes and most hollow items can be galvanized, inside and outside, in one operation. Where AESS is being installed in an exterior environment, it is critically important that all surfaces be coated. For HSS members this implies the additional coating of the interior of the shape, which means increasing the surface area for coating and increasing the cost.

Good member design for galvanizing requires:

→ means for the access and drainage of molten zinc
→ means for the escape of gases from internal compartments (venting)

It is important to bear in mind that the steelwork is immersed into and withdrawn from a bath of molten zinc at about 450°C. This temperature can cause distortion in thinner steels. If the intention to use galvanized coating is known early on during the design process, it may be decided to increase the thickness of the steel to prevent distortion. Any features that aid the access and drainage of molten zinc will improve the quality of the coating and reduce costs. With certain fabrications, holes that are generated for other purposes may fulfill the requirements for venting and draining. In other cases, it may be necessary to provide extra holes for this purpose. For complete protection molten zinc must be able to flow freely to all surfaces of a fabrication. With hollow sections or where there are internal compartments, the galvanizing of the internal surfaces eliminates any danger of hidden corrosion during service.

From a design perspective, it is important to understand the physical limitations of the galvanizer's facility. This concerns for instance the size of the bath. It is not usual to dip pieces that are 20m or more in length, but the limit must be verified, as it impacts member size, possibly resulting in a need for additional connections. Double dipping (one end of the element at a time) is not an effective solution.

Left: The Cirque de Soleil Headquarters in Montreal, QC, Canada, designed by Dan S. Hanganu, uses simple standard steel sections with a galvanized finish as solar control devices and also to provide visual interest to the façade.

Right: The thickness of the metal will limit the depth of the layer of galvanized zinc that bonds to the steel. The thinner the steel, the thinner and more vulnerable the coating. This diamond grating has been galvanized but is showing wear due to snow and deicing agents. The adjacent steel and fasteners are not galvanized but painted with a heavy zinc paint, which is not holding up well.

Left: Galvanized steel was chosen as the finish for the varied steel elements that were used for the Prince Edward Viaduct Safety Barriers, Toronto, ON, Canada by Dereck Revington Studio. The safety barriers are permanently situated in a harsh exterior environment and their location, hanging high over the Don Valley, makes it extremely difficult to carry out maintenance.

Right: A detail of the barrier illustrating the variety of sections that can be galvanized to ensure durability.

Left: Galvanized steel is used extensively on the LEED™ Gold Water Center in Calgary, AB, Canada, designed by Manasc Isaac Architects. The rugged material should obviate the need for excessive maintenance in this exterior application.

Right: Detail of the galvanized trusses showing how the color of the material works well with the exposed underside of the galvanized steel roof decking.

## METALLIZATION

Metalizing is a substitute for painting structural steel. It protects steel for significantly longer than paint alone. Steel of every shape and size may be metalized either in the shop before construction or on site as an alternative to painting. Metalizing is a very versatile and effective coating for protecting steel structures that are to be continuously exposed to weathering. It is more expensive than galvanizing.

The metalizing process begins with proper surface preparation. Next, aluminum wire or zinc wire is continuously melted in an electric arc spray or gas flame spray gun. Clean, compressed air strips droplets of molten metal from the wire, depositing these particles onto the steel, thereby forming the protective coating. This sprayed metal coating is a barrier coating and a galvanic coating in one. A single metalized coating can protect steel for 30 years or longer, depending upon the application, coating thickness and sealing. Metalizing is thought of as a cold process in that the aluminum or zinc is deposited onto steel by spraying rather than by dipping the steel into a bath of molten zinc as with galvanizing. The steel remains relatively cool at about 120°–150°C. This means that there is virtually no risk of heat distortion or weld damage. It also means that there is no size limitation as in the limitations of dimension for a galvanizing bath.

There are no Volatile Organic Compounds (VOC) in the metalized coating. There is no cure time or temperature to limit metalizing, which therefore may be applied throughout the year, virtually regardless of temperature.

Three types of wire are used to create three specific coatings:

- Sprayed aluminum is preferred for use in industrial environments, particularly where there are high concentrations of sulfur dioxide and other pollutants.
- Zinc provides greater galvanic protection than aluminum. Its greater galvanic power protects gaps in the coating better than pure aluminum. It is marginally easier to spray pure zinc than pure aluminum by some flame or arc spray systems.
- Zinc with 15% aluminum wire combines the benefits of pure zinc with the benefits of pure aluminum in the metalized coating. It is very often used as a substitute for pure zinc, because it is somewhat more resistant to chloride and sulfur dioxide than pure zinc, while retaining the greater electro-chemical activity of pure zinc.

## WEATHERING STEEL

Weathering steel has the unique characteristic that under proper conditions it oxidizes to form a dense and tightly adhering barrier or patina, which seals out the atmosphere and retards further corrosion. Other carbon steels, by contrast, form a coarse, porous and flaky oxide that allows the atmosphere to continue penetrating the steel. In many climates the oxidized layer on weathering steel does not consume a significant amount of steel in its formation. As it needs wet/dry cycles to form, this finish is not suitable for interior environments because it will not age very quickly. If desired, it can be pre-aged outside and then installed inside; otherwise, the final surface state will take many years to develop.

At the Pavilion of Light in Phoenix, AZ, USA by DeBartolo Architects weathering steel plate is used as a garden wall barrier. The depth of the plate steel has been chosen so that it also acts to retain the soil. The difference in the finish of the various panels is clearly visible. Gravel at the base of the steel absorbs run-off and masks the effects of staining.

Run-off of water from weathering steel tends to produce long-lasting streaks or other patterns of red oxide on materials located below. Special attention must be paid to the drainage of stormwater (or condensate) to prevent staining of surrounding structures, sidewalks and other surfaces.

After about two years the oxide skin will have developed a much darker and reddish brown color. As this is "living steel", the color will not be consistent from project to project or even within a project, so care must be taken that inconsistency is part of the design intention. In wet climates the red color cast of weathering steel will generally be more intensive than in dry climates. The final color will have a rich dark earthy tone and the steel will be low-maintenance, durable and attractive, provided it is carefully detailed.

Left: The Australia Pavilion at the Shanghai Expo 2010, China by Wood Marsh used a weathered steel cladding for its exterior. The finish varies where the exposure conditions are modified by the overhang.

Right: To control the sight of run-off staining the steel, the base of the building has been surrounded with large rust-colored rocks.

Weathering steel is not readily available in W shapes and HSS shapes in many areas. It may require sourcing and special orders. In terms of availability, few steel service centers will stock a large inventory of weathering steel because it is normally produced in shapes and sizes suitable for bridge construction. The wish to use weathering steel for a limited application usually represents low tonnage for a service center to order so might pose a problem.

Weathering steel is also available in sheets for roofing and cladding. It is low-maintenance and no painting or re-coating is required. Weathering steel must be kept free from debris such as leaves or pine needles, as these retard the wet/dry cycle necessary for weathering steel and accelerate corrosion. Also, if corrosion is accelerated the loss of material may be more significant and could cause perforations in very thin sheets. Weathering steel is not appropriate for eco-friendly roofs, as the thin layer of steel has low solar reflectivity and is therefore considered to be a "hot roof" and contributes to heat island effect.

The Luxembourg Pavilion at the Shanghai Expo 2010, China by François Valentiny uses weathered steel cladding. The water feature assists in absorbing any colored run-off from the structure. Weathered steel is also used for the horizontal walking surfaces for a very homogeneous aesthetic.

Weathering steel finish, a new coating now available for use, is a shop- and field-applied coating that gives the appearance of weathering steel but does not create the same durable oxidized layer as actual weathering steel. It is applied to standard structural steel materials and might be useful where certain sizes, shapes and thicknesses of weathering steel are not available, or for interior applications where weathering steel might prove difficult. If used, the coating must also be applied to site welds to achieve a uniform appearance. It produces virtually no rust run-off. Being only a coating, it will not be as durable as weathering steel and will need to be reapplied periodically. As the coating mimics the appearance of rust it will be difficult to assess failure prior to the evidence of oxidation on surfaces below.

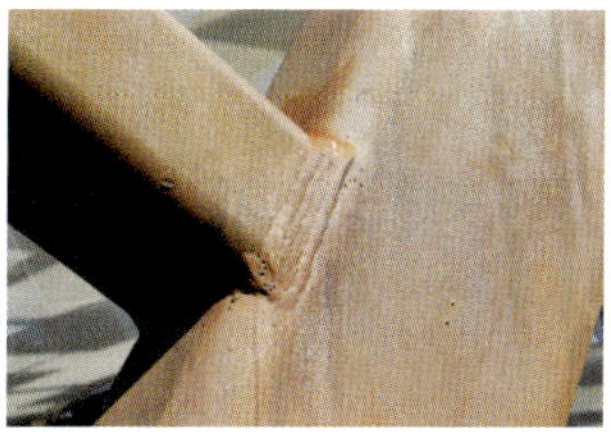

Left: Weathering steel coating is applied to the varied-sized steel members at The Springs Preserve in Las Vegas, NV, USA. This allows the use of a large array of steel shapes without the difficulty of sourcing the genuine material. Minimal staining shows on the concrete and walkways below.

Right: Weathering steel coating can also be applied on site to welded connections for a continuous appearance. Reapplication will be required, as the finish will degrade over time.

## STAINLESS STEEL

Although significantly more expensive than regular carbon steel, stainless steel is the most corrosion-resistant form of steel that can be selected for an architectural project. Stainless steel has the advantage of having its corrosion protection integral to the structural member. It has a remarkable finish and requires far less maintenance than regular steel protected through methods of galvanizing, metalizing or with painted or intumescent coatings. There are significant cost premiums for stainless steel beyond the cost of the material. From a structural perspective it requires a different set of calculations, as its behavior is very different from regular carbon steel. Only dedicated tools must be used to cut and finish the steel. Tools used with carbon steel will embed small particles of carbon steel in the stainless, causing rust spots to occur.

Left: The Exterior Domes in Robson Square, Vancouver, BC, Canada have recently been replaced with stainless-steel glazed structures. The damp exterior environment makes it worth the extra expense to provide such a corrosion-resistant, low-maintenance material.

Top: The beauty of the finish in stainless steel requires that extra care be taken in welding and detailing.

## *FIRE PROTECTION SYSTEMS*

Although steel is an incombustible material, it is subject to sudden collapse when exposed to heat during a fire. Although the specifics vary by jurisdiction (in terms of use, building height and access to fire-fighting equipment) steel is generally considered to need fire protection if expected to endure a fire for more than 45 minutes. In most fire codes, the focus of fire protection design is first to maintain the structural integrity of the building long enough to evacuate the occupants and second for the structure to remain intact after the fire has been extinguished. The larger and more complex the building, the more difficult this becomes. This means that the use of simple exposed painted structural steel is quite limited.

Fire protection can be achieved either by covering the steel with a material that will delay the heat damage for a period of time, or through the use of a fire suppression system, or with a combination of the two systems.

The pipe runs for this fire suppression system at the Palais des Congrès in Montreal, QC, Canada have been painted to match the exposed steel. The open nature of the structure allows for easy accommodation of the pipe runs.

### FIRE SUPPRESSION SYSTEMS

When designing a steel-framed building it is important to coordinate the pipe runs of the fire suppression system so they do not interfere with the steel structure. In buildings with exposed steel systems it is common to paint the pipe runs to match the structure in order to camouflage the system. The overall depth of the steel-framing system, the openness of the members and a possible suspended ceiling will all impact the level of difficulty of accommodating suppression runs.

Top: Spray-applied fire protection is commonly used where the structural steel will be given another finish, as in this office installation at the Bow Encana Tower in Calgary, AB, Canada. In this type of application, the steel deck can be protected during the same installation. A suspended ceiling will be installed and the columns furred out with gypsum board.

Middle: Spray-applied fireproofing is used in an exposed condition in this parking garage at the Vancouver Convention Center, Vancouver, BC, Canada by LMN Architects.

Bottom: These very large tubular columns at Pearson International Airport in Toronto, ON, Canada by SOM Architects have been filled with concrete to achieve their fire resistance rating.

## SPRAY-APPLIED FIRE PROTECTION

Spray-applied fibrous fire protection is commonly used in concealed structural steel framing systems. This method has replaced the use of sprayed asbestos fireproofing. There are three different compounds used in this method: gypsum plasters, cementitious plasters and fibrous plasters. The materials are spray applied to a requisite thickness in order to delay the rise of the temperature of the steel to its approximate failure temperature of 540°C.

Although not the usual solution for AESS installations, spray fireproofing could be used if the steel is located at a significant distance from view or touch. There need not be the same level of steel detailing required as for fine finishes. The surface is normally primed prior to the application of the product. The type of primer required by the manufacturer must be verified. If spray-applied fireproofing is used in exposed applications, it does tend to collect dirt and its appearance degrades very quickly. Remediation of this problem is not simple. It is also subject to damage by occupants, in which case the fire protection as well as the appearance can be compromised.

## CONCRETE

Concrete has long been used as both a fire protection method and a composite material for structural reinforcement of the building. Concrete can be either used to surround the steel, creating a depth of cover between the fire source and the steel, or to fill HSS sections, thereby increasing their resistance to fire. Filling provides less resistance than encasement. Filling prevents the hollow steel from buckling inward under load when it is weakened by the heat of a fire. Encasing slows the temperature increase of the steel.

## INTUMESCENT COATINGS

Intumescent coatings provide both a fire resistance rating and a painted appearance for exposed steel. They contain a resin system pigmented with various intumescent ingredients that, under the influence of heat, react together to produce an insulating foam or "char". The emerging char layer has low thermal conductivity as well as a volume many times thicker than that of the original coating. The char layer reduces the rate of heating experienced by the steel, thus extending its structural capacity and allowing for safe evacuation. As intumescent coatings can extend the fire resistance rating of exposed steel to a maximum of two hours it has become quite popular for use with AESS applications. The fire resistance rating is in part dependent on the type and thickness of the coating as well as the type of fire that has to be anticipated in the building use. Increasing the fire resistance rating is usually achieved by applying multiple coatings of the product.

The required thickness of the coating is in turn determined by the thickness of the structural steel member. Thin or light members will require more coats than heavier members. It is hence sometimes more cost-effective to increase the thickness of the steel so as to decrease the number or thickness of intumescent coatings. The increased cost of steel is significantly less than the extra cost to increase the thickness of the intumescent material. Structural steel is inherently a more sustainable material, so the reduction of the amount of coatings is preferable.

Intumescent fire protection application is preceded by the application of an approved primer. If the wrong primer is applied it may interfere with the successful application of the intumescent coating system.

The exposed steel in the atrium of the Bloomberg Building in New York City, NY, USA by Cesar Pelli is possible through the use of intumescent coating on the steel.

Left: The exposed steel at the Palais des Congrès is finished in a light grey intumescent coating. The slightly rough finish suits the more rugged bolted connections and the choice of standard W shapes for the trusses.

Right: The exposed steel at the Palais des Congrès in Montreal, QC, Canada, designed by Les architectes Tétreault, Parent, Languedoc et associés, Saia et Barbese, Ædifica, Hal Ingberg, is finished in a light grey intumescent coating. The columns that form the wind bracing for the façade have elongated circular cutouts whose edges have been reinforced by the addition of a plate welded to the inner diameter of the cutout. The structure is designed as a plain canvas that becomes brightly colored as light passes through the red, blue, yellow and green glazing of the curtain wall façade. The floor and wall surfaces are either grey or reflective, adding to the effect. When the sun's rays are perpendicular to the façade, shadows from the steel framing form dark lines on the floor.

Traditionally, intumescent coatings have been applied on site during the construction phase of the building. Today, in-shop application has become a more common practice as better control of application conditions has become possible: controlled venting as needed for solvent-based systems and better control of temperature and relative humidity for better drying (coated steel sections cannot be moved until they are hard enough to resist damage). In-shop coated members must be carefully handled during transportation and erection and any damage properly repaired, in order to preserve the integrity of the fire protection system.

Intumescent coatings are either acrylic- or epoxy-based. Acrylic coatings can be either water- or solvent-based and are field-applied. The water-based material is more ecology-friendly but takes somewhat longer to dry where humidity levels are high and temperatures are low. It is therefore mostly used for interior applications. Water-based coatings are typically applied when relative humidity is between 40% and 60%. If there is concern about the presence of high VOC levels on the project, a water-based product can be used if the humidity levels are kept low. It is important that the layers are allowed to dry thoroughly between coatings.

The solvent-based coating is more robust. Epoxy coatings are normally shop-applied and can be used on interior or exterior applications. They are more durable than acrylic coatings and can also be used to provide corrosion protection. Where access for finishing may be an issue, shop-applied epoxy coatings may offer savings. Solvent-based fireproof coatings can be applied with relative humidity up to 85%. Solvent-based products can dry faster but can also strike back to dissolve prior layers if insufficient drying time is permitted between layers.

The intumescent coating system can include a "top coat". This provides a hard protective coating to the product which otherwise is prone to fingerprinting and does not clean well.

The 27m-long legs of the addition to Ontario College of Art and Design, ON, Canada by Will Alsop were primed and coated with intumescent coating at the fabrication shop. This required great care in handling during transportation and erection. Some touch-up was required during construction, easily done using a lift truck. In spite of the necessity of some repair work this was superior to coating on site in terms of logistics. The high-traffic area subjects the coating to vandalism and so it needs continuous repair.

White or light colors will tend to yellow with time so if color matching is an issue this should be taken into account when mixing intumescent and painted finishes in a project. If combining intumescent and regular paint finished steel note that exact color matches are not possible. The nature of the intumescent finish will alter the color of the coating. It will be necessary to detail the structure to account for this slight change in hue or tone.

There are thin and thick intumescent coating systems. A thin coating is considered to have a range from 0.5mm to 6mm/.02in to .23in and a thick coating up to 13mm/.51in. Because the wet film needs to be relatively thick (several hundred microns according to the particular formulation), intumescent coatings are often thick to avoid slumping and runs while still wet. Several coats may need to be applied to build up to a total dry-coat thickness sufficient to give the required fire protection.

Although these coatings provide the appearance of a painted finish, the texture is not as smooth. Thin-coat intumescent systems will result in a finish that resembles an orange peel. The thicker system can conceal some of the finer details of the AESS connections. It is inappropriate to finely detail a connection that is to be protected with a thick intumescent coating. If badly applied, a thick system can give a very uneven, textured appearance. The use of thick intumescent coating often precludes the need for fine finishing, as it is thick enough to cover up surface imperfections that would be unacceptable if a standard paint finish were employed. If a very smooth high-gloss finish is desired this system requires additional surface treatment.

Care should be taken when using thick coatings in high- traffic areas or where they can be subject to vandalism. In case of damage intumescent coating must be properly repaired to maintain the required fire resistance rating. Color matching can also be an issue with repair.

*CHAPTER 8*

\- - -

# *CURVED STEEL*

\- - -

*CREATING CURVES IN STEEL BUILDINGS*

*LIMITATIONS ON CURVING STEEL*

*THE CURVING PROCESS*

*CURVED STEEL APPLICATIONS*

*FACETING AS AN ALTERNATE METHOD TO BENDING*

*CREATING CURVES WITH PLATE MATERIAL*

The large round curved HSS members of the pedestrian bridge at the Wells Fargo Building in Salt Lake City, UT, USA, designed by HKS Architects, provide a striking contrast with the glass box they support as well as the tower behind. Highly specialized processes are required to bend steel of this diameter.

# *CREATING CURVES IN STEEL BUILDINGS*

Curved structural forms and bent steel are to be found in many contemporary projects. There are three primary ways to achieve curved forms:

→ bend the steel
→ facet the building to give the appearance of curves while using straight members
→ cut curved forms out of plate material

The choice of which method to use is a function of the aesthetic desired, the budget and in some cases the physical size of the project. Curved structures are more expensive to fabricate and erect and require specialized expertise from the fabricator.

# *LIMITATIONS ON CURVING STEEL*

Bending and curving the steel is a specialized process that is normally done at a steel bending facility. The majority of fabricators do not bend steel. If bent or curved steel is required for a project the work is subbed out to a specialist. The maximum size of steel to be processed, in terms of its sectional properties, its shape, its weight and length, is a function of the capacity of the bender's equipment. It must be remembered that the straight material that is delivered via truck to the bending facility may not fit on the same truck for its continuing journey, depending on the degree of curve. If the revised shape of the steel exceeds the transportation limits, then splices in the piece that might impact the design will have to be considered.

Beyond the capacities of the bending facility there are other factors that must be recognized when choosing to include curved steel. There is a practical limit on the tightness of the radius. If the radius is too small, deformation of the section will occur. For tubular material the cross-sectional shape may warp. For wide-flange or channel material, the flanges or web may buckle. If a section is longer in one axis or not symmetrical, steel benders refer to the "easy" or alternatively the "hard" way to curve the pieces. Choosing the "easy" way helps to ensure a successful bend without deformation.

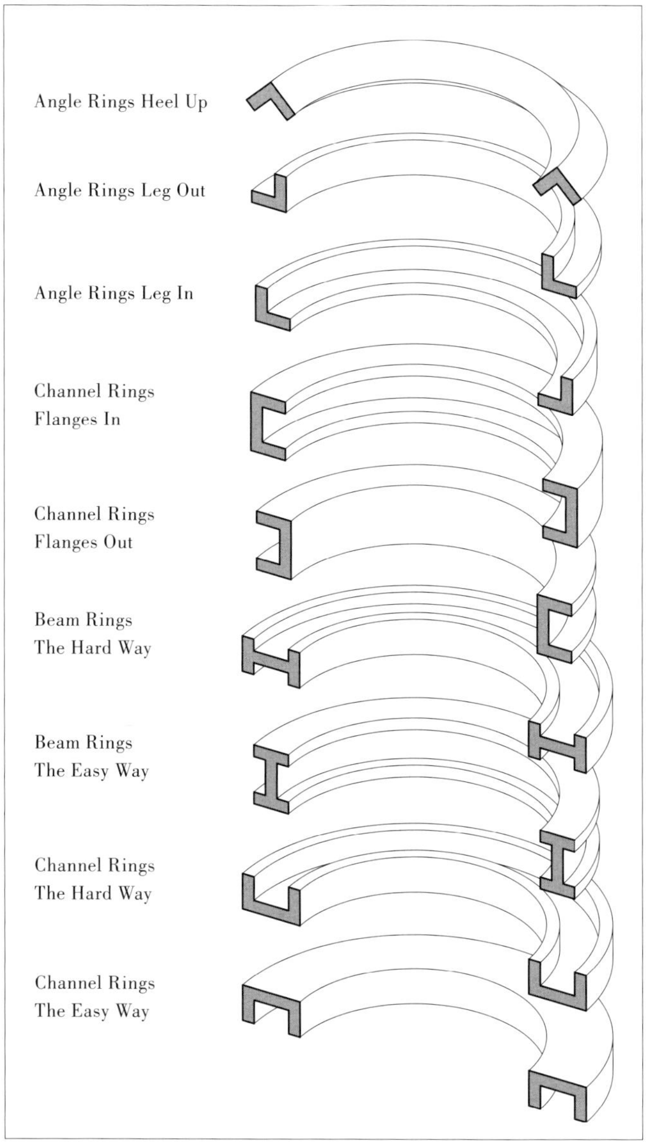


The "easy" and "hard" way of bending various steel shapes.

## *THE CURVING PROCESS*

**During the curving process the steel shapes are passed back and forth through a sequence of three rollers multiple times. With each pass the pressure on the member is increased and the member's radius becomes tighter.**

The straight ends on some curved square HSS sections. These will be cut off by the fabricator and the ends recycled.

This square HSS shape is being passed through the curving rollers at Kubes Steel's bending facility in Stoney Creek, ON, Canada. The rig is customized for each size and type of steel by replacing the rollers at the base that guide the steel.
There is some waste in the process, as the outer ends of the steel will remain straight, because there needs to be a length of steel that bridges between the first two rollers to hold the element in position and will never be subject to bending. These sections are eventually cut off and recycled.

A wide-flange section being curved the "easy" way. The roller fittings have been changed so that the shape fits the guide.

The smaller the diameter, the less pressure is required to curve the steel. The remaining straight lengths will also be much shorter.

These curved unequal-leg angles are not carbon steel. Benders will service all types of metal, including stainless steel, and aluminum. Care needs to be taken to clean the equipment, so that carbon steel does not come into contact with stainless steel as this would cause rusting of the stainless material.

**Plate steel is not bent using the same process. The specialty fabricator will use a brake press to form the steel. They will do this by marking the plate with a series of lines that will be used to determine the pressure points for the press. Regular and irregular curves can be formed this way.**

This steel plate is marked in preparation for insertion into the brake press.

The dimensions of the brake press will set the limit for the sizes of the pieces to be formed. Overhead cranes are used to position and hold the pieces during forming.

Large steel cylinders whose dimensions exceed available HSS sizes are created with break-forming. The pressure lines of the press show on the inside of the cylinder but they are not evident on the exterior. The resulting curve is surprisingly smooth.

# *CURVED STEEL APPLICATIONS*

Curved steel may or may not be used in an architecturally exposed fashion. If the curved steel is to be AESS, then it must follow the requirements as described in Chapter 6 on AESS. The choice to use curved steel adds to the cost of the project in terms of both money and time. If the overall form of the building is curved, then curving might be appropriate.

Left: The entry atrium at the Salt Palace Convention Center in Salt Lake City, UT, USA by Thompson, Ventulett, Stainback & Associates, working with Gillies Stransky Brems Smith Architects, uses curved rectangular HSS members to create the lace-like expression of this space.

Right: The radius of the curved steel sections used in the "arches" is quite tight. The bending needs to take into consideration the location of the HSS seam to hide it from view.

The Direct Energy Centre in Toronto, ON, Canada by Zeidler Roberts Partnership in Joint Venture with Dunlop Farrow Inc. uses curved sections to create the form of its exposed steel roof. The roof structure uses both wide-flange and paired back-to-back channel sections that have been curved the "hard way". Given the aesthetics and form of the roof, curving the steel was necessary as there were no interim or secondary members that would have allowed for faceting of the roof. The continuity of the members and the use of clean welded connections were part of the architecturally based requirements of the design.

Left: The curves used in creating the expression of the Experience Music Project by Frank Gehry in Seattle, WA, USA are not uniform and therefore create different issues for fabrication. The curves need to be broken down into smaller segments and connected, as the bending machine typically cannot create complex curves.

Right: The structural steel that gives form to the undulating roof is created by joining segments of curved wide-flange beam sections. As a continuous appearance was not a requirement, and additional tectonic expression desired, the curved segments are simply connected via bolting through plates that have been welded to the ends of the sections. It is evident that each section of steel exhibits a specific curve, and where there is a discontinuity, the pieces have been joined.

Curved round HSS elements are required in the fabrication of the pods for the Leslie Dan Faculty of Pharmacy (see Chapter 4), at least in the vertical orientation in order to define the shape of the pod. Many projects may use an economical combination of curved and straight segments, as was the case for Leslie Dan. Curving does add cost to the project. As the design of the pods allowed for the use of plate connectors, the problem of inline-joining the curved segments was avoided.

Plate connectors at the Leslie Dan Faculty of Pharmacy in Toronto, ON, Canada provided sufficient stiffness to the connection as well as constructability for the ironworkers.

Connecting curved segments can pose a problem if the connections must be concealed where there is insufficient space for the use of plates. Precise alignment of the connecting curves of the two segments is required. Additional material is added to the connection to increase stiffness as well as to provide material to be welded. This is sometimes done with round HSS members. The procedure is similar to connecting two straight tubes by welding a smaller section of tube inside the larger tube, thereby providing an overlap and a backstop to form the back of the weld. However, when round tubes are bent they tend to deform, so it is not a simple matter to create a smooth connection. There is also potential for imperfections in the weld as the containment of the weld is not as secure as a straight tube-to-tube connection.

The non-uniformly curved stairs for the Addition to the Art Gallery of Ontario used curved round HSS steel to form the base structure for the stairs. Even though the stairs were to be clad, it was important to keep the form as clean and tight as possible. Connecting plates would have added undesired bulk, so all welded tube-in-tube connections were used.

Left: The main stair that rises through the atrium of the Art Gallery of Ontario (AGO) in Toronto, ON, Canada by Frank Gehry uses round curved HSS as its base structure. The curved stairs at the AGO were fabricated by Mariani Metal of Toronto.

Right: The steel plate attached to the curved tubes to support the treads is also curved. Plate is normally curved via break-forming. This allows for the creation of complex curved shapes.

Left: The tube-in-tube arrangement of the connection is problematic in its geometry because of the curve of the tube and the angle of the slice. Problems arise when attempting to splice curved members, as not all of the deformations can be controlled. For a splice to be inspected, there needs to be some assurance that the welding method was successful. It is difficult to backstop the weld with the inner sleeve because small deformations in the sections occur unavoidably during the curving process.

Right: Looking up the center of the central steel stair one perceives the complexity of the curved forms as well as the permanent bracing. The weld marks reveal the joints in the prefabricated segments.

Left: With the stair cantilevered from the rear façade it was difficult to access the exterior to complete the welds. Scaffolding had to be erected to provide the ironworkers with stable access.

Right: The welded connections used to divide the curved stair into segments were sized for shipping and managing the erection and site-welding.

The curved stair on the rear face of the AGO cantilevers out from the main structure. This stair is clad in titanium and is also structured using a similar method.

## *FACETING AS AN ALTERNATE METHOD TO BENDING*

**Bending and break-forming are not always required for curving, depending on the needs of the project and the appearance sought after. If the curve is large enough, it is possible to use less expensive straight steel sections and simply facet the structure. This will depend on the function, intended aesthetic of the building and the budget.**

Left: The curved Bow Encana Tower in Calgary, AB, Canada, designed by Foster + Partners and Zeidler Partnership, uses the scale of the building to achieve the impression of curvature. None of the elements is actually curved. The building is faceted making use of straight pieces and the triangulation of the diagrid form to achieve this visual effect.

Top: A closer look at the suspension system that supports the glazing of the double façade reveals that the curve is comprised of straight sections that have been cleanly welded together.

Top: The University of Phoenix Stadium in Phoenix, AZ, USA, designed by Peter Eisenman, has a curved plan as well as an exterior that boasts multiple curves.

Left: Only straight segments of HSS were used for the Phoenix Stadium. The straight sections that approximate the curved form on the interior of the building are significantly longer than those used on the exterior to support the cladding. The interior-to-exterior curve is mediated by a truss-like structure. In fact, the exterior is faceted. The scale of the building made this possible. The angular look fit well with the exposed steel interior of the stadium. The horizontal banding of the cladding was an essential choice to making possible the use of straight sections.

## *CREATING CURVES WITH PLATE MATERIAL*

**Curved members can be created by using custom-cut sections in lieu of bending the steel. New CNC processes combined with plasma cutters can create very uniform flat-curved shapes using plate material. The limits on this type of process will depend on the capabilities of the fabricator and the equipment for cutting the plate. Larger sections can be assembled from smaller pieces that have been welded together and maintain structural integrity.**

The sleek exterior form of the National Grand Theater of China in Beijing by Paul Andreu required an innovative approach to detailing the curve of the exterior cladding, the glazing and the interior structure. While the large scale allowed the cladding to be faceted, this was not an option for the interior form.

Left: The curved truss sections were cut from very thick plate. The smaller truss segments (curved flange and straight web members) were cleanly welded together to create the seamless appearance of a large continuous truss cut from one enormous steel plate. The inner and outer elements of the truss are true curves.

Right: The structure is faceted in the plan direction. The curved plate trusses are connected by straight tubular members. This view shows the vague signs of the weld that attaches the plate sections that comprise the truss. These nearly invisible welds would have required significant grinding and filling.

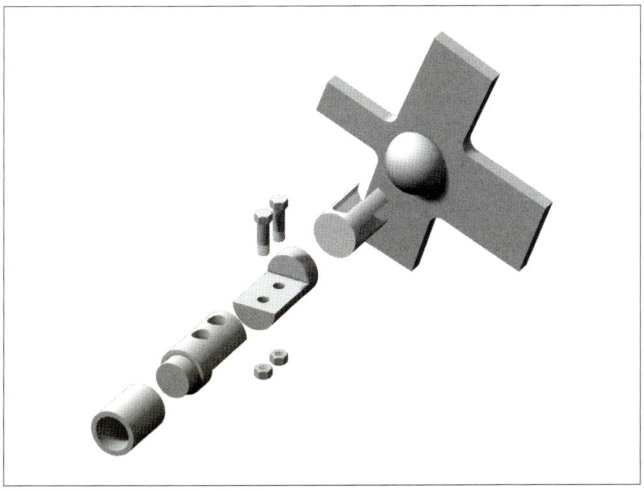

The design of the connection used to join the horizontal tubes to the ball joints of the truss was very innovative. The detailed view of the concealed connection shows the stub that is welded to the ball joint of the truss. The ever-changing geometry of the connection between the round horizontal members and the plate trusses is handled with a semicircular solid steel ball joint. A solid steel stub is welded to the ball joint. The change of geometry between the horizontal members and the plate trusses is accommodated when the stub is welded to the ball. The stub provides a bolted connection for the horizontal tube. Once bolted, the holes and voids are filled and painted to give the appearance of a welded connection.

**The lesson in approaching curved steel design is simply to innovate. There are numerous ways to solve a problem — some more efficient, some more costly. A serious discussion among all members of the design team is critical to achieving the optimal solution.**

*CHAPTER 9*

\- - -

# *ADVANCED FRAMING SYSTEMS: DIAGRIDS*

\- - -



The Bow Encana Building in Calgary, AB, Canada, designed by Foster + Partners with Zeidler Partnership and engineered by ARUP, uses an expressed diagrid structural system for this double-façade building.

20
19
18
17
16
15
14
13
12

# *TALL BUILDINGS*

The Council for Tall Buildings and Urban Habitat (CTBUH) defines a steel tall building as one whose main vertical and lateral structural elements and floor systems are made from steel. A composite system is defined as one where steel and concrete act together in the main structural elements. A mixed-structure building is one that uses different structural materials or systems above or below each other.

The use of steel as the primary structural system in tall buildings has declined significantly over the years. From the birth of the skyscraper to 1980, the predominant system of framing for buildings was a moment-frame tube in steel. Some later structures used either a bundled-tubes structure or the "diagonalized core system". A diagonalized core system relies on the addition of systems of diagonal members to the frame to achieve more resistance to lateral forces. After 1980 many buildings were constructed using the tube-in-tube system or core-and-outrigger system, which were normally constructed using cast-in-place concrete or a composite concrete and steel system. This followed marked improvements in the ability to pump concrete to great heights.

There is a variety of factors that contribute to the selection of a structural method in the construction of a tall building. Different methods simply work better with certain materials. Framed tubes, bundled tubes and the diagonalized tube are all more readily constructed in steel than concrete. There are also arguments that support increased structural efficiency in the strength-to-weight ratio through the use of a diagonal framing system. This type of system is normally only constructed in steel.

Geographic preference also plays an important role in the selection of a structural system. New York City and the American Northeast are home to a significant number of tall buildings, the majority of which continue to be constructed in steel — even down to the material choice for foundations — in spite of more global trends toward concrete, composite and hybrid structures. The availability of material as well as the influence of the trade unions affect material choices in this location. In the Middle East and in China there is predominant use of reinforced-concrete tall building systems, or composite systems. The availability of both material and skilled labor has influenced the material choice in these locations.

Tall buildings require specialized construction due to their increased vulnerability as a function of both wind and seismic loading. A major issue is the development of steel systems that assist with the resistance of wind loads. These systems can be extrapolated to structure a wide range of regular and irregular geometries, including highly eccentric loading situations.

The diagonal grid, as discussed below, emerged from an effort to make the tall building resist lateral (primarily wind) forces in innovative ways. The basic construction systems for tall buildings have been a key factor for the development of "diagrids" (the contracted form of "diagonal grid"). Portal frames were found to be insufficient in resisting the lateral forces for tall buildings. Rather than simply creating stronger wind-resistant framed connections, added diagonal members were found to be a more effective way to make the frame more rigid. Diagonal members were also found able to redirect loads and provide alternate load paths in instances of structural failure. The modern diagrid building evolved as standard framed buildings with supplementary diagonal bracing were extensively replaced by those employing an exclusive grid of regular diagonal members. In many cases there are no vertical columns. In some others, the vertical elements are there to supplement the load-carrying function of the diagonal members.

The structural steel skeleton for the tall building evolved to include diagonal members to increase stability, eventually giving way to a dominance of diagonal members. The "bundled tube" type provides added stability by allowing the base of the structure to be substantially larger than the decreased number of "tubes" toward the top of the building. The "belt truss" provides both stability and a place for mechanical floors. The "braced rigid frame" (also known as a "framed shear truss") concentrates wind bracing to a vertical band that runs up multiple faces of the tower. The "diagonalized core system" extends the diagonal members over the entire façade on each face, using the diagonals to supplement the vertical load path provided by the columns. The "diagrid" eliminates vertical columns and uses the diagonal members to support the floors while simultaneously resisting lateral forces.

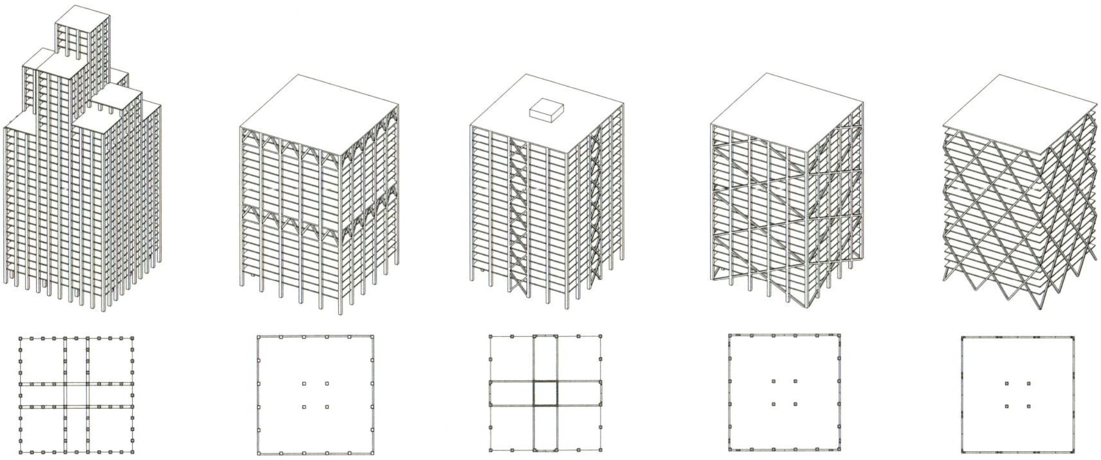

Bundled Tubes | Belt Truss | Braced Rigid Frame | Diagonalized Core System | Diagrid

## DIAGONALIZED CORE BUILDINGS

**Skyscrapers brought with them particular structural problems related to their height and the necessity to resist wind loads. A tall building is essentially acting as a very long cantilever. Early buildings used strong moment-resisting connections within a simpler framed system to resist bending in the structure. These major moment-resisting connections were hidden within the frame and so did not impact the design of the façade. Additional steel was added to the hinge-type framed connections to stiffen the joints.**

**As the design of tall buildings evolved architecturally, new structural systems were developed that chose to express wind resistance by exposing the diagonal braces in the façade. These diagonal braces reinforced a framing system that remained fairly consistent with the standard portal framing that had been developed in the earlier part of the 20th century.**

Left: The Millennium Tower in Dubai, UAE by Atkins Architects uses a modernized variation of the exterior diagonal bracing system on its exterior. The exterior extensions of the floor plate use a vertical K-truss to add rigidity. This is an example of a "braced rigid frame" or "framed shear truss".

Right: The 100-storey John Hancock Building in Chicago, IL, USA, designed by Skidmore, Owings & Merrill, expressed the diagonal reinforcing of its frame as an overlay to the rectilinear pattern made by its strip windows, column covers and spandrel panels. The tower also tapers toward the top in response to wind loads. This system is known as a "braced tube" or "diagonalized core system".

The Indigo Icon Office Tower in Dubai, UAE by Atkins Architects creates a variation of the X bracing system. The bracing frame is set outside the exterior cladding of the tower to exaggerate its expression. There are issues related to climate and temperature swing associated with the choice to set such a structural element outside the environmental/thermal envelope, as the exterior steel will experience thermal expansion differently than the interior structure. This sort of solution is only applicable in climates where thermal bridging is also not a significant issue.

The idea of exterior bracing as a means of both structural and architectural expression is widely used. This differs from genuine diagrid construction as here the diagonal bracing is simply used as an addition to fairly standard framing and as a means to give additional rigidity to the building and is not used as the primary structural system.

Left: The Quantam Nano Engineering Building at the University of Waterloo, ON, Canada, designed by KPMB Architects, uses multiple means of diagonal bracing on both the exterior and interior of the laboratory building. The extra resistance on this 5-story structure was required due to the nature of the labs and the processes contained.

Right: The AESS steel bracing of the Quantam Nano Building sits outside the curtain wall system. Different finishing is required for this steel in contrast to the painted steel structure on the interior.

Left: This residential tower structure in Dubai uses truss band bracing. Here two floors of truss structure are used with standard vertical columns supporting the four floors between. In this instance, the diagonals of the trusses will be incorporated into the cladding design and the spaces will be used as occupied floors. The trusses here are less obtrusive, as the design allows for a clear, column-free span from the core to the outside wall.

Right: The mechanical floor of the Bloomberg Tower in New York, NY, USA, designed by Cesar Pelli. This bracing floor is constructed of trusses, with the structural steel spray-fireproofed.

## TRUSS BAND SYSTEMS

The truss band system is a variation of other tubular systems. Bracing can also be provided to a framed structure by conceiving a number of floors of the tower as large truss structures. On the exterior of the building this is typically seen as a truss band. These floors are often planned for use as mechanical service floors, as the space is substandard for use as office space due to the interference of the many diagonal web members of the trusses that can exist within the plate area of the usable floor space. The frequency of the occurrence of these floors, and the depth of the trusses, are a function of the height-to-width ratio of the building, combined with local wind and seismic issues. Mechanical service needs will also impact the requirements.

## BUNDLED TUBE BUILDINGS

An alternate method of creating bracing for tall buildings was developed through the bundled tube. With this method, the plan of the tower is divided into a large grid. The volume is stepped back toward the top to reduce wind resistance while providing a larger and hence firmer connection at the base. This type of structure has allowed for some of the tallest free-standing buildings to be constructed.

Tower buildings are essentially cantilevers, requiring a substantial moment resisting connections at their base. Today variations of the initial construction as used in the Willis (former Sears) Tower extend the notion to include buildings that have an enlarged base and also step back toward the top. The Burj Khalifa in Dubai has a Y-shaped plan that provides substantial reinforcement at the base of the tower, stepping back significantly over its height to achieve a reduction of floor area for the top floors.

Left: The Willis (former Sears) Tower in Chicago, IL, USA, designed by SOM, maintains the appearance of rectangular framing but instead steps back the building in blocks to address increased wind-loading sway at the top and provide more stability at the base of the tower. This is known as bundled tube construction. It is presently, after the destruction of the World Trade Towers in New York City in 2001, the tallest steel skyscraper in the world.

Right: The Burj Khalifa in Dubai, UAE, designed by SOM (Adrian Smith Design Architect), is the world's tallest building as of 2010. It uses mixed construction, with the lower 80% of the building constructed of specialized reinforced concrete and the upper portion from steel framing. Wind testing for the tower, including the design of the steel top of the building, was conducted by RWDI in Guelph, ON, Canada.

## COMPOSITE CONSTRUCTION

Many tall buildings now use composite construction to assist in achieving height as well as in the creation of unique forms. Combining steel and concrete systems gives architects and engineers greater latitude. It has been considered routine for most tall buildings to use concrete for the construction of the central service core. In composite construction, floor, column and bracing elements may be made of either steel or concrete or a combination of the two materials to achieve strength.

The Burj Al-Arab in Dubai, UAE, designed by Atkins Architects, uses composite construction. Parts of the structure use a combination of steel and concrete systems. In this instance, a composite system supports the unusual shape of the building.

Left: In addition to using concrete for the interior structure, the overall shape of the Burj Al-Arab is braced by steel trusses that are exposed on its exterior. Not all tall buildings that use composite construction make such expression of the differentiated uses of their structural materials.

Right: The interior of the Burj Al-Arab clearly expresses the balance between the lightness of the steel systems and the heaviness of concrete. The view straight up the atrium shows the tensile steel framing that gives form to the large "sail" at the entrance side of the building, offset by the balconies and solid finishes on the hotel-room side of the structure.

## WIND TESTING

One of the key considerations in determining the structure and shape of a tower will be its ability to resist wind loading. Although Computational Fluid Dynamics (CFD) programs are able to do some predictive modeling that will help to determine form, most very tall or unusually shaped buildings are tested in a physical boundary-layer wind tunnel. The CAD drawings are put into a 3D printer and a very accurate model is created from resin. The resin model is fit with numerous small rubber tubes that are attached to sensors at the surface. These are able to record the wind pressures. The wind tunnel model will include scale models of the surrounding buildings so that the data is as accurate as possible. Obviously, if other buildings are constructed nearby at a later date, this can modify the results and in some instances may cause difficulties for existing buildings.

The wind tunnel model for the Burj Khalifa. Testing took place at the practice of RWDI in Guelph, ON, Canada.

The wind tunnel engineers will suggest changes to the shape of the building based upon their findings. The investigation will also look into the design of any damping systems that will be required to offset the potential sway at the top of the tower. The Tuned Mass Damping (TMD) systems must be accommodated into the plan and section of the building.

Extremely tall structures tend to be designed more aerodynamically. Testing is of high importance for new structures that are comprised of twisted or unusual shapes, as in this instance the engineering profession does not have any rules of thumb on which to rely.

Left: The 3D models of 53 Stubbs Road, Hong Kong by Frank Gehry, showing the mass of tubes that feed into the center of the model and that are attached to sensors on the surface of the model.

Right: When buildings are placed in the wind tunnel it is important that the terrain around the building be modeled as well as its immediate urban environment (boundary layer) in order to provide an accurate simulation of the resultant wind pressures.

# DIAGRID SYSTEMS

While the percentage of purely steel skyscrapers has diminished over the past two decades, there has been a distinct rise in the number of high-profile buildings that have chosen to use new variations of the diagonalized core system. The new "diagrid system" is used as a means to deviate from purely rectilinear construction aesthetics and also provide a highly stable structural system. The principle is to take the load path on an angle as a means to eliminate vertical columns and solve bracing issues at the same time. Whereas early applications of expressed diagonal bracing tended not to modify the base rectilinear shape of the tower (save by slight tapering as in the case of John Hancock in Chicago, as mentioned above), current applications of the diagrid are exploiting the ability of the triangulated "mesh-like grid of steel elements" to more easily distort and create curved or even more random geometric forms. The reference to "mesh" recalls 3D modeling language, where curved or irregular topographical forms are turned into a mesh to convert them into mappable triangulated shapes. Diagrids can use the diagonal support system to the point of eliminating all vertical support both on the exterior frame of the building as well as in the space between the exterior frame and the (normally concrete) core. In many cases the floor framing system will be able to span from the exterior diagrid frame directly to the core, thereby eliminating all interior columns. These thin plan buildings are excellent in achieving high levels of daylighting.

Modified diagonalized core system buildings, now known as diagrid buildings, began to appear in contemporary steel design around the year 2003. The three early examples – the Greater London Authority (GLA), Swiss Re and the Hearst Tower – were under development in the offices of Foster + Partners at the same time, and the engineering expertise of ARUP was part of all of the projects. Interestingly, all three use unique variations of the system by virtue of their three-dimensional geometry. The Hearst Tower is perhaps the most normalized, given the rectangular shape of the tower – modified slightly as the corners are indented in places. The shape of the Swiss Re building bulges at mid-height and tapers to a virtual point at the top (hence its nickname, Gherkin). Both Hearst and Swiss Re have eliminated vertical columns and have allowed the diagonal grid of columns to provide the load paths, with floor framing simply tied back to the elevator core. The GLA's backward-leaning egg shape again challenges the diagrid structure by adding further loading eccentricities (see page 139). A spiral ramp that winds up along the interior edge of the façade demonstrates the load-bearing ability of the diagrid structural type so that a regular flat floor-framing system tied back to a core is no longer needed. These deviations from the more symmetrical forms of Hearst and even Swiss Re provide other architects and engineers with the suggestion that the diagrid form can potentially support even more daring feats.

Diagrid systems have evolved to the point to be used today also in a range of innovative mid-rise steel projects.

The Hearst Building in New York City, NY, USA, designed by Foster and ARUP in 2006, was the first diagrid structure to be erected in the United States.

THE ADVANTAGES OF A DIAGRID OVER A MOMENT FRAME

There are a number of structural advantages that can be attributed to the use of a diagrid system over the typical moment frame tube or bundled tube system for a tall building. Where the original diagonalized core system laid a series of diagonal bracing members over a framed exterior support system, the current (standard highrise) diagrid system uses an exclusive exterior frame comprised entirely of diagonal members. This type of structure carries lateral wind loads more efficiently, creating stiffness that is complemented by the axial action of the diagonal member. If tightly engineered, these systems can use less steel than conventionally framed tall buildings.

A diagrid tower is modeled as a vertical cantilever. The size of the diagonal grid is determined by dividing the height of the tower into a series of modules. Ideally the height of the base module of the diamond grid will extend over several stories. In this way the beams that define the edge of the floors can frame into the diagonal members, providing both connection to the core, support for the floor edge beams, and stiffness to the unsupported length of the diagonal member. This aspect of the diagrid is often expressed in the cladding of the building. The modularity of the curtain wall normally will scale down the dimensions of the diamonds or triangulated shapes to suit the height of the floors and requirements for both fixed and operable windows.

As with any deviation from standard framing techniques, constructability is an important issue. Both the engineering and fabrication of the joints are more complex than for an orthogonal structure and this incurs additional costs. The precision of the geometry of the connection nodes is critical, making it advantageous to maximize shop fabrication to reduce difficulties associated with job site work.

There are two schools of thought as to the rigidity of the construction of the nodes themselves. Technically, if designing a purely triangulated "truss-like" structure, the center of the node need not be rigid and can be constructed as a hinge connection. Where this may work well for symmetrical structures having well-balanced loads, eccentrically loaded structures will need some rigidity in the node to assist in self-support during the construction process. In many of the diagrid projects constructed to date the nodes have been prefabricated as rigid elements in the shop, allowing for incoming straight members to be either bolted or welded on site more easily. As this type of structure is more expensive to fabricate, cost savings are only to be realized if there is a high degree of repetition in the design and fabrication of the nodes.

The triangulation of the diagrid "tube" itself is not sufficient to achieve full rigidity in the structure. Ring beams at the floor edges are normally tied into the diagrid to integrate the structural action into a coherent tube. As there are normally multiple floors intersecting with each long diagonal of the grid, this intersection will occur at the node as well as at several instances along the diagonal. The angle of the diagonals allows for a natural flow of loads through the structure and down to the foundation of the building. Steel has been the predominant material of choice for all diagrid buildings constructed to date.

Diagrid building and the design and detailing associated with the steel structural systems can be divided into distinct groupings:
→ Towers and tall buildings,
→ Curvilinear forms,
→ Crystalline geometry, and
→ Hybrid buildings with combined geometries.

## DIAGRID TOWERS

The most natural extrapolation of the diagonalized core tower is the diagrid tower. In this instance the regular portal frame is eliminated and replaced by a tube of diagrid steel that serves to carry all of the loads down the exterior face of the tower. The displacement of vertical columns by the diagonal members necessitates an increase in the density of these members, over earlier examples where the diagonal bracing was supplementary and therefore less frequent. Where the diagrid sits external to the envelope or curtain wall the cladding system is connected to the floor structure. Where the diagrid is internal, the cladding is connected to the diagrid. This tends to influence the design of the cladding system. Floor-connected curtain wall is typically rectilinear and diagrid connected-curtain wall is triangulated.

Left: Bush Lane House in London, England, designed by ARUP in 1976, was one of the first buildings to use an expressed exterior diagrid to eliminate the use of interior columns to achieve clear-span office space. It is constructed from stainless steel with cast nodes.

Right: The cast stainless steel nodes are connected back at each floor level. The curtain wall behind maintains a regular rectilinear pattern in contrast to the square diamonds of the exterior tubular structure, indicating that it is attached to the floors for support.

Left: Swiss Re in London, England by Foster + Partners and ARUP uses the diagrid to create a curved tower. The geometry facilitated a special ventilation system that spirals up the darker glass in the façade.

Right: The diagrid at the base of the building is framed out to create an arcade element.

One of the more challenging issues with oddly shaped diagrid buildings is devising a system for washing the building. For Swiss Re a mechanism was attached at the top of the building that would cantilever the cables for the equipment away from the surface of the building.

The cables are pinned to the grid and padded to prevent any sway in the equipment from damaging the façade. The darker coloring in the glazing denotes the location of the double façade portions of the envelope that are used for ventilation.

In some cases, where the floor plate size is large or the loads are eccentric, the external diagrid may supplement the support system provided by interior columns, in a similar way to a traditional diagonalized core system, but with more intensity. This is the case in the CCTV Tower in Beijing, designed by Rem Koolhaas and ARUP, where the exterior diagrid serves as additional support to the interior framed system. In this unusual pairing of tilted, connected towers there are vertical columns supporting the floors, on the interior of the plan as well as at the outside face, many of which extend the full height of the building. A heavily braced transfer floor at mid-height that is also a mechanical services floor was used to transfer the load of columns that could not align on a single vertical path. The internal columns are encased in concrete, which provides for 3-hour fire protection as well as additional strength. The diagrid system on the exterior acts as a tube that integrates the floors, columns and exterior structure. The "columns" of the exposed diagrid have the same exposed width with their depth varying to suit the load requirements. The diagonals are all 1m by 60cm/3.28ft by 1.97ft plate girders, with only the steel thicknesses varying according to differentiated load requirements. In a framed steel tower a triangular plate can be used at the intersection of a column and beam to create a moment-resisting connection. The CCTV building uses four of these plates at the major intersections of the perimeter columns, braces and beams to create a "butterfly plate" as a variation of a traditional moment-bracing plate stiffener.

At the CCTV Building in Beijing, China, designed by Rem Koolhaas of OMA with ARUP in 2009, the diagonal structure is expressed in the design of the curtain wall. However, unlike many diagrid buildings, the predominant pattern of the glazing in the project is rectangular. The range of density inferred by the diagonal patterning on the façade corresponds directly to actual variations in the internal structure. The diagonal grid system allowed for the construction of the large cantilevered sections of the towers without need of shoring. The vertical lines in the curtain wall follow the natural vertical alignment of the columns and floors on the interior.

The construction of this building would not have been possible without the added strength of the diagrid. The diagrid allowed for the construction of the cantilevering sections without the requirement of a major shoring tower to provide temporary support during construction.

The CCTV Building in Beijing was the first of the diagrid-based towers to significantly deviate from an easy-to-support form. Although diagrids had been used for odd geometries and extreme cantilevers on buildings below twelve stories, nothing quite like this had been attempted before. Just prior to the opening of the tower, the adjacent Mandarin Hotel was ravaged by a fire that gutted the building. As the two towers were connected below grade through foundation systems, the opening of CCTV was postponed while investigations were carried out in order to fully understand the structural interdependency of the two towers. There was concern that the demolition of the Mandarin Hotel might result in an imbalance to the CCTV Tower.

At the time of writing, the current most innovative use of the diagrid structural model is in the creation of "twisted forms". These can be seen in numerous tall buildings presently under construction, particularly in Asia and the Middle East. The "mesh" of the steel diagrid is capable of conforming to almost any shape that can be created using 3D modeling software. The diamond-shaped grids are easily further subdivided into triangulated patterns for curtain wall manufacture. Typically the twisted building shape will be combined with a substantial vertical concrete core that can provide straight-run elevator access throughout the building and arrange the offsets to hang from the core. Ring beams are placed around the perimeter of each floor and attach to the diagrid. These provide the connection point for the floor beams that will normally clear span from the outer diagrid framed wall to the core. Combining twisted and vertical elements requires extra engineering to assure the structural integrity of the building. There is also a substantial increase in fabrication and erection cost as a result of the decrease in repetitive design of the nodes.

Capital Gate in Dubai, UAE, designed by RMJM Architects in 2011, boasts a backwards lean of 18° – which is significantly more than the Leaning Tower of Pisa. A roughly elliptical concrete core extends up through the center of the structure. The white-diamond shape made by the curtain wall cladding expresses the location of the steel diagrid behind. Each diamond represents two floors. In order to balance the rear lean at the top of the tower there is significant structure that opposes this mass at the ground-floor level on the opposing side. In the lower sections of the building the diagrid is located very close to the concrete core on the backward-leaning side, while it is very close to the front of the building toward the top.

The curtain wall has been designed with triangulated operable windows. The actual diagrid on this building roughly forms a square.

The front (south) façade of the tower is shaded by a structural "sheet" of steel and steel mesh that appears to flow from close to the top of the tower down toward the base and then outward to form a large canopy at the ground level of the tower. The shading device is said to contribute significantly to a reduction in cooling load. The curved steel beams that give form to the shade structure are tied back to the nodes of the diagrid with round HSS members.

In response to the uniqueness of the curvilinear forms, a special round connection was developed to simplify the variations in the connection of the shading device to the primary structure.

# *PROCESS PROFILE: BOW ENCANA TOWER / FOSTER + PARTNERS AND ZEIDLER PARTNERSHIP*

Design Architect: Foster + Partners
Executive Architect: Zeidler Partnership Architects
Structural Engineers: Halcrow Yolles
MEP Services Engineer: Cosentini Associates
Constructor: Ledcor Construction Limited
Structural Steel Trade: Supreme Walters Joint Venture

The 59-story Bow Encana Tower is a joint venture between Foster + Partners and Zeidler Partnership of Toronto, ON, Canada. The lateral support system consists of a perimeter trussed tube. It is located inside the glazing line because of the severe cold winter weather in this climate region. The diagonal grid system consists of six-story-high diagonals along the curved north and south elevations. The southern face curves inward to allow for many of the sustainable design features, including a double glazed atrium and sky gardens. The south-facing diagrid is fabricated using AESS, while the north-facing diagrid is fabricated as standard structural steel, which will be concealed beneath fire-protective coverings.

The Bow Encana uses combined gravity and lateral systems. The gravity system is comprised of steel columns, structural steel beams and concrete-on-steel deck or composite slabs for the floors. The lateral system of the exterior diagrid on the north and south façades eliminated the need for interior concrete shear walls, thereby assisting space planning and architectural expression. The diagrid system takes advantage of the curved shape to increase its rigidity. The six-story-tall diagonal members are connected to each other via special nodes. The nodes on the exposed and non-exposed faces are quite different in their design and appearance. Link or ring beams at the tips of the diagonals further increase rigidity and provide the attaching point for the floor beams. It is estimated that this system represents a 20% saving in steel over a regular moment frame system.

A variety of systems was considered for the diagrid structure, but ultimately it was decided to custom-fabricate the members from built-up triangular plate sections. The engineers felt that the fabrication and erection of the diagrid system had fewer complexities than a fully moment-connected frame. This was due to well-selected node points that allowed for repetition of the components and connections. The choice to expose the diagrid on the south face did necessitate a much tighter level of tolerance for the fabrication and erection process.

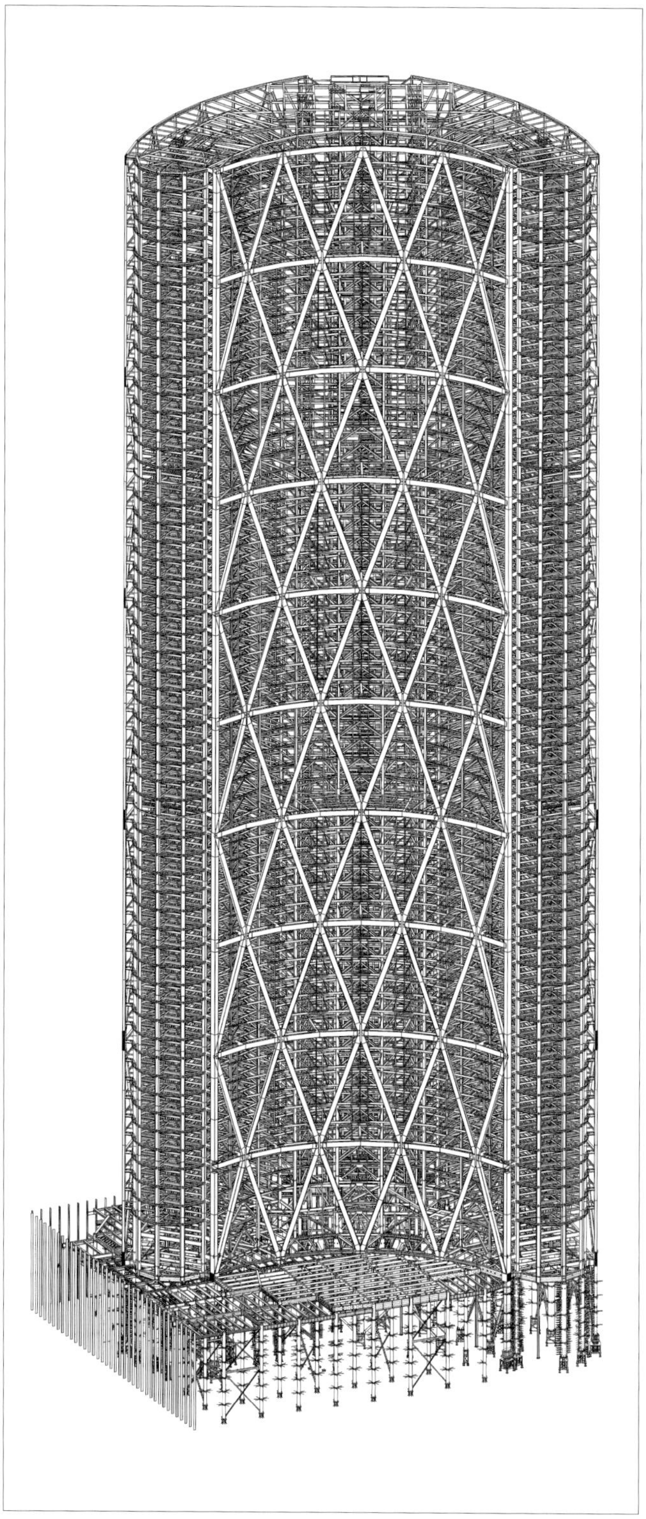

Overall structural isometric of the Bow Encana Tower in Calgary, AB, Canada as drawn by the fabricator and erector, Walters Inc. of Hamilton, ON, Canada. This drawing serves as an overall reference for the entire project. It shows every single piece of steel for the project.

Left: This digital model shows the ground-floor framing of the tower. The basement was fully constructed in steel. The yellow lines indicate the extent of the tower floor plate.

Right: This detail of the overall image shows the condition at the curved ends of the tower, where the front and rear diagrid structures meet. The color coding is indicative of the member types and is also used to describe aspects of the staging of the construction sequence.

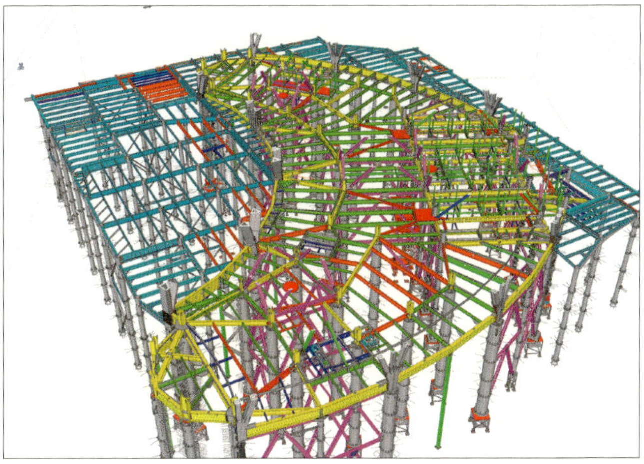

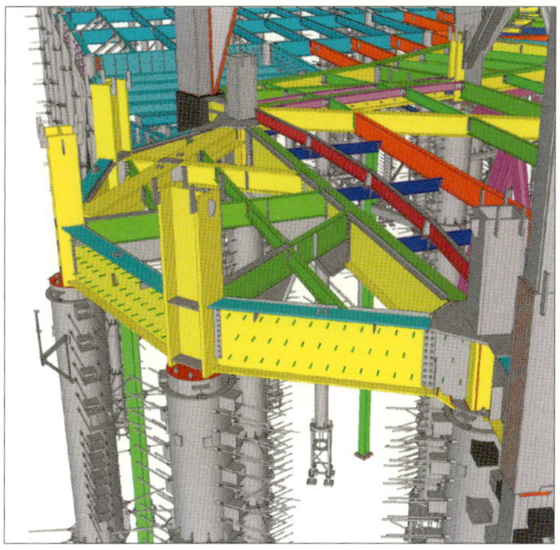

Left: The base of the diagrid must connect to the piling cap. This detail shows the sections fabricated from triangular plate to which the long six-story diagonal members will connect.

Top Right: Use of (green) temporary shoring during the erection of the nodes.

Bottom Right: The major diagrid members are shown in blue, with the temporary shoring in red and, in green, floor framing that must tie into the diagrids and complete the stabilization. The temporary supports were reused several times in the course of the project.

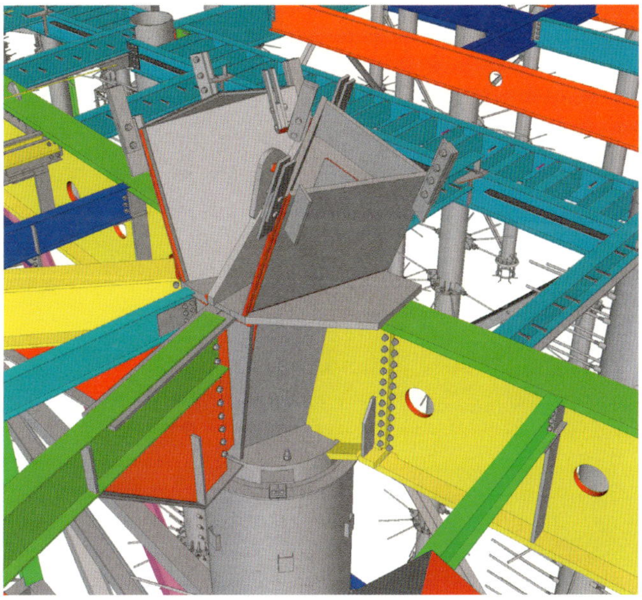

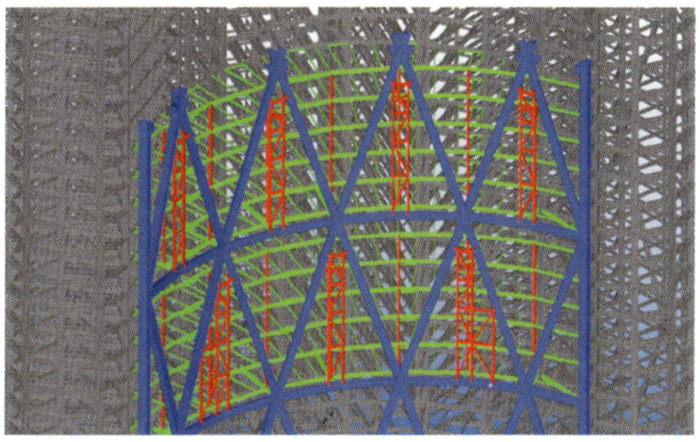

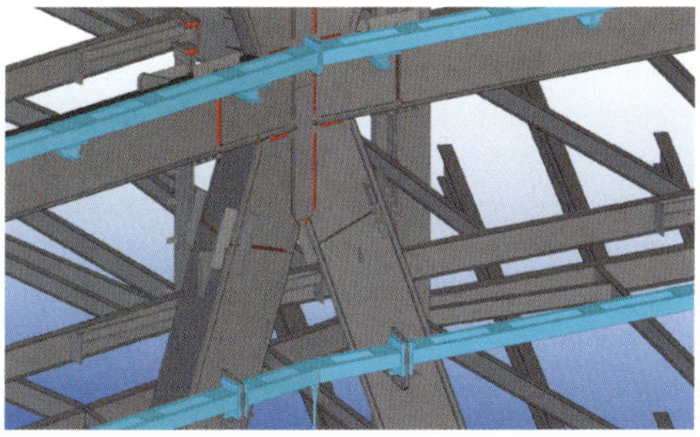

This image shows the connection to the ring beams at the atrium face. Although the face of the building is curved, these elements are fabricated from straight segments.

Two views of the same connection illustrate the precise correlation between the digital 3D model and the actual building. This is indispensable to maintain quality in this type of complex project. For cost savings, the back sides of the triangulated members, to be hidden behind the curtain wall, are not as finely finished as the exposed interior sides.

The diagrid is free-standing at the base of the building to accommodate a large atrium at the ground floor. On this façade it remains separated from the inner curtain wall, allowing for the construction of a double façade to assist with heat control. The horizontal steel rings at this level provide stabilization that in conventional construction would be given by the intersection with the floor beams.

One of the nodes in production at the fabricator's shop. The top face of the element is AESS and the rear face fabricated to be concealed. Temporary bracing members are attached to ensure that the node does not deform during transport, as there is little tolerance for dimensional error during erection. It is essential to do this work in the shop because a crane is needed to lift and turn the member to provide access for fabrication.

This view shows the thickness of the plate and the use of the internal plate for bracing both in situ and during shipping. The tabs are used to provide temporary bolted connections on site and are removed once welding is complete.

This is the semi-complete connection at the piling cap. The welds are finished and in the midst of being remediated to remove any trace of the connection process.

Ironworkers working on one of the nodes at the north face of the building. As this connection will be covered with gypsum board, member selection and connection methods are quite different from AESS diagrid members on the south side of the building.

Top: The steel decking and concrete topping are essential to complete the stabilization of the structure. The vertical column connections sit about 1m above the floor level.

Middle: The floor beams frame into the node on the north façade of the building, providing additional support.

Bottom: Temporary connection tabs remain on a diagrid member for the north face, as the welding has not yet taken place.

The curtain wall pattern on the north façade expresses the steel diagrid, while the primary pattern of glazing is rectilinear.

The United States Pavilion for Expo 67 in Montreal, QC, Canada was one of the first large-scale applications of Buckminster Fuller's geodesic dome. Although very lightweight, the form proved to be fairly static and as a result was not widely adopted as a support system for buildings.

## CURVED DIAGRID-SUPPORTED SHAPES ON LOW- TO MID-RISE BUILDINGS

Beyond the use for towers, the diagrid structure quite naturally adapts to supporting a wide range of non-rectilinear forms. When adapted to support spherical or curved forms, diagrids tend to replace the use of geodesic systems, which did not easily allow for variations on spherical forms.

The first high-profile application of the curved diagrid was in the Foster/ARUP design for the Greater London Authority Building in 2003. The diagrid was designed to create a stepped façade that would provide sun shading. A spiral ramp winds up inside the exterior wall, which interfaces easily with the geometry of the diagonal grid. Unlike many of the diagrids that are used in tower applications, the steel in this building was left architecturally exposed.

Left: The diagonal grid of the Greater London Authority (GLA), in London, England, designed by Foster/ARUP in 2003, reveals the welded tubular steel structure on the exterior through the articulation of the curtain wall system. The further subdivision of the glazing provides a glazing unit size that is suited to the scale of the building. The idea of the triangular "mesh" covering the building provides a way to break down the scale of the shape to one that is more human. The modularity of the glazing subdivisions is almost always much smaller than the steel structure.

Right: The egg-shaped building leans backwards to create a series of steps in the floors that assist with solar shading.

Left: The close connection between the curved curtain wall envelope and the round HSS diagrid members results in tight construction tolerances.

Right: The architectural exposure of the steel diagrid required a high level of care during the site fabrication of the all-welded structure.

On a circular structure the diagrid can also be used to handle less severely curved forms. Aldar Headquarters in Abu Dhabi is the first building using diagrid construction to have a circular/disk form. Two large curved round HSS tubes sit at the edge of the circle to define its form. The diameter of the circular exterior of the 23-storey building, constructed to LEED™ Silver standards, is 120m. The distance from the pair of rectangular concrete cores at its center to the façade is quite tight, creating very unique interior spaces. Steel ring beams, which span horizontally between the diagonal grid members, provide stability for the structure at the edge condition of each floor.

Although the face of the building is convex, the diagrid members themselves are created from straight segments. The curtain wall glazing is subdivided into a triangulated pattern that relates to the floor levels. This smaller triangulated "mesh" assists with fine-tuning the final curved shape.

The side view shows the relative thinness of the building. The symmetry of the form helps in balancing the loads as well as providing some economy in the engineering, fabrication and erection of the structure.

Aldar Headquarters in Abu Dhabi, UAE, designed by MZ Architects and ARUP in 2010. The white cladding lines expressed on the exterior delineate the location of the major diagrid members behind. The major structural nodes of the diagrid occur at the intersections of the white cladding. The vertical distance of each "diamond" contains 8 stories.

## CRYSTALLINE DIAGRID FORMS

Even though angular crystalline forms use the principles of diagrid construction, their structural resolution is quite different from diagrids used in towers or other more regular forms. To date, most crystalline applications of the diagrid have been used to create larger aggregated volumes, often with complicated intersections of their volumes. This has meant that much of the expression and formal impact of the angular steel supports can be seen on the interior of the building. Eccentricities and large cantilevers also require more strength in the nodal connections. In order for these structures to be supported during construction, either temporary support towers or cable stays are necessary before the concrete floor systems are poured to provide the necessary diaphragm action.

The diagonalized structure of the Denver Art Museum in Denver, CO, USA, designed by Libeskind and ARUP in 2005, created major structural cantilevers. The eccentricity of the diagonal members required significant use of shoring during construction to support the sections until the floors and other lateral bracing systems were in place.

Studio Libeskind's foray into diagrid design worked with the potential for the diagonal grid to facilitate extreme geometries, including severely crystalline forms and large unsupported cantilevers. The use of the diagrid expanded in a major way the angularity of their design for the Jewish Museum in Berlin, Germany, whose angular form was framed more traditionally.

One of the issues with both the diagonalized core building and the contemporary diagrid building is the architectural impact of the diagonal structure. Early office structures such as the John Hancock Tower in Chicago used extremely large diagonals, whose disruptions to the glazing in the curtain wall deny access to light on the exterior wall at major points of intersection. As diagrids normally eliminate interior columns, both vertical and diagonal, their use does not negatively impact interior planning. Where diagrids are modified to create more crystalline forms, the grid has ceased to be an exterior tube-like element and instead thoroughly permeates the volume and massing of the building. This means that there is significant impact of the diagonal columns and subsequent wall planes on the interior of the building. For buildings that are to serve as a functional shell and not as the primary object, increased dialogue is required to ensure that function, fitments and (in the case of museums) exhibits work with the skewed architecture.

The Seattle Central Library uses a very complex structural system that combines an articulated concrete core with a diagrid envelope and glazing system. The steel diagrid allows for extensive cantilevers with minimal structural interference, thus maximizing the extent of glazing on the envelope. The specific use of diagrid framing in this project varies from many others in that the dimensions of the grid correspond exactly to those of the curtain wall system it supports. Additionally, the diagonal grid is supported by large steel members that have been inserted into the structure as needed at erratic intervals rather than in a predefined pattern.

Left: The Seattle Central Library in Seattle, WA, USA, designed by Rem Koolhaas/OMA in 2004. The steel diagrid that supports the exterior glazing is comprised of panels of wide-flange sections that have been prefabricated in large "sheets" at the shop. These are joined together on site via bolting.

Right: The expanses of the panels span between larger steel beams that break up some of the larger span requirements of the planes of the exterior form.

Left: At seemingly erratic instances, diagonal steel columns provide additional support to the span of the glazing support diagrid.

Right: Where the angled steel column supports meet the diagrid, the grid is doubled up to better distribute the loads to the diagrid frame.

## HYBRID SHAPES

The benefits of diagonal grid systems have been exploited in a wide range of projects that may be seen to use variations of the methods proven in more regular diagrid buildings. Multiple layers of diagonals, often three-dimensional, are used to create complex forms with irregular, often curved geometries. As the structure is often left exposed, this requires a higher level of precision and workmanship in the fabrication and finishing of the structure. Such a system was employed in the design of the National Stadium in Beijing, China, designed by Herzog and de Meuron and ARUP with Ai Weiwei. The desire to emulate the texture and form of a "bird's nest" required multiple layers of seemingly random diagonal steel members.

Top: Although the structure of the Beijing National Stadium in China, designed by Herzog & de Meuron/ Ai Weiwei/ARUP in 2008, may have an outward chaotic appearance, there was significant modularity and specialized sequencing in the design and erection process of the members.

Right: All of the members are custom-fabricated box sections, prefabricated to their maximum size in order to minimize site welding. Temporary clips, similar to those used on the Bow Encana columns, were used to hold the sections in place during site welding. These were removed and their connection points ground to diminish any telltale marks prior to applying the finish coating. All of the welds were done with the intention of achieving a flush, seamless appearance.

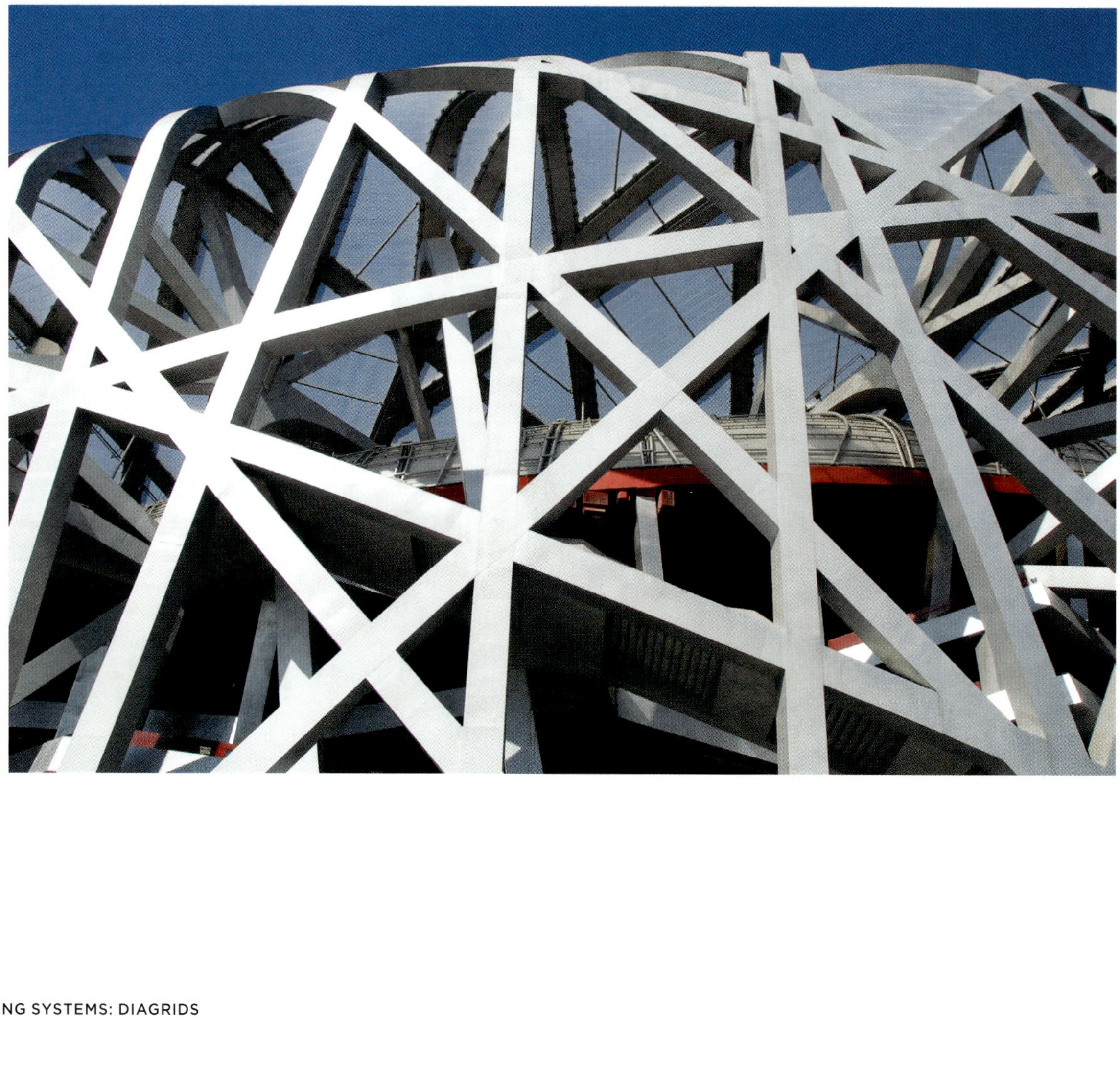

Left: A view up one of the primary three-dimensional trusses. These were erected first, then subsequent layers of diagonal members and then filled in for additional support.

Right: Traces of the weld from the removed temporary clips and the connection between segments.

The evolution of the diagonalized core building systems toward the modern diagrid continues to facilitate an ever-growing variety of applications that vary in terms of scale and geometry. The steel detailing of these systems is based on the same basic principles of connections as for framed systems. Where a building like the Bird's Nest may on the surface appear to be quite irregular, but in fact be supported by quite regular patterns of underlying geometry that combine to create complexity, buildings like the Canadian Museum for Human Rights in Winnipeg, MB, Canada, designed by Antoine Predock are using diagrid framing to support a structural geometry that is indeed irregular and unconventional.

The Canadian Museum for Human Rights in Winnipeg, MB, Canada, designed by Antoine Predock, uses diagrid framing to create a series of irregular volumes that will eventually be topped by a spire-like tower. The steel diagrid is surrounded in part by large curved round HSS tubes which support large expanses of glazing that are intended to mimic the wings of a bird. (Image as of May 2011.)

The façade framing will be quite separate and supported by these HSS tubes on the upper and lower ends of custom-designed trusses. The clips to which the glazing trusses will be connected are visible. Each is set at a unique angle to coordinate with the requirements of the glass. The use of BIM is critical to ensure proper coordination and alignment. Only the exposed portions of the steel that will be designated as AESS have been primed.

Given the high proportion of eccentric loads, some of the nodes that serve to transfer loads through the building are very complex and make use of a variety of steel shapes. As this node will be concealed, the choice of members has been left to best suit the structural requirements.

These types of systems truly exploit the tensile strength of steel, particularly in terms of its ability to support lateral and eccentric loads. Although not specifically discussed, many of these projects exist in seismic zones, and earthquake resistance was built into the design of their diagrid systems.

# *CHAPTER 10*

*- - -*

# *CASTINGS*

*- - -*

*HISTORIC AND CONTEMPORARY CASTING*

*BASIC TYPES OF CAST CONNECTORS*

*TENSILE CONNECTORS*

*BASE CONNECTIONS*

*BRANCH-TYPE CONNECTIONS*

*PROCESS PROFILE: UNIVERSITY OF GUELPH SCIENCE BUILDING / YOUNG + WRIGHT ARCHITECTS*

Pudong Airport in Shanghai, China by Paul Andreu uses a variety of steel shapes to create the undulating curved roof over the terminal. Custom castings are used to transition the differing geometries of the roof beams and of the angled supports of the tree-like columns.

18
17
16
15
14
13

# HISTORIC AND CONTEMPORARY CASTING

When the word "cast" is associated with iron and steel construction, images of intricate details and ornamentation immediately come to mind. Casting seems synonymous with ornament. Early cast iron and steel were used very deliberately to increase the level of decoration in projects, at first to help them fit with more traditional forms of architecture and later to create their own unique organic forms.

Left: Cast iron was chosen over wrought iron for the Bibliothèque Ste. Geneviève in order to increase the amount of detail and achieve some economy through industrialized repetition. In contrast, wrought iron of the period was very plain in appearance.

Right: The original entrances to the Paris Métropolitain, designed by Hector Guimard, have become the "poster children" for Art Nouveau style. The use of cast steel was integral to the production of these organic forms, making them durable in the outdoor environment (if not completely resistant to graffiti).

Historic cast iron was very brittle and not suitable for welding. Modern cast steel has very different properties and many of the larger connecting elements are designed specifically with welding in mind – although this does vary from application to application.

If casting was selected in the past specifically for its ability to *increase* the level of detail and decoration in projects, the current reasons for its rise in popularity are precisely the opposite. Casting is now chosen as a means to simplify the appearance and geometry of connections that must accommodate the convergence of multiple structural elements. Castings are employed to smoothen out the connections, simplify potential geometry in welding, and make load transfer paths through connections more reliable and more resistant.

Modern steel castings are higher in strength, weldable and more ductile. Castings are used in conjunction with cable and glass structures, and in complex tubular joints for buildings or in bridges. While they bring with them the added advantage of handling complex, curved geometries without the difficulties found in using multiple combinations of tubes and plates, they do require a different level of engineering and testing expertise. Economy is found in the mass production of elements. One-off castings or small runs can be very expensive.

In order for castings to be cost-effective, certain conditions should be met. Foundries are disbursed so travel and shipping will be factors. Repetition of elements can amortize the cost of the mold. If many elements are joining at a restricted point, or the stress through the connection is very high, then castings make sense. A rough rule of thumb is that if the connection starts to cost four times as much as the material it is made of, then steel castings start to be economical.

The casting process will use either an expendable or non-expendable mold. Smaller repetitive elements, such as those used in glazing and tension systems as connectors, will use a non-expendable mold and will typically be die-cast. Larger, unique, non-repetitive units will normally use an expendable mold – a mold that is broken to remove the casting. The casts are made by pouring molten metal into a mold cavity formed out of natural or synthetic sand. The sand is bonded together using clay, chemical binders or polymerized oils. The sand can be recycled to create another mold. Sand-cast steel generally has a rough surface that will not match standard steel. Special finishing will be required if a seamless final appearance is sought between the casting and the adjacent tubular member. For higher levels of AESS categories this can mean significant grinding and filling to smoothen out the rougher finish of the casting or remove casting mill marks.

Castings can be formed hollow or solid. Solid castings are usually to be found in smaller connectors like the clevises that are used to form the terminus of tension rod-type structures. Hollow castings are used for larger members, as solid castings would have difficulty in achieving uniform cooling. Non-uniform cooling can create internal stresses. Non-destructive evaluation of each large casting, including 100% ultrasonic testing, should be considered as a minimum.

When selecting a caster, be sure that the foundry will perform appropriate testing. Large specialty castings require specific testing to ensure that they are properly designed and capable of resisting stresses. Cast steel exhibits isotropic properties, making it quite suitable for transferring forces through the connections in a reliable manner—i.e. being able to resist shear, moment and torsion stresses. This is achieved by working the geometry as a function of variations in wall thickness, independent of the finished form of the exterior. Unlike fabrications made from tubes or plates, the interior dimensions of the void in a casting do not have to match the exterior form of the object.

## *BASIC TYPES OF CAST CONNECTORS*

Where historic steel structures would cast entire elements, including columns, beams and trusses, modern cast steel is normally only used for the connection point or node. A more standard structural steel element is then connected to the node. This is more economical than either casting the entire member or constructing a complex connection using modified or agglomerated standard sections. As was seen in the giant 11-tonne gerberette castings of the Centre Pompidou, the restriction on size is a function of the casting facility and the ability to transport and erect the element. Castings can be quite small and fairly standard, as are found for tensile connectors, or quite large and unusual, for larger structural applications. Solid castings are effectively used in seismic installations.

Cast ConneX® High-Strength Connectors™ are standardized, high-strength end connectors for use in combination with round HSS members. They are used in a variety of mission-critical applications (i.e. earthquake-resistant or blast-resistant construction), where the structural steel connection must be as strong as the connected HSS member in tension and/or compression. They are very commonly applied in AESS, as fabricated connections with similar high-strength capabilities would have to be heavily reinforced with steel plate, angle or channel elements and are thus rather unsightly. The connectors are shop-welded to the HSS elements to which they connect; the connector HSS-assembly is subsequently bolted in place on site (via double-shear bolted connection to a gusset plate). Current sizes accommodate round HSS with outer diameters ranging from 102mm/4in to 219mm/8.625in.

Left: A cast High-Strength Connector™ produced by Cast ConneX® Corporation of Canada. The solid casting is welded to the incoming tubular component. Multiple holes are drilled through the plates to provide a rigid connection.

Right: Earthquake-resistant braces equipped with Cast ConneX® High-Strength Connectors™ that are ready to be bolted in place.

Left: An earthquake-resistant brace equipped with Cast ConneX® High-Strength Connectors™ installed in an office building with a steel-braced frame structure.

Right: A large hollow universal pin-connector-type casting produced by Cast ConneX®. It will be welded to a hollow steel section or pipe member. A pin connection will be drilled with a single hole to permit rotation in the joint. Pin connections do not necessarily need to be solid, as they are not transferring the same kind of load as a high-strength connector.

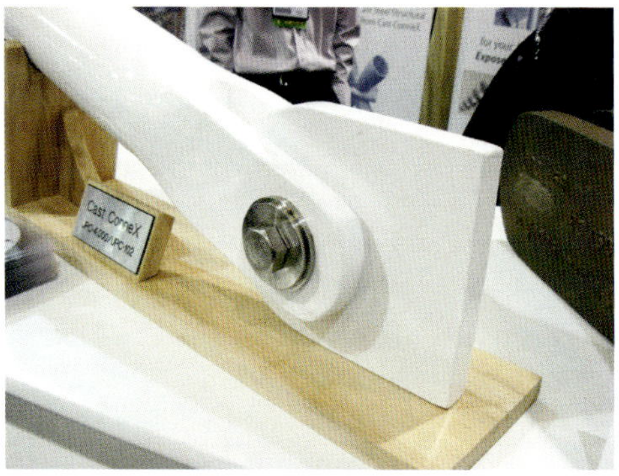

A Universal Pin Connector™ produced by Cast ConneX®. The solid cast end is welded to a tube or a rod, depending on the size of the connection and the detailing. A single hole provides for flexibility in aligning the geometry of the joint.

Left: Two 324mm/12.75in diameter HSS columns fitted with Cast ConneX® Universal Pin Connectors™. The elements have been finished to achieve a seamless transition between the HSS member and the cast steel connectors.

Right: A Cast ConneX® Universal Pin Connector™ applied at the base of an inclined exterior column which supports an overhanging canopy. The detail provides a seamless-looking member.

## *TENSILE CONNECTORS*

Tension structures often use very slender members, as there is no requirement to resist compressive forces and hence no need to stiffen the section through an increase in section properties. This leaves very little perimeter to facilitate joining (welding) the rod or cable at its end point. A suite of basic connection types is used that attach to the slender structural members either by threading or welding, depending of the member size and loading requirements. As tension members normally require tightening after erection to ensure that they are taut and ready to work, the members themselves must be installed "loose". In cases where threading on the ends of the members does not provide sufficient ability to tighten the system, interior elements like turnbuckles are installed mid-section. Turnbuckles may also be required if the end connector is welded to the rod or section.

Left: The cast clevis-type end connector uses a single point of rotating connection and typically provides a thread for the connection of the rod to the clevis. In this instance a cotter pin-type attachment is used rather than a single bolt.

Right: The cast steel connector based on a standard turnbuckle is used to tighten a tensile rod. The rods are threaded and tightening is achieved by rotating the connector.

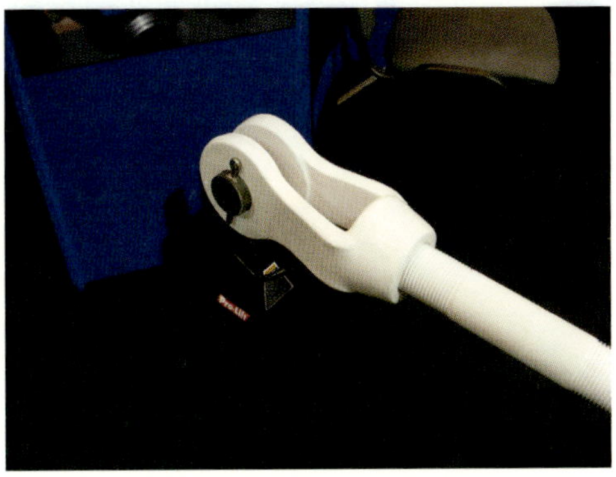

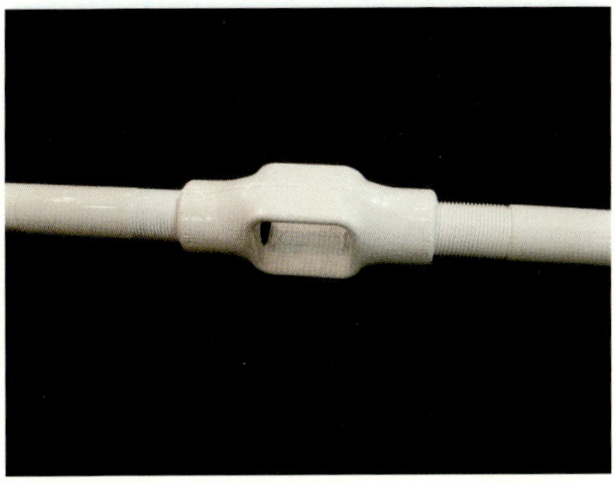

**Cast connections are typically used in tensile structures, as they provide for an easy-to-fabricate transition between cable or rod-type tension members and the bolted connection to the compressive elements. Some of this connection language has been derived from suspension and cable stayed bridge detailing. Some also has evolved as an economical simplification of the more elaborate custom detailing to be found in early High Tech architecture (see Chapter 5: AESS: Its History and Development).**

The circular dome of the Reichstag Building of the German Bundestag in Berlin, Germany, designed by Foster + Partners, uses a spiral plate-steel ramp as the primary circulation path by which to ascend or descend the glazed dome. Although the steel in the project is predominantly created from custom-made curved and welded steel plate, cast connections play an important role in the dome's tensile stabilization system.

Left: The upper viewing platform is connected to the triangular welded plate steel ribs via clevis-type tension connectors. These connections use standard cast end-point connectors.

Right: The curved steel ramp is connected to the triangular ribs via similar clevis-type tension connectors. This connector has been cast as a variation, allowing two rods to be joined through one connector, thereby simplifying the geometry of the connection that would normally see the use of two separate connectors.

# *BASE CONNECTIONS*

**Non-tensile connectors have a slightly different associated tectonic language. Where the base connection can be a hinge and need not resist moment, the connection can be designed to allow some rotation and, if desired, not provide defined rigidity.**

Left: The Richmond Speed Skating Oval, BC, Canada, constructed for the 2010 Winter Olympics, uses an interesting mix of wood products and steel in its design language.

Right: Custom-fabricated galvanized steel end connectors are used to join the glue-laminated struts to the exposed concrete foundation piers. The connectors have been galvanized to ensure weatherability in the damp climate. Stainless steel bolts are used for the same reason, as well as to add interest and material texture to the detail.

Left: The Ludwig Erhard Building in Berlin, Germany, designed by Nicholas Grimshaw, makes use of some unusual cast connections to complete the details on this building of the Chamber of Industry and Commerce.

Right: The "feet" of the large curved stainless steel sections of the Ludwig Erhard Building are created from cast stainless steel.

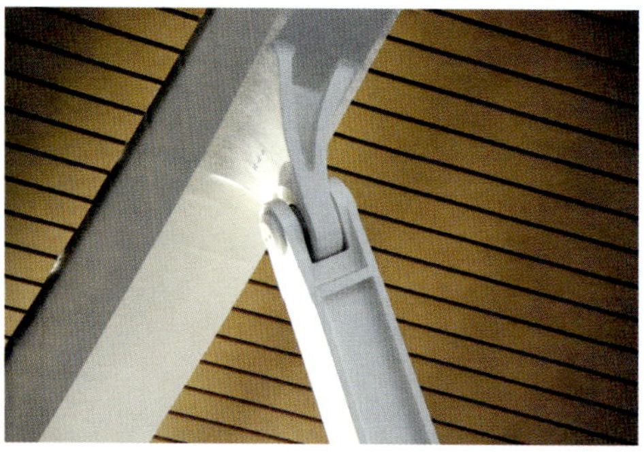

Left: The curved geometries of Pudong International Airport in Shanghai, China require a range of methods to create the various steel components.

Right: The connection of the branch to the curved beam is accomplished through a cast connection that is integrated into the beam. This accommodates a twist between the alignment of the beam and that of the tree branch.

Left: The curved beams at Pudong Airport are in part stabilized by lightweight trusses that are integrated into the form. Clevis and turnbuckle attachments are used with the rods to tighten the components.

Right: A turnbuckle-type joint is incorporated into this T joint in the light tensile truss.

# *BRANCH-TYPE CONNECTIONS*

**Cast connections can be effective aesthetic and economical solutions when joining multiple structural members. They can simplify the geometry of the connection and make for smoother transfer of loads through the connection. Even custom-made castings can be mass-produced, thereby creating economies in erection and labor as well as materials. Comparison studies can be carried out to provide a project with alternative approaches.**

Each project requires a differentiated approach as a function of:

- → number of members incoming
- → access to the connection for erection
- → desired aesthetic
- → decision to reveal or expose the transition between members
- → decision to mask or reveal the different surface textures of the casting and the structural section
- → structural load path requirements for either a hinged or a moment-resisting connection
- → budget

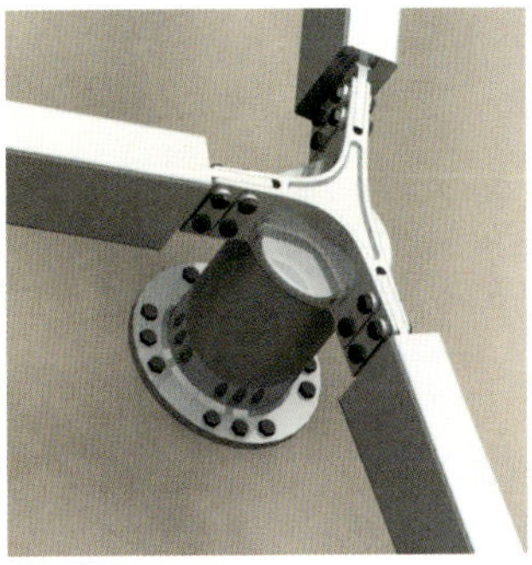

Left: This custom-made steel connection for the Quantum Nano Building at the University of Waterloo, ON, Canada is created from a large number of welded parts. Hundreds of identical elements cover the façade of the building.

Right: Proposal for an alternative connection for the Quantum Nano Building (courtesy of Cast ConneX®) that would not have altered the design of the rectangular HSS elements but would have greatly simplified the erection and fabrication of the hub.

**The size and complexity of a connection and the incoming members, as well as load paths, may benefit from the use of castings to create a strong yet elegant solution. Mass fabrication remains a prerequisite for cost savings.**

Left: Large cast end connectors are used in conjunction with custom-made AESS steel to create these large branch connections at Heathrow Terminal 5 in London, England by Richard Rogers. The connections accept the load of two large roof struts, simultaneously connect to the front wall of the terminal, and transfer the loads to the floor many stories below through sloped columns.

Right: Part of the rationale not to use a fixed central cast connection in this instance would have been issues of access for erection and site welding as well as some requirements for pin and hinge connections in the load paths.

Left: The custom-made connectors that attach the HSS tubes to the hinge have unusual inset bolts. This avoids site welding while at the same time providing a unique look to this specialized piece. The diameter of the recesses is sized to allow bolt tightening.

Right: Various other castings were also used at Heathrow Terminal 5, including a large cast column base to receive the incoming angled column, as well as a clevis-type attachment to support part of the bracing system for the exterior wall. Again, the size of the building meant that economies were achieved by the production of multiples of the various casting types.

While many of the Heathrow castings were designed as hinge-type connections, the castings used at Hauptbahnhof Station in Berlin were working to achieve moment-resisting load transfer. The aesthetic also looked for a very smooth suite of connections, contrasting greatly with the lightness of the glass and steel systems in the balance of the station.

Upper left: This unique set of cast connections at the Hauptbahnhof Station in Berlin, Germany is designed to transfer the load from four points, down through diagonal tubular members and into a set of four braced columns below. A decision was made to reveal the change in material between the casting and the hollow round member by expressing a single line and planar change along the element.

Lower left: The upper inclined members are resolved into a cast connection that transfers the load to four joined hollow columns. The unity of the connection serves to brace the columns at their upper end. The joint between the parts is expressed.

Right: The column cluster's length is braced quite discreetly with welded plate connections in-between the columns at multiple points along the height that tie the elements together and reduce the unbraced length.

Castings can also elegantly solve highly unusual branching connections due to odd geometries that would be difficult to detail using standard bolted or welded connections.

Left: The nine-story atrium of the Caisse de dépôt et placement du Québec in Montreal, QC, Canada by Architects Consortium Gauthier Daoust Lestage / Faucher Aubertin Brodeur Gauthier / Lemay Associés made extensive use of custom castings to resolve the unusual intersections of the components of the vertical trusses.

Right: The base connection for the tripartite column allows the columns and their load paths to be simply resolved to a single point. Aspects of the intersection of the casting and the HSS members were also concealed by careful welding, grinding, filling and finishing.

Left: The structural elements were fabricated from straight round HSS members. The tapered end fittings achieve a lighter look. The connection between the node and the large vertical support is expressed by a change in diameter of the members.

Right: Although there were many variations on the cast connection geometries and loading considerations throughout the project, a uniform tectonic language was achieved.

## *PROCESS PROFILE: UNIVERSITY OF GUELPH SCIENCE BUILDING / YOUNG + WRIGHT ARCHITECTS*

Architects: Robbie/Young + Wright
Engineers: Carruthers & Wallace Ltd.
Steel Detailing, Fabrication and Erection: Walters Inc.

This steel tree structure at the University of Guelph highlights the ability of cast connections to provide a seamless appearance or the illusion of no connection at all. This application of cast connections created a higher level of AESS finishing than possible by any welded connections, even with the highest level of finishing. This type of connection is also able to create a very seamless transfer of forces, including moment, through the joint. It requires a high degree of precision in the design and fabrication of the casting, including testing, to ensure that there are no flaws in the casting as a result of problems in the casting or cooling process.

As a seamless appearance was desired, and cast steel has a naturally textured finish due to the use of the sand-casting process, it was necessary to do extra grinding and filling of the casting itself to make its finish match that of the structural branches. Mechanical pipe was used instead of HSS, as it also has a more textured appearance, is seamless (so no grinding of HSS weld seams would be required), and its physical properties for strength and welding better suited the site fabrication restrictions and requirements. It is to be noted that it was possible to use mechanical pipe, as this is not a seismic application.

Left: The tree structure that forms the support system for the triangular atrium space of the University of Guelph Science Building in Guelph, ON, Canada, designed by Robbie/Young+Wright Architects, had the unique design requirement to create a seamless-looking steel structure, tree-like in form.

Right: Compounding the requirements for this AESS structure was a desire for the use of a high-gloss paint finish – guaranteed to reveal any imperfections in the final finish of the product.

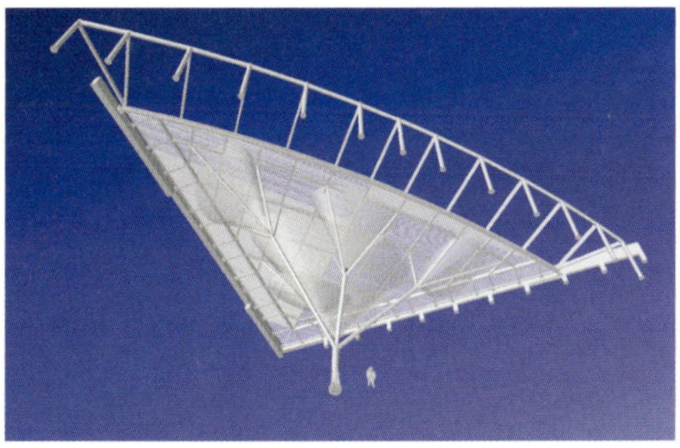

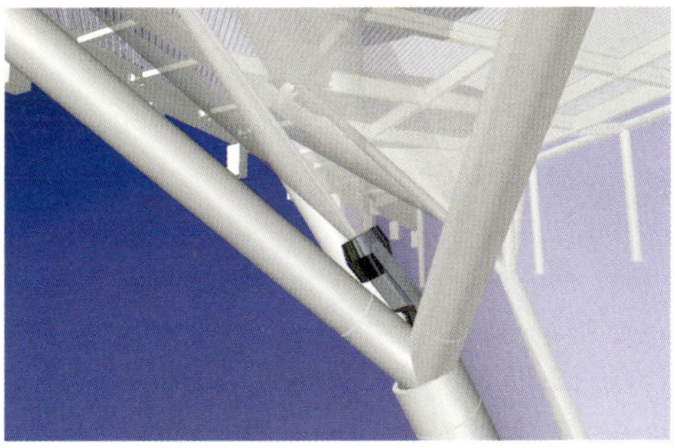

Left: The form of the atrium and tree were studied as 3D digital models.

Right: Details of the member-to-member connections in the 3D model provided the basis for the design of smoother cast connections.

The initial wall thickness for each node was chosen based on the results of the finite element stress analysis. As is typical in the design of castings, the casting was thicker at the bottom than the top (by a factor of approximately two). German foundry Friedrich Wilhelms-Hütte GmbH in Mülheim an der Ruhr was selected to produce the cast steel nodes, as they were able to provide high fabrication standards and offered a wide range of material and structural testing, including non-destructive testing (visual, ultrasonic, liquid penetrant and magnetic particle examination) as well as tensile, bending and notch toughness (Charpy) testing of the cast material. The steel used for the casting had to be modified to one that would allow welding of the node to the branch. In other cases where castings are used in bolted or threaded applications, a different kind of steel can be used.

The amount of carbon in steel affects its weldability. The higher the carbon content the more difficult the connection is to weld and the more likely special procedures such as preheating, interpass temperature control and postheating are necessary. Heating of the adjacent material is required to prevent rapid cooling during or after the welding process. This would result in problematic stresses in the joint. It is easier to apply local heating in a controlled shop environment than it is in many site situations where access is often already difficult.

The steel specified for the casting had to meet ASTM International A27 Grade 70/40 with a modified chemistry to ensure that the casting could be welded to the pipe branch with minimal preheating and would require no post-weld heat treatment for stress-relieving. Although the casting would be shop-welded to one end of each branch/trunk and the seam finished, site welding would be required for the opposite end. Site conditions would make both pre- and post-heating difficult.

Different foundries use different fabrication processes. The most common methods for structural steel components are die-casting and sand-casting. In die-casting molten steel is injected into a steel mold at high pressure. The method can be used for precise, highly repetitive elements. Sand-casting is used for a wide range of larger elements that can be less repetitive. Unique sand-casts can be made for each connector. Sand-casting was used for these connectors. A 3D physical model, based upon the digital 3D models created for simulation and design, were used to make the sand-cast.

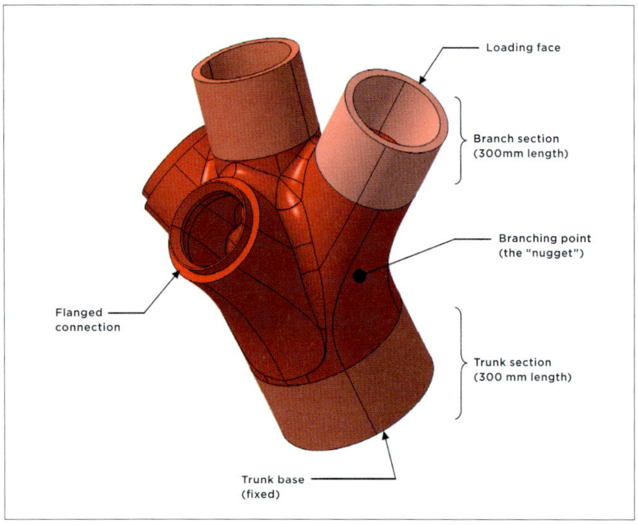


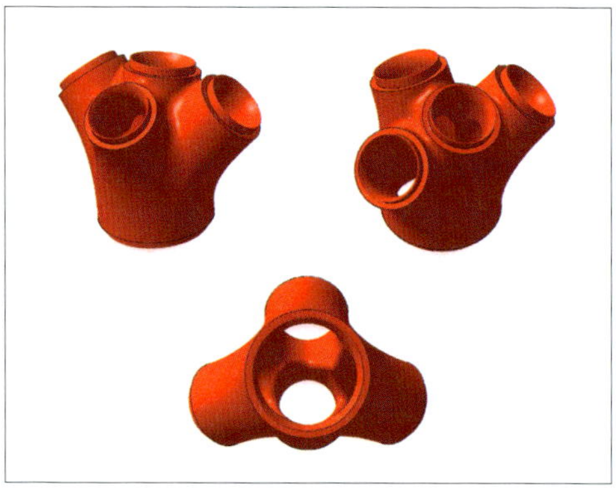

Left: The parts of the connector and their technical terms that must form the basis of conversation among the fabricator, engineer and foundry.

Right: The castings are studied as 3D models to ensure that each satisfies the aesthetic requirements of the connection.

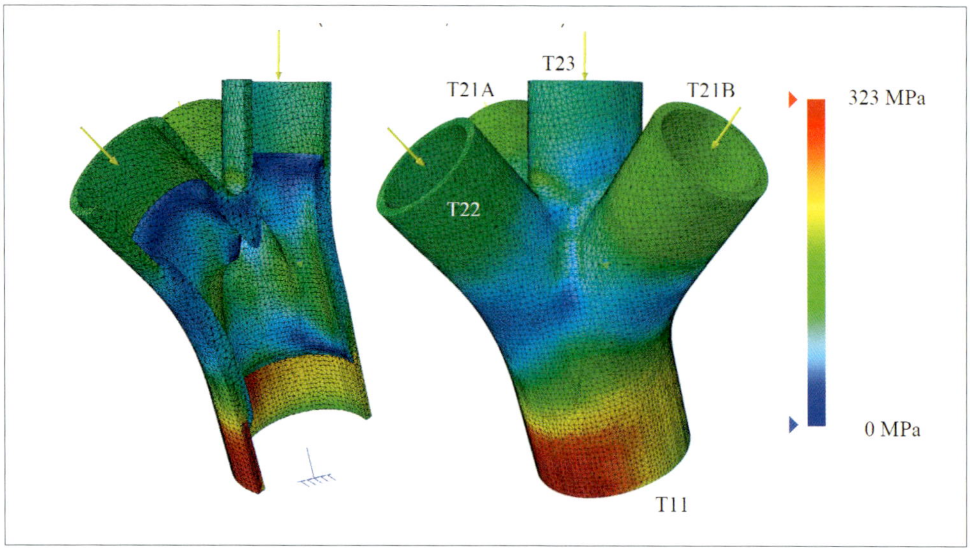


Stress simulations are used to predict potential failure modes and to determine where additional steel thickness is required in the casting.

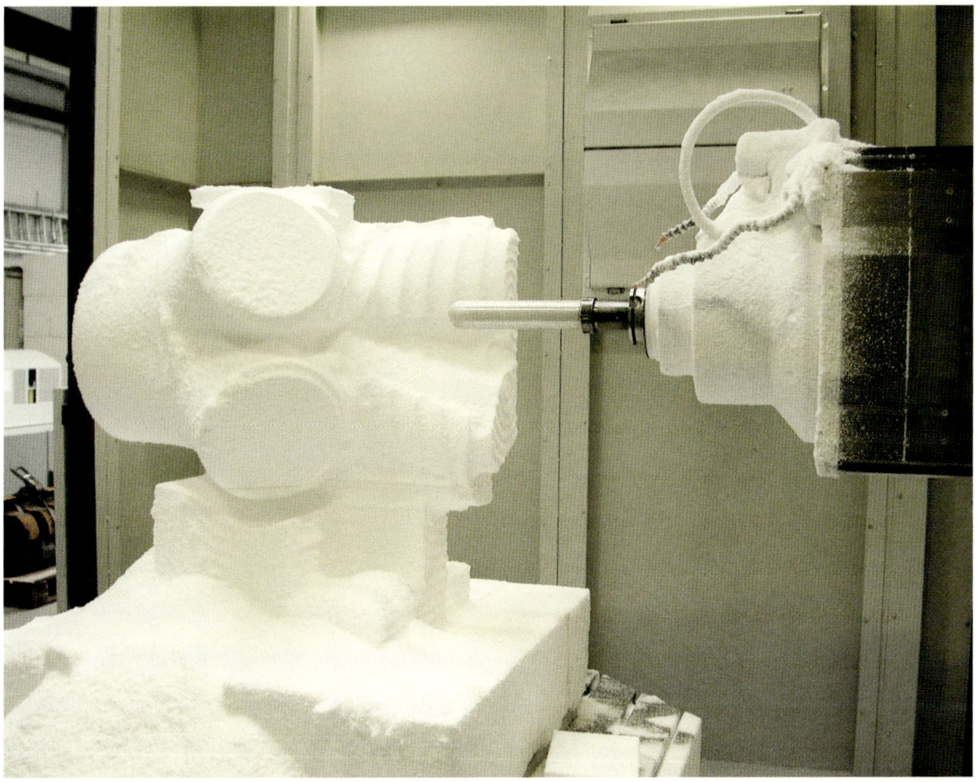

The digital model informs the CAD/CAM process which shapes the base for the casting.

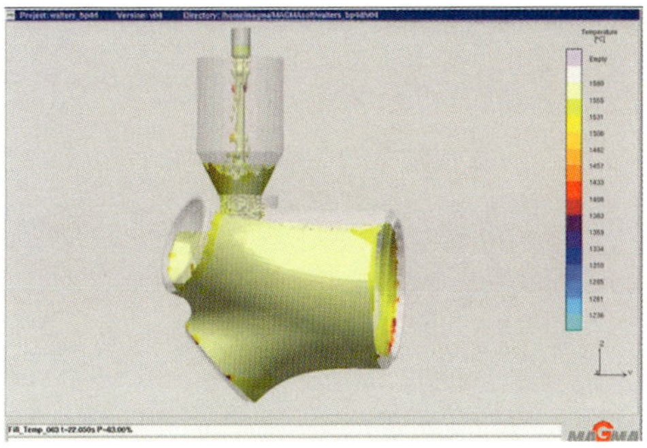

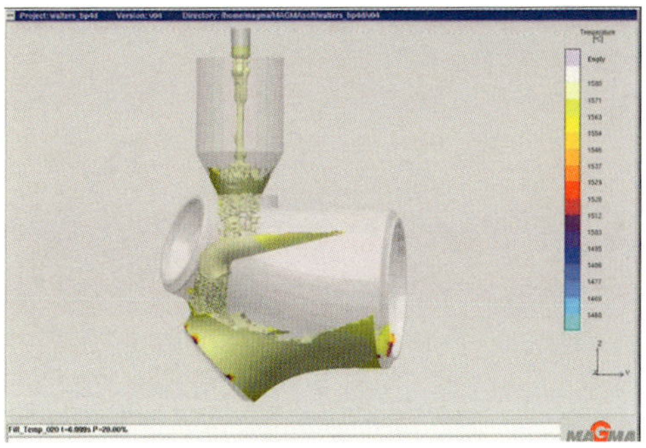

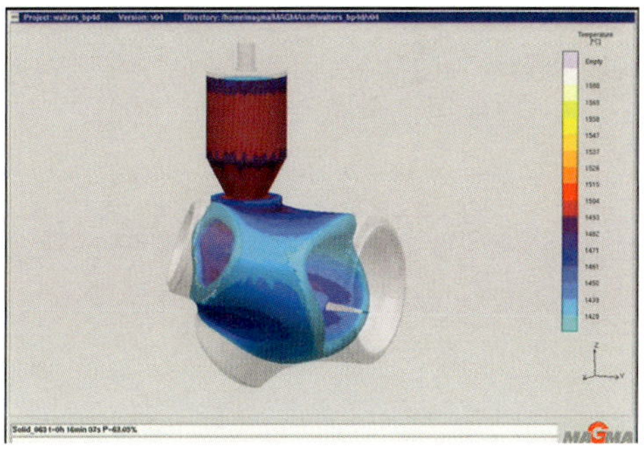

These stills from a simulation video illustrate how the molten steel is poured into the void of the sand mold. The gradient shows the temperature of the metal. The wall thickness of the mold will directly influence the cooling pattern of the node. The cooling needs to be slow and consistent and without pockets of either extreme heat or cool, as this would cause stress in the metal. The first two images show the hot steel being poured into the mold and the third the cooling process.

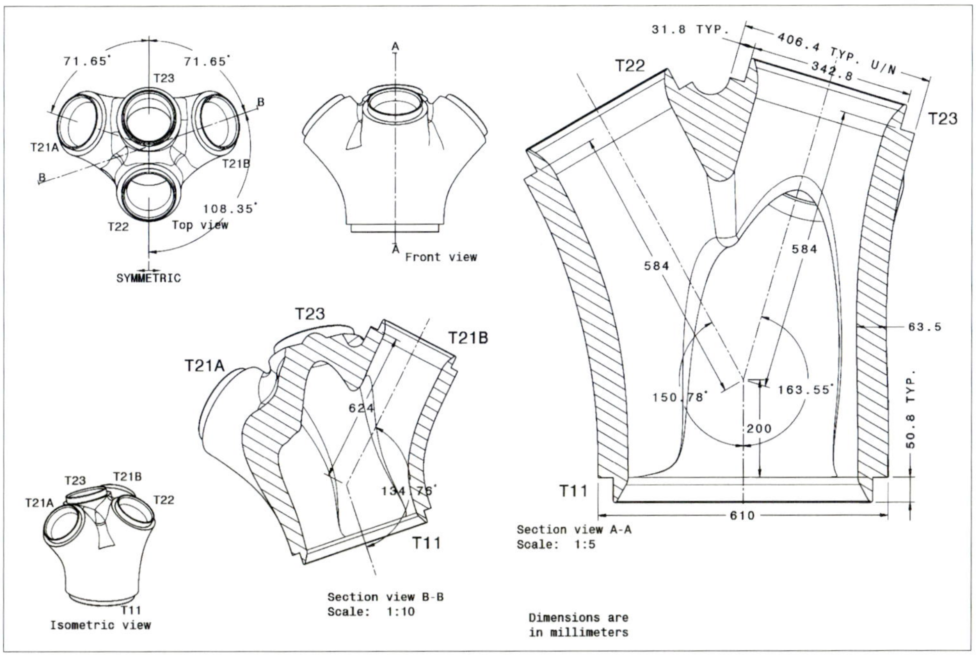


Each node is laid out in a detailed shop drawing to provide exact specifications for the dimensions and to allow coordination with the steel pipe branch fabrication.

Left: When the node is first removed from the casting, its appearance is rough and remediation is required to remove burrs and excess steel.

Right: The rough casting is ground and polished prior to being primed, the weld edges being left clear of primer.

To limit the amount of welding that needed to be done on site, each node was connected to its respective base branch in the shop. This allowed for more controlled heat and finishing. Multiple weld passes were required with additional grinding and filling prior to finish applications.

Left: Steel tabs are welded to the openings in the casting to allow for easier site fabrication. They are placed at the top edge of the opening to assist in aligning and then holding the incoming tube to be connected. An additional section of tube is secured inside the opening to backstop the welding.

Right: The main node with one branch connected. Large groove welds will be required. The alignment tabs and interior tube are also visible.

Temporary shoring must be provided. This is often required when welding moment-resisting connections, as they have little or no self-supporting capabilities until the welding process is 100% complete. The shoring for this project was quite extensive, as it had to support the multiple branches as well as provide a working platform at each node to facilitate the erection process and access for welding.

Left: The steel shoring frame can be seen surrounding the tree. A lift is in process. Padded slings are used to prevent damage to the primed steel during erection.

Right: The tree branch, complete with shop-attached node, will rest on this padded temporary perch to maintain its position while the joint below is welded.

A view looking at the emergent tree as a support system for the atrium roof. The sloped branches carry the roof loads down through the moment-resisting cast nodes.

A pin connection at the top end of the branch satisfies load transfer. It also provides a nice-looking bolted connection to ease the installation of the top piece and eliminates the need for additional site welding.

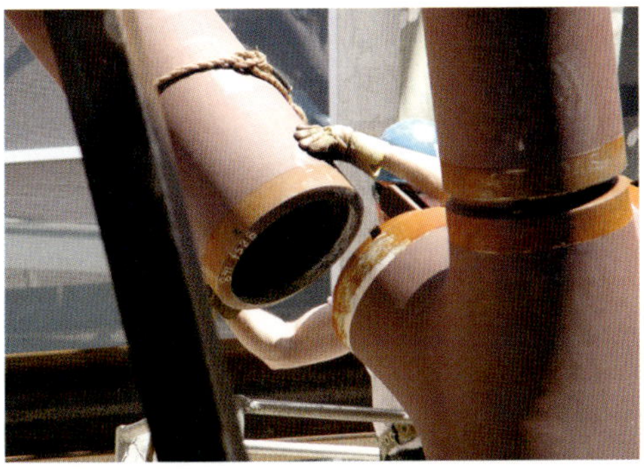

An ironworker guides the pipe onto the cast node. As the priming has been held back from the connection, the oxidation will be removed prior to welding and finishing, after which the node will be primed before being painted.

Successful installation of the last branch requires that tight tolerances have been maintained throughout the fabrication and erection. Minimal force may be used or the surfaces could be damaged. The ironworkers are using come-alongs to urge the piece into place. Padding is required to prevent damage to the tube.

*CHAPTER 11*

---

# *TENSION SYSTEMS AND SPACEFRAMES*

---

## *TENSION SYSTEMS*



## *SPACEFRAME SYSTEMS*



Tensile fabric structures are able to exhibit amazing feats of architecture and engineering that are only possible using highly articulated steel structures and connections. The glass, fabric and steel roof of the Sony Center at Potsdamer Platz in Berlin, Germany by Helmut Jahn creates a theatrical semi-enclosed public space.

# *TENSION SYSTEMS*

The technology and detailing behind architectural tension systems is derived from that used in the rigging of tall ships, as well as more simple applications of indigenous tent structures. In the post-war period the experimental projects of engineer Frei Otto began to look seriously at the potential that such systems had for architectural applications. Otto's design for the German Pavilion at Expo 67 is considered equivalent in impact to the work of Buckminster Fuller for the USA Pavilion at the same event. The Olympiastadion designed for the Munich Olympics in 1972 by architect Günter Behnisch and Frei Otto was the largest-scale application of this technology to date and provided the inspiration and precedent for others to follow.

The Olympiastadion in Munich, Germany by Günter Behnisch and Frei Otto used large tower masts to support a large-scale roof created from tension cables and acrylic glass.

Architecture that features elaborate use of tension members as a focus of the design parti did not truly appear until the emergence of the High Tech movement in the 1970s. The exposed steel systems associated with the style tended to be very lightweight and largely comprised of "assembled" hinge or pin-type connections. The assemblage process tended to reduce the use of site welding in favor of quicker-to-erect bolted systems. Concrete was minimized on the job site, which also tended to compromise the inherent stability of the structures and their ability to create a diaphragm action. X bracing was used in lieu of concrete shear walls.

The hanger system developed to suspend the glazed walkways off the Centre Pompidou front façade makes clear differentiation of the tensile versus the compressive members through their contrasting diameters.

The three primary forms of tension systems that emerged through High Tech development (see Chapter 5: AESS: Its History and Development) are:

- lightweight X bracing (Centre Pompidou) for stabilization
- a means of supporting/hanging larger cantilevered sections (Oxford Ice Rink). This is a variation of a stayed bridge structure and may include a mast or the adjacent building or structure could provide the compressive support.
- the substitution of rods or cables for structural sections in force-differentiated structural systems

While X bracing was necessary as a stabilization device for the new lightweight, hinge-connected, framed structures, the exaggerated mast-support-type systems were employed as an alternate method to support flexural members such as beams, trusses and cantilevers. In the Oxford Ice Rink by Nicholas Grimshaw, the mast system provides a center support for the beams to clear-span the rink and acts rather like a cable-stayed bridge. In the Centre Pompidou, the tension supports are used to assist in the hanging of the glazed walkways from the front frame of the building.

Force-differentiated structural systems must determine the location of the tensile members that can take advantage of the lightness of rods or cables. Compression members will use heavier sections that work in visual contrast. These systems are most easily applied to trusses whose members are normally designed for purely axial loads. In most situations the bottom chord of a simply supported truss acts in tension, so that the member selected for the bottom chord needs not respond to compression forces, and slender member types such as rods can be employed instead of the usual HSS or W shapes.

These early tension systems developed a language of specialty connections for use in securing rods. Rods are more commonly found in architectural applications and cables in bridges. More recent buildings have begun to explore a more finely differentiated application of tension members, highlighting the differences in the forces in trusses and similar structures.

## TENSION CONNECTORS

Specialized connections are often required when attaching tension members to an exposed steel system. These can be custom-designed and fabricated to match the architectural language of the project, or they can be selected off the shelf. There are four primary considerations when designing tension connectors:

→ that these typically form pin-type connections, so transfer no moment
→ that the rods or cables are normally quite small in diameter and must be securely fastened to resist pull-out due to tension
→ that the type of connector will vary as a function of the use of a cable or rod: rods can be machined to have threads, which is not possible for cables
→ that these systems are normally installed loose and must be able to be tightened in order to secure, tension and plumb the systems.

Today, many tension connectors are made from cast steel and mass-prefabricated at competitive costs, as the demand is quite high. A wide variety of available connections and connectors is shown in this chapter as well as in Chapter 10: Castings.

## CROSS BRACING

In contemporary construction, tension members find their most common use as lightweight cross bracing. Steel framing, particularly in assembled or framed buildings, incorporates only the transfer of horizontal and vertical loads through the connections. The respective connections are referred to as hinge joints, not because they necessarily appear as hinges like those on a door frame but because they are designed without the stiffness that is required to resist any bending. If a building uses a rectangular frame and lacks any triangulation (triangles forming an inherently rigid shape), then some sort of bracing is required to stabilize the building. In more ordinary applications of concealed structural steel, bracing is often accomplished through the use of cast concrete shear walls. Large steel plates can also be used. Alternate means had to be found when the early forms of expressed steel in High Tech architecture sought to minimize the use of concrete in an attempt to increase the long-term flexibility of buildings.

The all-glass façade of the Munich International Airport, Germany by Koch and Partner provided structural rigidity by using lightweight steel cross bracing rather than solid panels.

At Munich International Airport, the pairing of cross bracers is worked geometrically into the front and back sides of the receiving connections. The incoming rods are threaded to connect with the castings, which in turn are received by a round steel plate of diameter adequate to resolve the geometry. Slender turnbuckles along the rods allow for tightening of the braces.

These kinds of braces work by triangulating the structural frame. Only half of the brace is functioning at a time. As the building moves due to loading, typically wind, the tension member acts to triangulate the frame. As the loads shift to come from an alternate direction, the load shifts to the other brace and the other rod relaxes. Details must be worked out for the connection of the braces to their end points on the frame, and also a detail for the point at which they cross in the middle of the brace. Tension connectors must be installed slack and tightened in place. The design of the connections must allow for this to take place.

This simple galvanized steel ring connector sits at the center of a cross brace. The threading of the rods and bolts allow for the tightening of the rods.

In order to keep the diameters of the bracing rods used at the Kant-Dreieck light, two sets of rods are used, connecting through specialized attachment points created by threading the rods through slightly larger tubes and bolting on the exterior face.

These lightweight braces, used to stabilize the structural separation of two parts of the office, are revealed in the exhibition lobby of Tate Snyder Kimsey Architects in Las Vegas, NV, USA. The physical separation is highlighted by the glazed link, and the lightweight galvanized steel X bracing provides an interesting detail.

The exterior bracing on the Kant-Dreieck in Berlin, Germany by Josef Paul Kleihues uses a light system of rods to brace the round HSS grid frame.

Larger bracing formed from wide-flange sections is used to reinforce the exterior wall of the Quantum Nano Engineering Building at the University of Waterloo, ON, Canada designed by KPMB Architects. This floor of the building will not have glazing, and the nature of the program requires extra structural protection around the laboratories.

Not all bracing is light. In some instances quite heavy members are used, particularly in concealed steel construction. One of the problems with bracing that is used to completely cross the structural frame is that it can impede circulation through the space as well as view to the exterior. Larger braces formed from heavier structural steel sections can be used more selectively and in key locations in the building to minimize interference in planning.

**Cross bracing is also used in seismic situations — either installed in the building as part of the design or increasingly added as part of a retrofit and upgrade.**

The Bennett Building in Salt Lake City, UT, USA is a good example of X bracing that is integral to the framing of the building, in response to a local seismic condition. The round HSS braces are exposed on the ground floor in a decorative way and set back behind the glazing on the upper floors. The seismic retrofit was under the direction of GSBS Architects.

**Cross-type tensile reinforcing need not be confined to use in the wall plane. Bracing can be used in quite innovative ways throughout the building to resist horizontal and vertical shear loads.**

The Offices for the APEGBC in Vancouver, BC, Canada, designed by Peter Busby and Associates, maintain a very light glazed appearance in spite of the local seismic condition. Special steel braces are used to support the exterior shading devices.

Left: The central point of connection uses small round HSS members through which the rods have been threaded, and a bolt at the end serves to both tighten and adjust the tension in the rods.

Right: The APEGBC building uses rod-type bracing in conjunction with some decorative "sails" in the ceiling plane to add stability. Short compression members serve to push the central connection point for the rods down from the underside of the steel decking, creating an almost truss-like action.

## INNOVATIVE FORCE EXPRESSION IN TRUSSES

**The slenderness of the tension elements in a building or structure can be used to contrast the required stoutness of the compressive elements. This need not be limited to elaborate canopy structures, but can also inform the selection of members for discrete elements within the building. In truss design, for instance, very slender members can be used for the tension members of the truss.**

Left: This variation of an extremely lightweight king post truss at the Picower Building at MIT in Boston, MA, USA, designed by Charles Correa, clearly differentiates the compression and tension loading in the truss by using heavier round steel sections for the compression members.

Right: The tension members connect to the base of the post. The members have been paired to divide the load and allow lightness in appearance. As buckling is precluded, the forces are resisted in proportion to the cross-sectional area of the member. Multiple thin members can be used to replace one that is more stout.

Left: The modified king post truss at Pearson International Airport in Toronto, ON, Canada, designed by SOM Architects, uses a curved wide-flange profile for the top chord. A pair of rods is used to create the tensile bottom chord.

Right: Designing the member connections can be exciting when the loading type can be differentiated. In this hall of Pearson Airport, the roller connection at the base of the post transfers the force to the tension rods. Web stiffeners are used on the beam to stiffen the member at key loading points.

Left: The truss system at Pudong International Airport, Terminal 1, in Shanghai, China, designed by Paul Andreu, uses tensioned rods to create the bottom chord of the trusses that clear-span the terminal.

Right: The connection between the bottom tension chord and the multiple compression posts on the truss is resolved quite innovatively by the use of a steel "ball" to secure the members into alignment.

This innovative king post truss at the Kempinski Hotel Airport Munich, Germany, designed by Helmut Jahn, uses a curved structural steel top chord as its compression member, with a round HSS center post.

The Kempinski Hotel atrium roof differentiates clearly between the tension and compression members. Tensile connectors are used to attach the rods to the top chord.

**Trusses need not always be oriented in standard fashion. Much innovation in the overall design of the structure can be achieved by questioning and challenging standard procedure. The truss can be inverted or placed on the reverse side of the envelope, pushing the form into place rather than merely supporting gravity loads.**

Left: The language of the steel in Hauptbahnhof Station in Berlin, Germany, designed by von Gerkan, Marg und Partner, uses the lightness of the tension trusses for the train shed to contrast with the heaviness of the steel used for the orthogonal tower blocks.

Top: The tensile truss system at Hauptbahnhof Station that is used to assist the curved beams that span the station is used on the interior and exterior of the train shed. Here the trusses are placed on the outside on the lower portion of the roof. Lightweight steel X bracing and outer tension chords contrast with the heavier sections used for the compression posts and chords that are integrated with the primary structure of the curved roof.

The canopy beneath the Grande Arche at La Défense in Paris, France was designed by the team of Johan Otto von Spreckelsen, Paul Andreu and Erick Reitzel. The regular plane of fabric sections is pushed and pulled into place by a series of cables that tension the canopy back to the building and platform. A strut-and-cable system forms a series of very lightweight (both in mass and appearance) trusses that act alongside the canopy to modify its geometry. These trusses are created from a series of tension members and round HSS web members that can act in compression and push the fabric roof.

The tubular truss compression mast of the Sony Center in Berlin, Germany, designed by Helmut Jahn, is used to separate the tensile layer forming the sloped "dome" roof from the cables that tie back to the three-dimensional truss ring that defines the perimeter of the structure.

The geometry of the base of the center post must accommodate the connection of multiple incoming cable attachments. The plates that connect to the center post must be thin enough to allow space for welding. The steel is thickened where the rods connect to provide additional material to resist pull-through forces.

The bowstring trusses that support the glazed roof at the TGV Station at Charles-de-Gaulle Airport in Paris, France, designed by architect Paul Andreu and engineer Peter Rice of RFR, illustrate a clear inversion of the placement of the tension and compression chords of the truss. The double round HSS bottom chord is subjected to compression, and the top chord to tension in this style of truss. The truss is supported at the top tension chord, making it appear to be hanging.

**There are numerous variations in the design of trusses that begin to play with the tensile capabilities of steel. Not all can be neatly classified or fall into straightforward variations of the typologies discussed in Chapter 3. It is essential for the designer to have a good feel for the compression and tension forces that the truss will be subjected to, as well as substantiation of the same through structural analysis. Only slender members must be subjected to tension forces.**

The diagonal trusses along the exterior of the Burj Al-Arab in Dubai, UAE, designed by Atkins Architects, use tensile cross bracing for stiffening.

The connecting plates for the tension members have been minimized at the Burj Al-Arab to the extent of making them virtually disappear when viewed at a distance. The plate dimensions for the connecting tabs still need to be adequate to resist shear forces for pull-through and provide adequate volumes of steel between the holes at the central connector.

## SIMPLE CANOPIES

Tension systems were used during the 19th century to assist in the support of canopies. After the invention of the Bessemer process, the new capabilities of steel had greatly enhanced the tensile capabilities of the material. The detailing of these was initially relatively primitive. One of the major structural concerns with this sort of support system, and one that prevails today, is to ensure adequate connection and support to the primary structure of the building to prevent the withdrawal of fastenings. In cold climates this can pose a problem, as it usually results in a thermal bridge through the insulation. It is possible to minimize conductivity by detailing paired steel plates that are connected through the insulation layer via bolts. The geometry of the tension connector will influence the amount of load that needs to be carried. The shallower the angle of support, the greater the load on the cable or rod. This is the result of the dead load being split into its X and Y components. Simple canopies usually do not require additional cable bracing to prevent sideways movement due in part to the rigidity of the supported canopy and due to the limited size and therefore wind loading.

Top: The entrance canopy for the offices of Tate Snyder Kimsey Architects in Las Vegas, NV, USA uses a variation of a suspension system to secure the roof back to the structure of the building. The canopy is tied back above and below the projected support beams as an innovative way to brace the steel beams. The rods have turnbuckles at their mid-point as the means to adjust the length/tension.

Bottom: The heavy steel canopy structure at the Clay and Glass Gallery in Waterloo, ON, Canada, designed by Patkau Architects, uses steel rods that are secured back through the brick veneer to the primary structure of the building. The horizontal beams are also supported toward their rear by steel struts, to decrease the effective length of the cantilever.

## CABLE-STAYED SYSTEMS

Cable-stayed bridges and their support elements and systems have served as a precedent for the lateral transition of this structural system into architectural applications. The basic elements of the system consist of the vertical mast (compressive element), the stays (these can be fabricated from cables or rods, as a function of the design and scale) and the anchoring systems for the top and bottom connections. In a bridge, the forces at the top connection are normally balanced, so that there is an even number of stays on either side of the mast with equal loading. The physical connection at the top must be sufficiently strong to resist pull-out of the stay from the tower. Likewise, the connection at the base of the stay must be ballasted and also resist pull-out.

Left: The Poplar Station of the Dockland Light Railway (DLR) in London, England uses a cable-stayed system to suspend the tubular pedestrian walkway over the rail tracks. The walkway is connected at either end to an access stair. The cables are attached to a support system that sits beneath the walkway. The walkway must be stiff enough to span between the support "slings".

Right: The top detail of the compression mast, which has been fabricated from round HSS sections, shows the clear balance of load that has been created by the connections. The fan-shaped boxes allow for adequate material around the cable attachments to meet the physical requirements of the connection and to resist the load.

Cable-stayed systems need not be symmetrical. The imbalance can be handled by the inclination of the tower(s) combined with the balance of the load on either side of the tower. Sometimes the mass of the tower itself can be used to balance an eccentric load. Such systems can be used to support quite unequal loads that are designed to appear as cantilevered elements, e.g. canopies, when in fact the material is incapable of self-supporting at the desired thickness or weight for a given distance.

Left: The glazed canopy at the Aria Hotel at City Center in Las Vegas, NV, USA, designed by Cesar Pelli, uses a rear-inclined tower from which to suspend its large curved glass canopy. The horizontal members that appear to be cantilevered are assisted by both larger round HSS members that tie them back to the mast as well as smaller stainless steel ties. The cantilevering structural members are also seen to tie back to the roof to provide more stability.

Right: The vertical masts and cantilevered support members are comprised of a series of finely crafted plates that have been welded together to create a composite section. Steel sections have been added as spacers to increase the lightness of appearance without compromising the strength. Lateral bracing interconnects the major supports and helps to support the spanning ability of the smaller round HSS sections from which the glass canopy is hung.

Trusses are not exclusively used as spanning members. They may also be designed to take compression loads. This is often done where a tower or mast element is required to support a cable-stayed roof system. The advantage of stabilizing the mast with cables lies in the ability to design the base connection of the mast as a pin connection rather than require a more substantial moment-resisting cantilever-type connection. This allows the overall structure to be lighter and simplifies construction.

The entrance canopy over the roadway at the Beijing International Airport, China uses a truss column as the compression mast from which to suspend the roof.

The glass and fabric canopy at the Munich International Airport, Germany uses triangulated compression masts, created from round HSS members, from which to suspend the roofs.

The masts are connected back to the adjacent buildings via paired tension rods to stabilize the structure.

The three HSS members of the truss mast are resolved at the base detail into a unified pin connection. The welding has been neatly done and no attempt has been made to grind or conceal the processes.

## TENSEGRITY STRUCTURES

One of the most innovative uses of steel tension systems is the creation of a tensegrity-type structure. In a tensional integrity structure a balance is sought between tension and compression members, such that compression members are exclusively joined to each other with tension members. Although most of the applications of this have been realized through artistic sculptures, there have been some architectural applications. The Phoenix Public Library uses an innovative tensile system to support the roof on its uppermost floor. A net-like system of cables, akin to a tensegrity structure, combined with round HSS struts, is used to transfer the load from the roof to the concrete columns below. This tensile system allows the roof system to be visually and virtually structurally detached from the primary concrete support columns.

The Aviary at the London Zoo, England, designed by Lord Snowdon in 1964, has been constructed as a modified tensegrity system. The compression triangular frames are used to separate a series of cables from which the mesh has been hung.

Left: A tensile fabric shading system is used on the façade of the The Phoenix Public Library, AZ, USA designed by Will Bruder. The lightness of the tension system contrasts with the relative solidity of the side walls of the library, and allows for control of the daylighting and solar gain in this very hot, arid climate.

Right: A tensile system is used for the Phoenix Library to separate the top of the tapered concrete columns from the underside of the steel-framed roof. The structural purpose of the members is clearly expressed, with cables used for the tension members and round HSS sections for the vertical compression members.

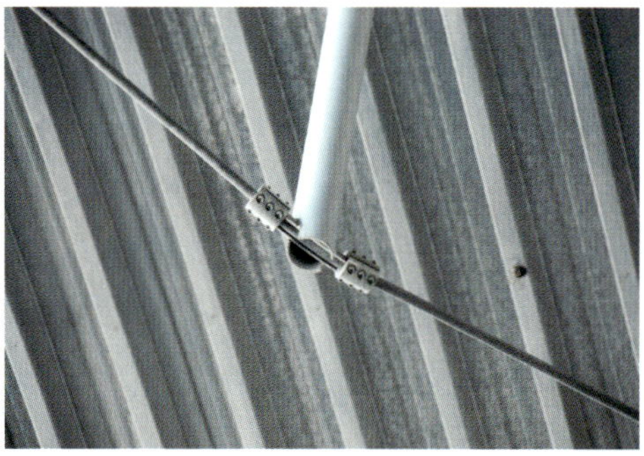

Left: A fairly straightforward language of connection is created to articulate the tension elements. Small clamps connect the cables to the top of the vertical HSS compression members.

Right: At the base of the strut, a similar connection method is used to essentially clamp the cable and ensure that it does not slip under fully loaded conditions.

This playful net sculpture called "Her Secret is Patience" by artist Janet Echelman, hangs suspended over a downtown park in Phoenix, AZ, USA. Its tower-and-cable system uses modified tensegrity to create its arrangement of structural elements.

The cable tiedown to the concrete foundation pier is achieved with this cast connection which attaches to a plate whose design is a scaled-down version of the larger mast base.

One of the unusual and challenging aspects of such a structure is to understand and control its erection sequence, given that the major mast/compression elements are hinged at their base and inclined.

A close view of the base connection for a major mast. The hinge connection has been created with heavy steel plates. Small triangular plates are welded to the connection to provide additional rigidity. The three bolts that attach through the joint have been welded to fix their position and prevent tampering.

# *SPACEFRAME SYSTEMS*

Spaceframes are considered to be the architectural invention of Buckminster Fuller and appeared experimentally in structures in the 1950s. Spaceframes were more common in architecture during the 1960s and 1970s, being used in new building typologies such as convention centers, exhibition buildings, airports and other single-storey uses that required long column-free spans. They fell out of favor in deference to the use of more custom AESS solutions during the 1980s and 1990s. Spaceframes are seeing a resurgence in some recent projects related to their modularity, speed of erection and ability to be customized.

Spaceframes are typically proprietary systems comprised of a set of straight steel members that are easily connected by custom-fabricated ball joints. The modules are based upon a triangulated grid for stability. Loads must be transferred at the nodal points, similar to truss systems, in order to maintain exclusive axial loading. A spaceframe can span roughly from 6 to 36 times the length of its module and can cantilever up to one-quarter of the length of the span.

The support system for the expansive glass roof at the Vancouver Law Courts in Vancouver, BC, Canada, designed by Arthur Erickson, is supported on a custom-made steel space truss fabricated from round HSS members. All of the connections are welded. The loads are transferred to the concrete frame via inverted pyramid-type supports, effectively reducing the span between supports. This type of pyramidal support is commonly used as a means to achieve span reduction.

The decision to use all-welded connections changed the appearance, speed of erection, as well as the ultimate cost of the Vancouver Law Courts. Given the building type and high-profile nature of the project, it was likely justifiable.

The Baltimore Washington International Airport in MD, USA uses a spaceframe technology to support its walls and roof.

The nodes of the airport structure are capable of resolving a large number of incoming members.

## NON-PLANAR SPACEFRAMES

**Spaceframes or spacegrids need not be planar in their design. It is possible to use extensive three-dimensional frames to create a multitude of shapes — from column structures to roofs. Curved shapes do imply that all of the member lengths are less uniform, creating a more complex design than in a rectilinear system.**

The Philologische Bibliothek der Freien Universität by Foster + Partners in Berlin, Germany uses a curved spaceframe to create a climate-modifying double envelope. One advantage of the spaceframe lies in its ability to create the ovoid form without requiring significant increases in costs that might be associated with a custom welded HSS system. Another advantage is its lightness, which reduces the self-weight of the structure. The composite skin is intended to be translucent, so that the minimal density of the light tubular steel was an asset.

A view through the interior glazing to the spaceframe system. This intersection illustrates the corner detail of one of the operable panels in the outer shell that is used to naturally ventilate this double façade.

The application of steel in the library is not quite AESS, although it is partially exposed to view, given the placement of the transparent panels both on the exterior and interior of the double envelope.

Left: Ferrari World Theme Park in Abu Dhabi, UAE, by Benoy Architects uses a spaceframe to create its 205,000m²/2.2 million sq ft roof structure. The vast scale and longspan requirements of this project would have made the use of any other form of structure impractical.

Right: The theme park roof is supported in part by curved rectangular towers that are fabricated from the same system of proprietary parts.

Left: Large tapered hollow structural members pick up the load from the spaceframe roof. The supports are resolved into a base connection that accommodates four members. Plates are welded to the bottom of the angled columns to create pin connections.

Right: The space grid uses classic ball-joint connections to connect the round HSS members. The loads are transferred to large sloped round HSS columns. Load transfer always occurs at a node, to ensure that the frame is only subjected to axial loading. The profiled steel roof can be seen to be bearing on beams that in turn transfer the load to the frame at nodal points.

Left: The Beijing International Airport, Beijing, China designed by Foster + Partners and ARUP uses an expansive double curved spaceframe system to create the roof over the terminal. The modular system is based on a unit size of 4.5m/14.75ft and resulted in 76,924 connecting members with 18,262 joints. Given the short time frame to have the facility open for the 2008 Olympics, this system was a more logical solution over a standard welded or bolted truss system as it allowed for maximum prefabrication and quicker assembly. The hollow steel columns have been separately tuned to account for potential sway in the instance of an earthquake. The terminal measures 800m/2,625ft at its widest point.

Right: The architectural language of the project deftly merges three steel systems at the exterior glazed façade at the passenger drop off zone. The 2m/6.5ft diameter hollow steel columns support the spaceframe roof. The finely welded and finished AESS trusses provide wind loading for the curtain wall façade. The detailing creates a virtually seamless transition from interior to exterior on the ceiling plane. The minimally obstructed height of the glazed wall enhances daylight penetration to the interior of the terminal.

Bottom: The passenger loading zone is protected by a substantial cantilevered canopy that extends across the entire face of the terminal. The spaceframe system easily accommodates this significant a cantilever as the forces within the spaceframe are shared, resulting in a very stiff system subject to smaller deflections than a standard truss spanning in a single direction.

Eden Project uses a hybrid between a geodesic dome and spaceframe, interlocking three domes of varying size to create a series of climate-controlled greenhouses. The base structure is created from hexagonal units, rather than the smaller equilateral triangles as more typically used by Buckminster Fuller. The poles and nodes were fabricated off site and arrived in flats to be fully site-erected. A substantial scaffold was required to erect the domes, which are 125m/410ft across and 60m/197ft high. ETFE cladding was chosen for its durability and very high level of solar transparency as this would help to ensure good light for the plant specimens to be housed within.

The exterior of Eden Project in St. Austell, UK by Nicholas Grimshaw shows the pillow nature of the ETFE cladding as it pinches together at the sides and presses out at the center of each panel.

Larger steel truss arches were required at the intersection points of the domes in order to resolve the geometry and stabilize the structures.

The steel structure closely resembles the system used to create spaceframe structures. The opened sections show the level of visual transparency of the ETFE material. The relative sizes of the steel tubes and rods that comprise the outer structure of the dome can be seen against the smaller members that create the three-dimensional bracing layer on the interior. Services such as wiring, fire protection and air to maintain the pressure in the skin run tightly along the hexagonal steel grid to conceal the systems.

## IRREGULAR MODULES

The National Aquatics Center for the 2008 Beijing Olympics was the first structure in China to use an ETFE membrane. The idea for the structure was based upon the geometry of soap bubbles. This transformation of the combination of a spaceframe and geodesic structure into one that included large variations in the relative sizes of the units added significant complexity to the design, fabrication and erection of the structure. The polyhedral spaceframe is comprised of 22,000 individual elements and 12,000 joints. Its form is highly earthquake-resistant.

Whereas earlier uses of this sort of structure worked with spherical geometry for the shape of the building, the Watercube creates an orthogonal building with an irregular-looking, three-dimensional polygonal steel framework of uniform thickness. The framework is clad on the exterior and interior with ETFE membrane bubbles. The 197x197x35m/646x646x115ft building was digitally "carved" out of a theoretical 3D model of a solid block of Weaire-Phelan Foam. The geometry of foam, seen as a perfect array of soap bubbles, served as a model to subdivide the three-dimensional space of the frame into a continuous bubble-like structure that could be transformed into a steel-framed system. Because of this means of form generation, the roof and wall structures are continuous. This also led to a decision to site-weld the steel components.

Rectangular HSS steel members are used on the interior and exterior faces of the wall to provide the proper geometry for the attachment of the ETFE membrane. Round HSS are used between the faces to work more easily with ball-joint-type connectors.

The National Aquatics Center (Watercube) in Beijing, China was designed by CSCEC, CCDI, PTW and ARUP for the 2008 Olympics. The polyhedral spaceframe geometry is fitted into a very precise rectangular building type. This marriage of geometries, combined with the ETFE cladding, creates a highly innovative enclosure system for the building. For solar control the ETFE is coated with an aluminum frit that varies to block the transmission of 5 to 95% of visible light, as a function of the solar orientation.

Top right: The member sizes of the polyhedral spaceframe vary as a function of their span and loading characteristics. A corridor penetrates the system to allow for an organic connection between spaces.

Top left: Viewing from the interior through into the enclosed structure reveals the density of the steel framework as well as some of the attachments and service systems. The translucency creates a ghost-like aesthetic for the space.

Bottom Left: Unlike other spaceframe buildings, which make predominant use of threading and bolted connections, many of the connections for the Watercube were site-welded. A view to the interior shows the combined use of rectangular and round HSS members and ball joints.

CHAPTER 12

---

# STEEL AND GLAZING SYSTEMS

---



The highly technical tensile glazing system at the Louvre pyramid in Paris, France, designed by I. M. Pei and Peter Rice, characterizes the extreme contrast between the limitations of load-bearing masonry and the possibilities of steel glazing systems.

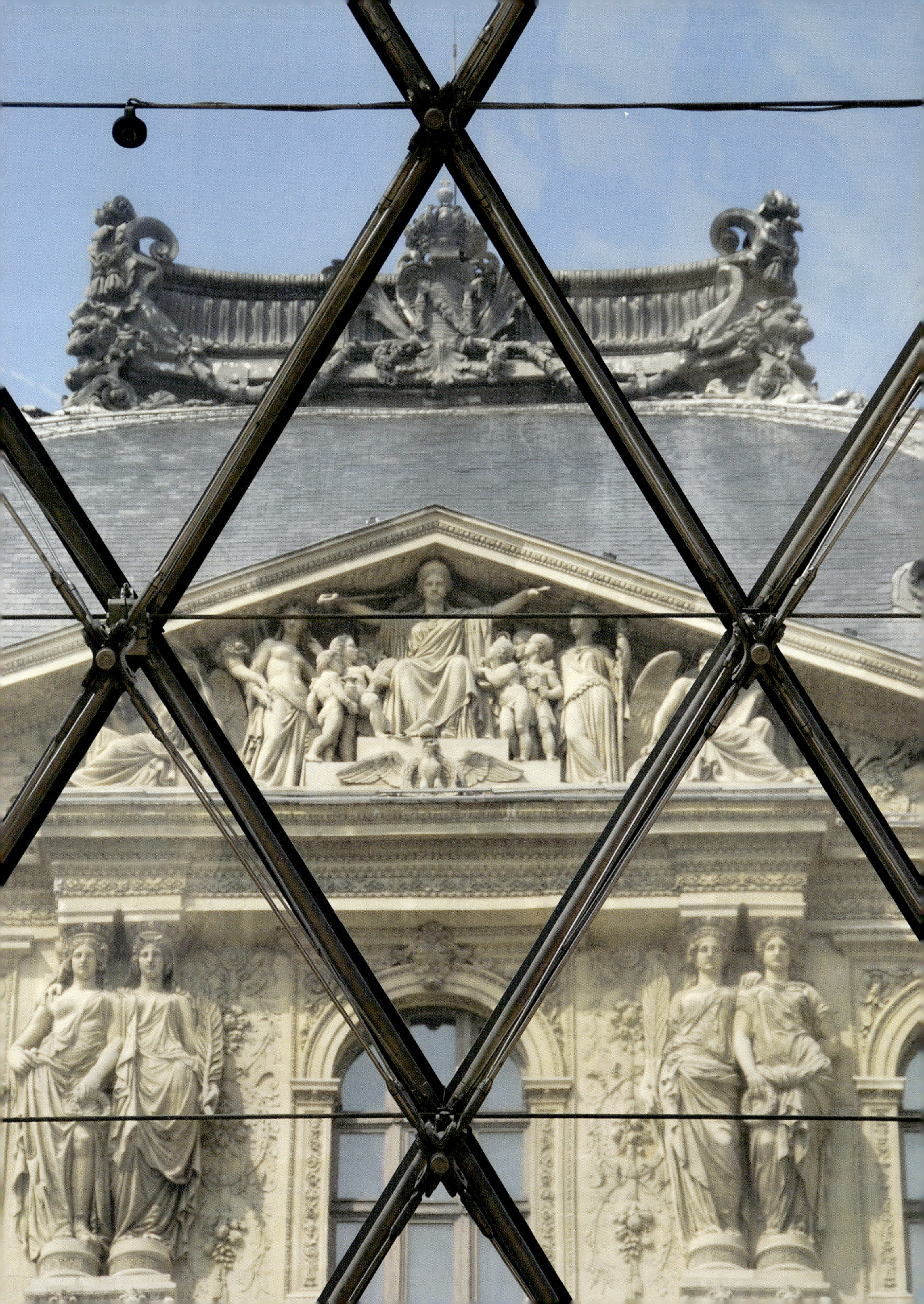

# *EARLY STEEL AND GLASS BUILDINGS*

Iron and glass were both children of early 19$^{th}$ century architectural progress. The timing of their advances in technology was complementary. Each allowed the other to reveal its advantages and propel alternatives to traditional load-bearing systems. Early iron framing revolutionized architectural design in that its strength and slenderness permitted the use of wide expanses of glass. This break from load-bearing masonry removed pre-existing limitations on window size, creating a significant paradigm shift. In these early buildings where thermal separation was not a consideration, the glass was normally housed within the steel frame of wall glazing, arcade roofs and skylights.

Toward the end of the 19$^{th}$ century steel framing became the basis for the construction of multi-storey buildings and skyscrapers. The ability of steel to carry loads under a cantilever condition allowed the expression and function of the exterior wall to be separated from the structural frame.

The Reliance Building in Chicago, IL, USA, designed by Charles B. Atwood and John Wellborn Root, constructed from 1890 to 1895, is considered to be the first true skeleton-frame steel skyscraper. The interior structure is concealed under fire-protective materials. The exterior glass and terra cotta skin is light-looking, with a substantially increased glazed surface compared to earlier load-bearing structures.

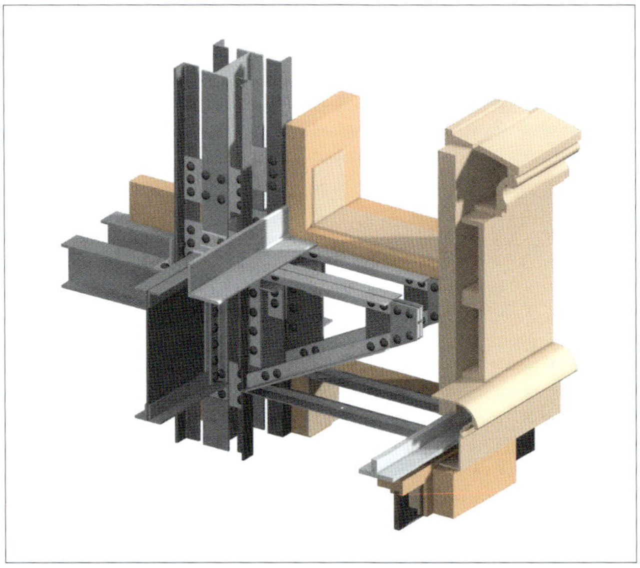

The Reliance Building uses cantilevered steel elements to separate the exterior wall or skin from the structural frame. both functionally and visually. This simple technique provided unprecedented freedom in envelope design. A typical steel frame was built up from smaller elements.

Developments in curtain wall construction, particularly the use of aluminum façade systems, along with the widespread availability of mechanical air conditioning, spawned a wide range of approaches to skyscraper envelope design throughout the 20$^{th}$ century. Early glass façades were most typically of a curtain wall type, the glass being supported in an aluminum framing system, which was tied back to the structural frame. As designers sought more creative solutions in glass, mullion-less curtain wall was created. This still relied on an aluminum curtain wall system behind the glass but replaced the mullion cap system with concealed fasteners. Although this chapter will not address these systems in detail, it is important to recognize the freedom that steel framing systems have provided, resulting in an increased use of glass in building façades.

Where steel skeleton framing initially allowed for a marked increase of expression in glazed façades, the International Style and the Modern Movement during the better part of the 20$^{th}$ century did little to take true advantage of the dynamic potential of the mix of the two materials. In part this was due to fire regulations that entailed the complete covering of interior steel to achieve the required fire ratings and in part to the restrained detailing of the "less is more" aesthetics.

Expressive combinations of steel and glass arose during the High Tech and then Postmodern periods of the 1970s and the early 1980s (see Chapter 5: AESS: Its History and Development). Architecturally exposed steel, plus a move away from standardized aluminum curtain wall systems, and the increased use of large glazed walls and skylights provided rich grounds for experimentation with the combined media. Whereas curtain wall systems chose not to express the wind bracing, High Tech and Postmodern architecture highlighted connections and bracing techniques.

An external truss system is used to suspend this flat glazed skylight at the Dubai Mall in the UAE. The differential temperatures between the conditioned space and the exterior must be accommodated in the design of the interface of the structures. As hot air rises, the temperature differential at the ceiling will be less extreme.

In spite of liberation in formal tendencies from the 1980s onward, two persistent technical issues in the detailing of steel and glass systems must be accounted for at the outset of concept design. First, what are the fire code issues associated with the exposure of the steel to be used to frame the glass? Is exposed steel permitted, and if so, what sort of protection systems are required (see Chapter 7: Coatings, Finishes and Fire Protection)? Second, if the element is part of the building enclosure system, how must the façade or skylight element deal with climate issues? There is much more flexibility permitted when designing for temperate climates, to the point in some cases of paying no heed to thermal bridging and enjoying complete freedom to place the support structure on the exterior. In severe climates, both hot and cold, thermal bridging and the insulating value of the enclosure are likely to be very important. This may require the use of insulating glass and different support systems.

## *TECHNICAL ASPECTS OF COMBINING STEEL WITH GLASS*

Although the focus of this chapter is on the selection and detailing of steel systems to support glass, it is important to be familiar with the technical characteristics of glass. Tempered or toughened glass is most commonly used in large-scale feature applications. Tempering with heat can produce a pane of glass four or five times stronger than annealed or float glass. Further protection against breakage can be achieved by laminating multiple layers of glass with thin plastic interlayers. This type of glass has been used successfully as flooring or stair-tread elements. Tempering not only enhances the strength of the glass, but also alters its characteristics should it break. Tempered glass will crumble rather than break into shards. If any holes are desired in the glass to accommodate fittings, these must be drilled prior to tempering.

The laminated glass used in the Shanghai Apple Store in China is joined using stainless steel connectors. It requires no additional support. All holes and cutouts were created prior to tempering and laminating.

For most situations where thermal control across the exterior wall is important, insulating sealed units that may be double- or triple-glazed will be employed. These can use tempered or laminated glass and accommodate argon fill, low-e and other selective coatings. The glazing layers will be joined by an edge spacer, preferably non-conductive. Until recently, insulating glass units were not drilled to accommodate penetrating fittings, but instead were always secured into frames. More recently systems such as the Pilkington Planar™ line offer fittings for supporting insulated structural glass assemblies. The glazing layers must be drilled prior to tempering and assembling into sealed units.

Increased concerns about terrorism have resulted in the requirement for blast-resistant glass construction for airports, rail stations, embassies and certain types of office buildings. Often this requires different detailing, the use of laminated glass and framing systems that are resilient upon impact without losing structural integrity. Cable truss support systems have been able to respond to the criteria.

Steel and glass production methods have different tolerances. When designing systems that mix these materials it is important to make allowances. Glass requires higher precision, with tolerances of +/- 2mm / +/- 0.08in, while steel tolerances are in the range of +/- 5mm / +/- 0.2in. These differences have to be accommodated during installation in order to keep the glass panels properly aligned. Where steel is to be welded it needs to be recognized that welding, in the heating of the steel, may result in distortion. This is less of an issue on short members, but for very long supports with eccentric welds this can be a problem as it could result in bowing of the member. Dimensional accommodation in the connection between the glazing panels and the steel is indispensable, particularly at the mid- section where the bow might be the greatest.

The vertical steel wind braces at the Leslie Dan Faculty of Pharmacy in Toronto, ON, Canada by Foster + Partners are five stories tall. The curtain wall is attached with slip connections to accommodate vertical alignment. The welded steel box sections are symmetrical, which assists in preventing bending due to the heat from welding.

The steel support system for the glass can bear on the floor, be suspended from the floor above, or span across the width of the glazed façade and transfer the loads to adjacent columns or vertical trusses. Some more recent horizontal support strategies have used tension cables. Cold climate applications will normally place the steel support system on the interior of the glazed wall to limit fluctuations in temperature and thermal movement and also to protect painted steel from weathering. Some temperate and hot climate situations will permit the steel structure to be located on the exterior of the building. Thermal movement will not cease to be an issue when detailing such systems. Environmental deterioration due to climate will also continue to be a concern. Finish and fire-protective coatings will be a consideration when choosing to detail steel support systems for interior versus exterior applications.

The glazed wall of the Salt Lake City Public Library, UT, USA, designed by Moshe Safdie, is supported by a cable tension system. The vertical HSS members that form the compression chord of the truss are pin-connected to the underside of the ceiling/roof. Additional horizontal cables provide stiffening. The wind-bracing system only supports direct loading to the glass.

A substantial amount of movement must be accommodated in the design of steel-supported glass systems. Glazed façades are often subjected to high levels of solar gain, which results in different thermal movement in the steel and glass. Wind loads result in unequal deflections at the center of the spans versus the top, bottom or lateral support points. The overall dimensions of the spans and points of support will impact these deflections. If the design uses a variety of panel sizes, detailing will need to accommodate these dimensional differences.

Steel and glass systems will be subjected to different loading conditions during and after construction. Loading conditions due to seasonal changes — wind, rain, snow and temperature loads — must also be accommodated. Systems will normally need to use vertical slip joints to allow for vertical movement due to deflection while limiting lateral movement.

As concerns about energy efficiency and the prevention of unwanted heat gain continue to grow, the glazed façade may also need to support external shading devices. The load from larger exterior shades will need to be tied back through the glazing to the steel support system. Smaller, more frequent shades can simply be an extension to the normal mullion cap system and might not require additional strength in the steel support system.

Left: The support system for the front wall of Heathrow Terminal 5 in London, England by Richard Rogers uses horizontal elliptical tube sections to minimize the visual impact of the large sections in front of the glass. The exterior shading devices connect through the horizontal mullions of the façade and tie back to the tubes.

Right: An additional suspension system on the exterior of the building is used to hang the shades from the roof structure.

## *SUPPORT SYSTEMS FOR GLAZING*

The type of glass traditionally used in buildings has been held in place in a "frame", thereby subjected almost only to major wind load stresses, minimal ponding due to rain and some snow loading. This has been addressed in part by increasing the thickness of the glass as a function of the load and the pane size. Curtain wall and skylight systems can adjust also to movements of the frame due to temperature, wind and seismic loading. New technological developments have both increased the options available and reduced the difficulties in designing, detailing and erecting steel buildings of all sizes with increased amounts and advanced geometries of glass. Much of the current use of glass in buildings bears little resemblance to historic models, and as a result requires significantly different detailing.

Stainless steel glazing support systems can be used in conjunction with AESS feature elements constructed from regular carbon steel. Stainless steel is used frequently to connect and support large glazing walls, often with quite innovative custom-made systems that are used to attach the spider connections to the steel. Such systems require even finer tolerances in order to achieve the proper fit.

There are three basic ways to consider how steel acts as a support system for expansive glazed applications:

→ The steel framework is used simultaneously as the main structure and the substructure holding the glass in place, whereby the glass is almost in the same plane as the steel. A slim aluminum cap system is often used in conjunction with this type of framing, the alignment holding tight to the plane of the exterior face of the steel.

→ Larger steel members are used directly behind or in front of the glass system to provide wind bracing. These structural steel sections, trusses or cable systems can be installed vertically or horizontally at the mullions and usually do not support the floor loads above.

→ The steel structure sits back from the glass to provide the lateral support, creating a separate, unique structure of its own. An interstitial support system (often cables) is used to connect the glass to the steel.

Top: The fritted glass roof on this small exterior skylight at the University of Houston, TX, USA is directly supported by the steel framing below.

Middle: Triangular trusses welded from round HSS members span the full height of the passenger side of the Beijing International Airport in China, designed by Foster + Partners and ARUP. The curtain wall is sized to span between the support points. The triangular nature of the truss limits the span of the curtain wall in the horizontal direction. The curtain wall connects to the truss at the respective panel points to better accommodate movement.

Bottom: The all-glass atrium at Tower Bridge House in London, England, designed by Richard Rogers, uses an exposed steel structure to create the form of the atrium. The mullion-less structural glass is attached to the steel with stainless fittings that penetrate the glass. The glass panels are sealed to each other using structural silicone.

Traditionally the steel systems designed to provide both support and wind stiffening for glass have been constructed from rigid members designed to AESS standards. More recently cable truss systems and cable net systems provide support that allows for increased transparency. They are effective also where blast resistance is required.

Each system entails a different method of attachment of the glass to the structural steel, depending in large part on whether the application uses insulating glass or solid structural glass. Structural or single-thickness glass allows for more options, as it may be held in place with attachments that simply penetrate the glass or by other perimeter systems (holes must be drilled prior to tempering the glass). Insulating glass can most easily be held in place at its perimeter, while drill-through technologies are more expensive. Where the glazed units are held in a frame, e.g. in a curtain wall, the steel support system should only connect to the frame at its intersection points, e.g. the corners, so that any differential movement can be accommodated by the frame and does not translate into the glass at mid-span. If this is not possible, connections can be made to the vertical components, as these are designed to accommodate movement. The connection should never be made at a horizontal mullion, because this would result in direct load transfer to the glass leading to fracture.

The spaceframe wall at Baltimore Washington International Airport, MD, USA, connects to the curtain wall at the corners of the frame to make sure that movement is translated into the frame and not the glass.

Carbon steel and aluminum must not come into direct contact, as this would result in an electrolytic reaction. These materials have to be separated either through the use of stainless steel fastening systems or by coating the carbon steel in Teflon. PTFE washers are also used.

The development of structural silicone systems has led to a blurring of the need to detail glazed roof and wall elements differently. The smooth exterior surface allows for easy drainage of water. Many contemporary buildings exploit this attribute resulting in continuous geometries.

Glass and steel systems can be subdivided into those that use rectangular geometries versus those that use curvilinear geometries. Approaches to considering the support of glass with steel systems differ as a function of the overall geometry. The fabrication of curved glass is expensive and hence uncommon, particularly where more energy-efficient double- and triple-glazed systems are required. In these cases the curved geometry is achieved through the triangulation or faceting of the supporting steel system. Glass unit sizes will vary as a function of the scale of the curved surfaces.

## *SELECTING THE APPROPRIATE SYSTEM*

The various methods of supporting glass with steel systems provide the designer with a range of possibilities. Beyond the initial concerns of budget, there are other factors that will influence the choice of system. The following is a checklist that can form a starting point:

Is preventing thermal transmission through the assembly important?
- Yes – use insulating glass with thermally broken frames or connectors
- No – structural glass with through fasteners may be used

Must the assembly be fire-protected?
- No – exposed steel connection systems can be used
- To a degree – adjacent fire suppression or intumscent coatings can be used
- Yes – for high-risk exposure, exposed steel systems may not be suitable

What is the impact of climate?

*Temperate:*
- → Little concern for thermal resistance
- → Supporting structure may be on the inside or the outside of the glass

*Severe cold:*
- → Insulating glass
- → Concern for differential expansion of the glass and steel
- → Steel structure on the inside of the glass

*Severe hot:*
- → Insulating glass (in extremely humid climates condensation may occur on the outside of the building due to air conditioning of the interior)
- → Some concern for differential expansion, dependent on the elevation and exposure conditions

*Shading:*
- → Small, even frequent shading devices can be incorporated into the design of curtain wall framing
- → Large or deep shading devices must be tied back to the primary structure for support
- → If a high level of shading is required, this negates the need to detail highly transparent assemblies to support the glass

What is the size of the glazed panel?
- → How frequent are the primary supports (columns or floor level attachments)?
- → How frequently can the glazing bracing elements be placed?
- → How do the panels connect to each other? Frame? Structural silicone? Stainless connectors?

What sort of lateral loads like snow, wind or blast must be resisted?

This impacts a synergistic question of glass thickness (strength) and support spacing – the larger the panels and less frequent the desire for supports, the more challenging the problem

What is the desired level of transparency?
- → High transparency – implies the use of mullion-less glazing and lightweight cable systems
- → Mid-level transparency – may use a denser suite of structural elements to provide wind resistance for the glazing
- → Normal levels of transparency – aluminum curtain wall framing may be used in conjunction with steel bracing systems

What is the desired aesthetic of the glazing feature?
- → How does the detailing and selection of the steel support system work with or complement the framing of the adjacent structure?
- → Is it a key architectural feature?
- → What is the budget?

What type of steel support system is to be used?
- → In line with the glass
- → Support system that sits behind the glass and connects directly to the glass
- → Support system that uses specialized stainless connectors to attach to the glass
- → Do standard structural or HSS systems fit with the aesthetic? Are planar or 3D trusses acceptable?
- → Will the supports run vertically or horizontally?
- → Is there a desire to use tension systems, cables or cable nets? Tension systems must tie back to the structure to complete their load path
- → Does the system use structural glass fins?

How is differential expansion and movement due to loading, thermal expansion and contraction accommodated?

Will the system use spider connectors and clamps?

Yes – be sure that this coordinates with insulating glass and that the penetrations are mapped out prior to tempering

## SIMPLE CURTAIN WALL SUPPORT SYSTEMS

In many steel structures there is no need for additional wind bracing. The frequency or shape of the structure is sufficient to provide support. Of primary concern will be the physical attachment of the glazing and its framing to the structural steel system. Ideally, loads should be transferred at the panel points of the glazing system so that no deflection is caused in horizontal framing members. This would be liable to cause cracking in the glazed units. Typically, aluminum curtain wall framing systems are used in these applications. In these, the steel framing is fitted with tabs created from plate steel that must align to matching tabs in the curtain wall system. Both vertical and horizontal adjustment will be necessary in the connection to allow for dimensional differences in the erection of the systems. Movement due to loading is normally accommodated in the curtain wall frame system.

A simple connection at the Brown Center, MD, USA by Charles Brickbauer typifies the normal connection between AESS support systems and curtain wall.

## SIMPLE WIND-BRACED SYSTEMS

The most common method of bracing oversized curtain walls is through the use of a vertical support system. This allows for the use of thermally broken frames and insulated glazing units that can employ more energy-efficient fenestration such as triple-glazed, argon-filled low-e coated glass. As the glass is held in frames, there is no need for penetrating connectors. The design of the system must allow for differential thermal expansion of the aluminum curtain wall and the steel support system. The steel wind bracing will expand differently as a function of the orientation and solar exposure. Such braces do not normally support roof and floor loads.

The bracing is usually installed vertically, and can bear on the floor or hang from the structure above, or be pin-connected at the top and the bottom. This bracing is normally created using AESS truss or solid members.

The vertical wind-bracing system for Reagan Airport is simply pin-connected at the base. The spacing of the horizontal mullions for the upper section of glass is set at half intervals to align with horizontal shading elements on the exterior face of the glass. The interior steel supports assist in creating shade on the interior. The frequency of the horizontal mullions in the upper half of the glass reflects the addition of external shading louvers, with half the spacing of the vision glass at pedestrian level. The curved vaults of the departure hall are acknowledged through the addition of curved lateral bracing of the vertical wind supports.

The wind bracing at Reagan International Airport in Washington, D.C., USA, designed by Cesar Pelli, creates a truss-like support from a pair of round HSS members that have been joined with steel plates. The connecting plates are aligned with the horizontal window mullions. The intention of this system is to create a visual texture. The vertical supports are placed at every window mullion. The change of color from yellow for the structure to white for the glazing supports highlights the different functions of the systems and also allows for a lighter feel to the glazing support system, in spite of the texture required to achieve both support and shading.

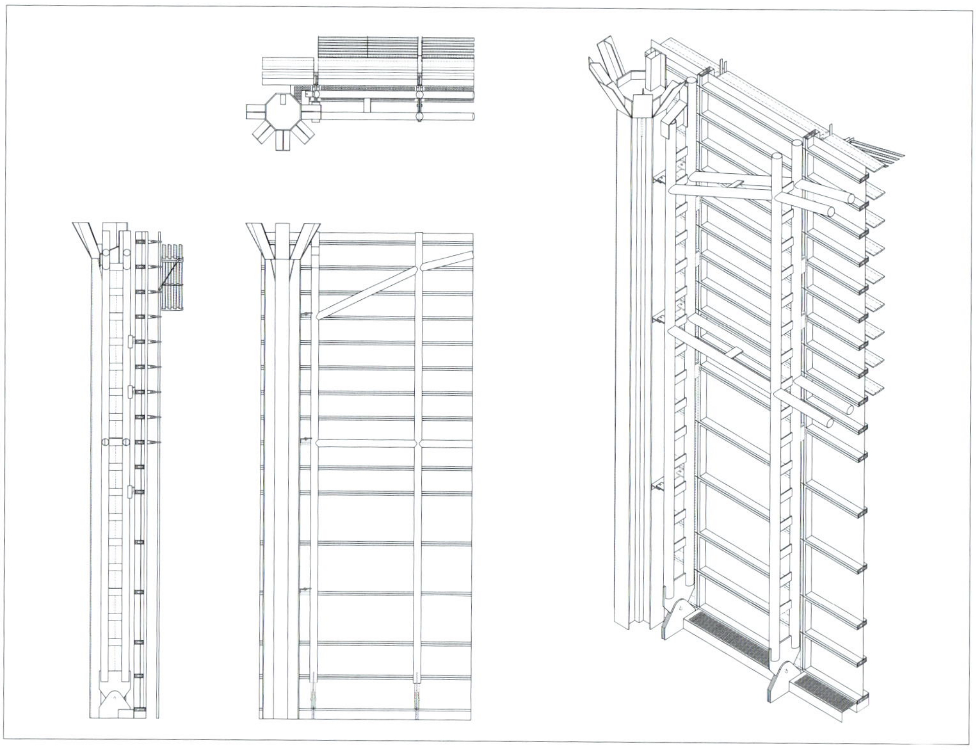

Large curtain wall installations can also require the use of more elaborate lateral support systems to resist wind loads. These are often found in airports, whose very high spaces frequently require large expanses of glass for daylighting.

The glazed end wall at Pearson International Airport in Toronto, ON, Canada, designed by SOM, uses a modified vertical truss system to provide bracing for the curtain wall.

At Pearson Airport, vertical trusses with arm-like extensions are connected to horizontal steel sections. The curtain wall is attached to these horizontal braces at each panel point. The use of the arms reduces the visual impact of the trusses, keeping the lateral bracing system in the same visual line as the aluminum framing.

## *CABLE-SUPPORTED STRUCTURAL GLASS ENVELOPES*

The spring support that is used to accomodate movement from deflection at the Serres of the Cité des Sciences et de l'Industrie in Paris, France, designed under the direction of Peter Rice from 1981 to 1986.

The first noted use of large glass panels that did not use a framing system was the Willis Faber + Dumas office building, designed by Foster + Partners from 1971 to 1975. The solid glass panels used a drilled connection in combination with reinforcing plates to assist in transferring the loads from the glass to the structure behind. The joints between the glass panels were sealed with silicone. Peter Rice took this early technology and transformed it into a new system of components to achieve the design objectives of a fully transparent enclosure for the greenhouses ("*serres*") at the Cité des Sciences et de l'Industrie at the Parc de la Villette in Paris. Key modifications in the nature of the stainless connector and an interstitial cable truss support system that connects the glass wall back to the primary structure form the basis of all subsequently developed systems.

Rice realized that an interstitial system was required to connect the façade glazing to the steel structure in order to distribute and absorb loading on the glass. Lightweight stainless steel cable systems that are pretensioned mediate between the glass and the structural steel. The trusses sit horizontally between the vertical steel support systems. Connectors from yacht rigging were either used or modified in the stainless steel assemblies. Stainless steel connectors are normally used, as they are easily attached to holes in the glass panels and their shank configuration and method of attachment to the primary structure are easily customized. Many of these connectors are fabricated from stainless steel that has been cast into these articulate shapes.

This diagram of the steel and cable support system for the Serres illustrates the hierarchical suite of steel members to transfer the load from the glass to the primary support structure.

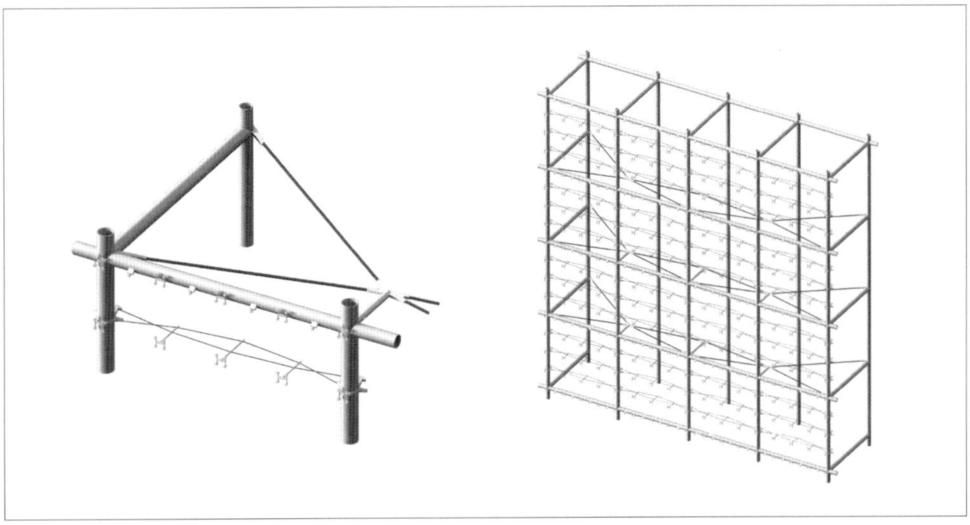

## CABLE NET WALLS

In contrast with the intense hierarchical sequence of truss systems used to support the glass boxes at the Serres, cable net systems appear structurally very simple. The first cable net installation of note was designed in 1993 by Murphy/Jahn Architects to create the front and rear walls of the lobby for the Kempinski Hotel at the Munich International Airport. Whereas the Serres system can be used to create glass "boxes", simple two-way cable net systems are limited to planar applications, as the loads from the vertical and horizontal cables must be transferred directly back into the primary structural system of the building. No additional members perpendicular to the plane are employed to distort or force the geometry. The base structure of the building must be designed to withstand the tension loading of the cable-net wall, including varied conditions during the installation and tensioning of the system, variable wind loads and forces from thermal expansion and contraction of the cables. It is desirable for the perimeter structure and the connections to the cables to be stiff to compensate for the flexibility of the cable net itself.

The requirements for the glass will vary as a function of the location/use, climate and local codes. Generally these façades will use heat-strengthened, tempered glass to increase their resistance to breakage, but laminated glass has become a more popular choice due to its durability. Tempered glass is also used in conjunction with a laminated application for added strength against breakout. The fastenings that are used to attach the cables to the glass tend to avoid drilling the glass (as is required for spider connectors), instead using a clamping technique referred to as a patch plate at the corners. This allows the connector to be smaller and hence more discreet. Drilled connections must place the holes at a distance from the corner, thereby increasing the size of the connector. This would work against the high level of transparency that is desired in this method.

Special fittings are required at the end points to attach the cables to the structure. The connectors are either swaged or speltered to the cable. Swaging is a process whereby the fitting is mechanically pressed onto the cable end. The spelter-socket connection takes the splayed wires of the cable and binds them with resin or zinc to a cone-shaped terminus. The swaged connection is the more commonly used, as it is very slender and complements the lightweight objective of the system. Cables are either galvanized or made of stainless steel. As most cable nets are installed on the interior of the glass, corrosion resistance is mostly important during construction. Untreated cables are not used.

Cable net systems must be designed to accommodate large deflections due to wind loading. The maximum design deflection is approximately L/50. The differential movement between the adjacent panes of glass at the center of the span is not as great as the movement between the glass and the adjacent structure at the boundary condition. Deflections and rotations in the center of the system are accommodated by a neoprene bearing pad between the glazing and patch plate.

The Kempinski Hotel Airport Munich, Germany, designed by Murphy/Jahn Architects, uses a cable net system to create the front and rear façades, achieving an extremely high level of transparency.

The cable net support system requires that the tension loads of the two-way system be resolved at its perimeter, limiting the application to planar installations. The attachment of the upper edge of the Kempinski façade is resolved by adding a paired plate between the diamond shape of the plate and the tensile roof truss system to accept the swaged cable fittings. This plate also forms the completion of the environmental separation of interior and exterior.

Left: The cables align directly behind the silicone joints of the glass. The slender swaged stainless steel end connectors at the base of the wall are barely visible. Butterfly-shaped patch connectors are used to connect the glazing to the cable system. These make it possible to avoid drilling the glass.

Right: The rear of the patch connector showing how the vertical and horizontal cables pass by each other and are clamped into position. The neoprene pad that absorbs the wind-induced rotation of the glass is also visible.

## STAINLESS STEEL SPIDER CONNECTORS

There are a number of methods of connecting the glass panels to the structural supports. The most commonly used is the spider bracket, which has one to four arms coming out of a central hub. Bolts penetrating the glass panels are secured to the arms, and the brackets are attached to the support structure. The holes in the glass are drilled to be countersunk on the outer face. An aluminum washer with a separating PTFE or thermoplastic liner layer is used to soften the load transfer between the stainless connector and the glass. Direct transfer of the load from the steel to the glass would result in fracture. Most systems will use an articulating bolt, which essentially has a ball at the point of intersection with the glass. This allows for some rotation due to loading without fracture of the glass. The articulating bolt was developed for the Serres of the Cité des Sciences et de l'Industrie under the direction of Peter Rice.

The spider connection developed for the Serres, shown here in exploded view, formed the basis for the design of connectors used today. The ball shape at the intersection of the glass can allow up to 10° of rotation, depending on the specific detailing for the project.

The stainless steel connectors at Richard Rogers' Tower Bridge House in London, England connect two panels back to the HSS steel support system behind. The structural glass elements are interconnected using structural silicone. A fully transparent corner is achieved.

The rear view of this connection between square HSS bracing and an exterior canopy shows the ability of the connectors to adjust for dimensional differences between the glass and the steel.

Stainless steel angle brackets, single brackets, pin brackets or clamping devices are all alternatives used on occasion. The panels are usually secured at the four corners, larger panels with an additional pair of bolts in the middle of each side. In Europe, bolted systems are slipping from favor and designers are tending to use a clip system where the panels are supported on the side, removing the need to drill holes in the glass.

The exterior glass on this double façade office building in Berlin, Germany, designed by Petzinka Pink Architects, uses a clip system that is secured back to spider connectors attached to a structural steel armature. In this instance the choice to use a clip connector complements the venting strategies for the façade. A sealed system was not desired.

## CABLE TRUSS SYSTEMS

Cable truss systems use trusses that have been created from cables that sit perpendicular to the plane of the glazed wall to resist wind loading. The compression members of the trusses are normally formed from stainless steel posts, as these are strong enough to withstand the loading but maintain the slender appearance of the cables. These attach easily to the spider connectors that are used to connect the glass. As the tensile forces in the trusses need not be as high as would be found in planar cable net systems, the cable truss system can be adapted for use in a variety of geometries. The loads from the trusses are normally restrained by architecturally exposed steel members that form part of the structural hierarchy of the system.

The Rose Center in New York by Ennead Architects (formerly Polshek Partnership), the largest suspended glass curtain wall in the United States, uses a prestressed cable truss system connected back to the primary steel structure for tensioning the glass. The prestressed cables are separated by solid stainless steel struts. This dual system works much like cross bracing: if movement in the system causes one cable to relax, the load is easily transferred to the other.

The 28.96m/95ft cube of the Frederick Phineas & Sandra Priest Rose Center for Earth and Space in New York, NY, USA by Ennead Architects (formerly Polshek Partnership) has 736 glass panels measuring 152.4 x 320cm / 5 x 10.5ft, fastened with 1,400 spider connectors. The tubular steel framework is here also used to support the roof.

Left: Pretensioned cable trusses run horizontally between the vertical tubular steel trusses that support the roof. A triangular tubular truss resolves the geometry of the corners of the building.

Right: This detail of the Rose Center shows the connection of the glazing system to the main structural steel system for the building. Stainless steel spider connectors attach the silicone-joined glass panels to the main framework behind. Stainless steel tension connectors provide additional support between the spider connectors. The stainless spider connectors are connected vertically by stainless steel cables. The design challenge is to create a language of connection detailing that is applicable to both the structural and the glazing elements. This image demonstrates the interdependence of the systems.

Lightweight cable tension systems have also been used on non-rectangular geometries, although this does present different issues in tying the tension system back to the primary structure. Adaptive changes for the curved façade at Channel 4 News in London, designed by Richard Rogers and engineered by Peter Rice, use a two-way cable net system to support the curved geometry. The tensile stresses must be held in a complete boundary condition rather than simply by a line of vertical support members. This means that instead of a linear arrangement of the connections of the cables back to the base structure, the tensile members create a three-dimensional web reflective of the non-planar shape of the wall. This impacts the location of the support steel in unique ways, as can be seen in Channel 4 News by Richard Rogers, where trusses cantilevered out from the roof level in a curved fashion are used to support some cables while others criss-cross the atrium to tie the curve back to the floor plates of the balconies. While the façade of the Serres in Paris employed spring connectors at the mid-support levels to absorb and prevent deflective transfer from panel to panel, the curved glass of Channel 4 News employs a substantial spring system at the top edge of the suspended glass wall that is hung from steel members cantilevering out from the top floor of the building. Curved glass applications will also require the use of softer silicone to absorb wind deflections with even higher flexibility.

Channel 4 News in London, England by Richard Rogers and Peter Rice. The web-like articulation of the cable net system can be seen through the façade. Spring connectors similar to those used in the Serres project by Peter Rice are used to hang the glass from the top (red) rail.

Many of the cable truss or cable net systems mentioned above use a criss-cross technique, similar to that used in cross bracing, to control the changing transfer of forces through the system under different loading conditions. When one cable is slack, the other will be in tension. The cable support system in the Newseum in Washington, D.C. uses horizontal pairings of straight cables that are tied back to substantial trusses that run the full height of the façade.

Top: The Newseum in Washington, D.C., USA, designed by Ennead Architects (formerly Polshek Partnership), uses various approaches to glazing the façade – the primary feature being the cable-supported structural glass at the center of the façade that daylights the central atrium.

Bottom: The cable support system of the Newseum employs spider connectors as well as vertical stainless steel plates to interconnect the parallel sets of cables.

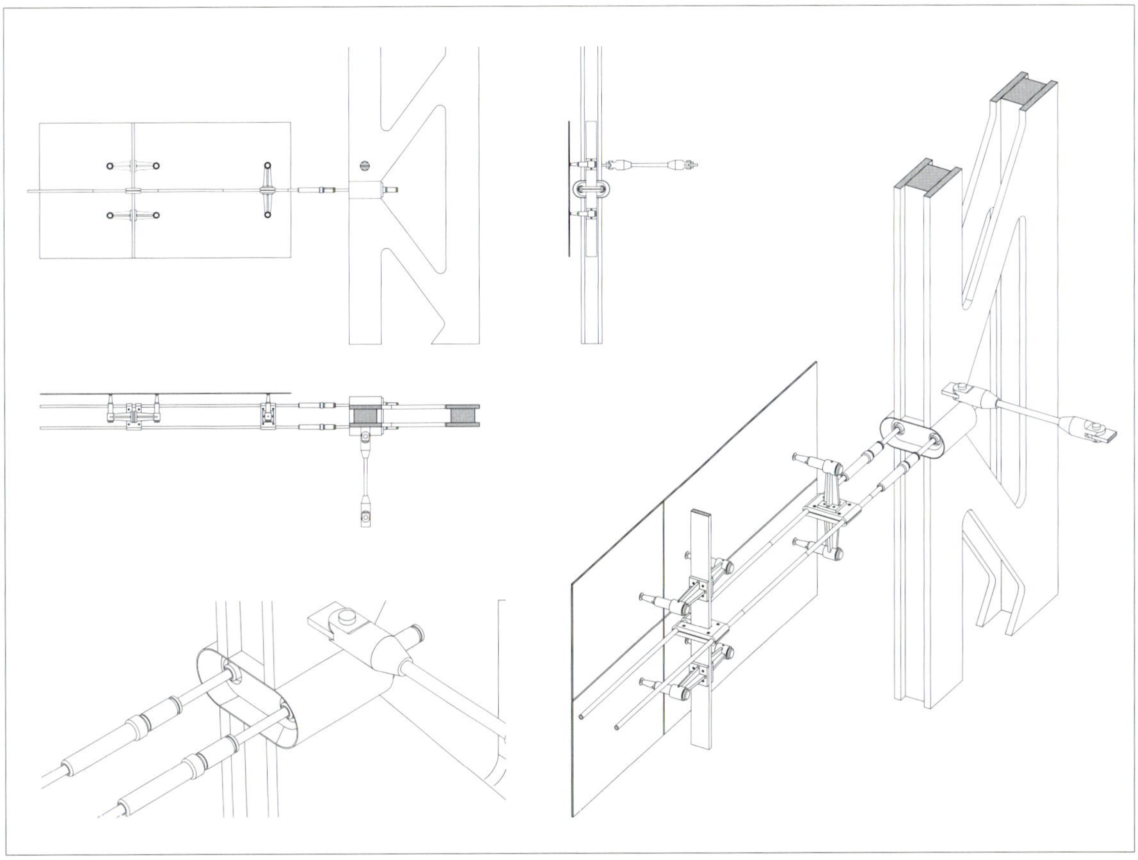

Right: Detailing of the cable brace system for the Newseum: slender turnbuckles provide for discreet tension adjustment in the system.

The design of the TGV Railway Terminal at Charles-de-Gaulle Airport in Paris pursued the intention to keep the side walls of the station as transparent as possible. It uses spider connectors in conjunction with a vertical steel structure that cantilevers from the foundation to support the walls. A gap between the cantilevered glass wall and the glazed roof provides natural ventilation. The masts are braced to resist twisting by a system of prestressed cables set close to the glass.

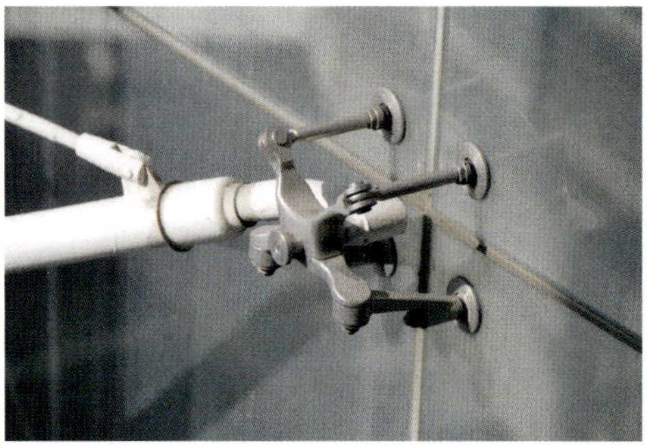

Left: The TGV Railway Terminal at Charles-de-Gaulle Airport in Paris, France was designed by Paul Andreu and J. M. Duthilleul with the engineering group RFR under Peter Rice. The large, croissant-shaped steel bow trusses that support the fritted glass roof are staggered against the masts to make it obvious that the masts are not supporting the roof. The masts in turn vary in height as they decrease according to the slope of the station roof. This modifies their geometry. As the primary round HSS members are placed "in line", hence unable to resist lateral forces along the wall, they are interconnected and braced between members with cables.

Right: The spider connector that attaches the glazing to the structural arms of the masts of the TGV station is a variation of the La Villette/Serres type.

## COMPLEX CABLE SYSTEMS

The variations in the detailing of the cable-based systems for the large and small glass pyramids at the Louvre in Paris highlight different solutions depending on scale and application. The large pyramid, which forms the enclosure system for the new entrance of the museum, has a marginally less transparent feel due to the density of its structure. Its joints are silicone-sealed for environmental reasons. The main structure of the pyramid must be substantial enough to span across the space as well as support the load of the glass and climate-related live loads.

The structure of the large pyramid is quite complex. The outer layer that sits directly adjacent to the glazing is comprised of round stainless tubes connected to a cast node. The diamond tube lattice sits about 50mm/2in away from the framing system for the glazing. A round tubular strut connects the lattice to the system of tension rods that forms the inner edge of the structure. The connections all facilitate tightening and alignment of the structure.

Left: The interior of the large Louvre pyramid is a column-free space. A custom-made cable and strut system creates the physical pyramid shape, whose only means of support is along the perimeter.

Right: The triangular geometry of the large pyramid at the Louvre in Paris, France, designed by I.M. Pei assisted by Peter Rice and RFR and completed in 1989, has been resolved into diamond-shaped glass panels.

Smaller, inverted pyramids were designed as a focal feature of the interior space and used a different approach to detailing. They form a "luster" or chandelier to reflect daylight into the subterranean floor. The glass top of the pyramid, supported by a separate cable tension truss system, is relatively flat to withstand weather, precipitation loads and occasional foot traffic. The structure beneath consists almost entirely of cables, relying on the mass of the glass to maintain the tension (having no larger structural members against which to pretension the system).

The inverted pyramid, hanging from a concrete frame, is supported by a stainless steel primary structure, with a suspension system to which the glass is attached. The joints between the glass panels are left open.

The stainless steel cable system that forms the small pyramid structure is resolved in specially cast nodes. These allow for tensioning of the members. Although designed with a clear hierarchy of systems and members, the visual impression of the finished piece is more light and lace-like, due to choices in member size and the materiality of the stainless steel.

One of the unusual aspects of the small, inverted Louvre pyramid is that it creates an enclosed space, so that access for assembly was not possible from both sides of the glass. Special spider connectors were created that clip the glass from both sides, facilitating erection. Although pads are used at the stainless-to-glass connection point to prevent cracking, there is not the same need to resist rotation for this interior application.

Paul Andreu used a variation of a cable truss system to support the water-covered atrium skylight below the large pond in front of the National Grand Theater in Beijing.

Left: National Grand Theater in Beijing, China. A view towards the ceiling of the atrium space. The primary span of the cable trusses is across the width of the space. The columns are positioned between these spans and a transverse series of cables is used to interconnect and provide lateral stability to the entire system.

Right: Although the structure of the atrium space skylight might appear as a more independent, tensegrity-type installation, the struts and tension members are integrated into the frame that supports the glass. The nodes show very vague signs of being welded to the straight, V-shaped glazing framing members. Fine diagonal wire braces crisscross the entire plane of the glass to provide resistance to cracking. This installation makes predominant use of rods over cables in order to preserve the smoothness of appearance.

Not all applications of complex cable systems fit neatly into a typology from which to derive details. Many structures use variations and combinations of more standard detailing. This is typical of the majority of those tensile-based steel structures in which glazed envelopes are used in lieu of fabric. Such is the case of the Hauptbahnhof train station in Berlin. The design of Hauptbahnhof creates a highly articulated family of details, the characteristics of which are shared by the structural system and glazing support system. The steel arches of the station use a supplementary tensile truss system to both strengthen and lighten their appearance. This language is translated into the requirements to reinforce the glazing. The curved, barrel-vaulted roof structure is divided into predominantly square glazed panes. As a square shape is not inherently strong, and a triangulated geometry was not desired, added stability was provided through the addition of two pairs of light steel cross braces in each glazing panel.

Hauptbahnhof Station in Berlin, Germany by von Gerkan, Marg und Partner, completed in 2002. The curved steel arch beams are fitted with a cable truss system at their underside. The curved beam forms the top compression chord of the structure with the truss system forming the bottom chord and web members. This detail illustrates an expansion joint in the structural system, where two such arch trusses support adjacent sections of the building.

The rectangular steel frame that supports the glass is reinforced with very fine paired tension cables that act as a fine mesh of cross bracing across the roof. The glazing sits very tightly to the steel grid. Custom connectors are used at the intersections of the cables and to attach these to the supporting beam.

The lightweight truss that reinforces the curved beam is comprised of cable sections that are clamped with custom connectors that in turn transfer the loads to the vertical struts. The connectors for the cables must permit tightening.

The design of the elements of the Hauptbahnhof structure creates a clear hierarchy of dependency and load path. The plate members that form the support grid for the glass feed into the curved wide-flange beams that form the intersection of the barrel vaults. The largest member visible is the top chord of the main curved steel section that clear-spans across the station.

A modified language of cable truss bracing is used to reinforce the structural glass façade at the entrances to Hauptbahnhof station. Laminated glass is used as compression struts for the assembly.

The Arcade Building at Potsdamer Platz complex in Berlin, Germany, designed by Renzo Piano Building Workshop. The steel and glass roof and walls are intended to open almost fully in good weather to naturally ventilate the space.

## OPERABLE STEEL AND GLASS SYSTEMS

Technical improvements to early, greenhouse-type venting systems have evolved as reliance on natural ventilation has resurged. The greater the percentage of operable panels, the more stiffness is required of the supporting steel structure. This creates challenges in keeping the structure light in appearance so as not to conflict with the requirement for increased transparency.

The Arcade Building at Renzo Piano's Potsdamer Platz complex in Berlin has the added challenge of combining a very lightweight steel structural system with a glazed roof and glazed end walls that are fully operable, thereby adding instability to the assemblage. The roof uses lightweight steel trusses to span across the space. The trusses are fabricated from a combination of plate and rod members that make dominant use of bolted type connections. Rods are used along the length of the roof to provide lateral support between the trusses. X bracing using thin cables is provided in alternate bays for added stability. The concept responds to a relatively mild climate not completely devoid of snow accumulation.

Top: A view along the steel roof truss of the Potsdamer Platz Arcade Building. The bottom chord of the truss is comprised of parallel plates, allowing the vertical web members to be interconnected. The diagonal web members are pin-connected through cast connections. The curved gears for the operable roof are visible.

Bottom: Steel tension cables connect the lightweight trusses that support the exterior wall. The vertical elements of the truss use a pair of thin steel plates. The glass is positioned at the midpoint of the truss that straddles the line of enclosure.

A view up the glazed entrance wall of the Potsdamer Platz Arcade Building. The mechanisms for the operable panels on the façade must be stabilized by the lightweight steel structure that runs up the façade.

# *HANDLING CURVES*

**Curving steel is a specialized process and might not be possible for all types or applications of structural elements, budgets notwithstanding (see Chapter 8: Curved Steel). Curved buildings will normally use flat glazing that is set in a geometry providing the impression of the curve. In some instances the structural steel framing will be curved, in others it will be faceted, like the glass.**

This subway entrance for the London Underground, England, is a rare example of the use of curved structural glass panels in conjunction with a curved steel support system. The aesthetic and scale required curving.

The approximation of a curved form by straight geometries may be part of the design intent. Such is the case in the Institut de la Mode et du Design in Paris, France by Jakob + MacFarlane.

The curved form of the Institut de la Mode is achieved by creating a welded steel framework from a series of straight pieces. The geometry is divided into small enough sections so that the curve appears fairly smooth when viewed at a distance. This permits the simple attachment of flat glass sections to a series of horizontal steel plates welded to the horizontal round HSS members.

Even a building that appears to create a smooth set of curves, like the National Grand Theater in Beijing, China by Paul Andreu, is actually comprised of straight cladding elements. The sheer scale of this building makes it appear to have been constructed from curved elements when viewed from a normal distance.

The custom connection for the curtain wall clip to a hole in the steel plate of the frame has been designed to allow for some tolerance between the two systems. Precise fabrication methods to cut the steel using CNC are of significance in preventing issues of misalignment during erection.

The curved dome of the Reichstag Building of the German Bundestag in Berlin, Germany, designed by Foster + Partners from 1992 to 1999, marries a curved support system on the interior of the dome with a faceted glazed exterior. This is in part functional, as the shingling of the glass panels allows for the intake of fresh air into the dome.

The structural steel framing that sits between the curved triangular steel ribs of the Reichstag dome and the flat glass panels is used to mediate between the geometry of the two systems. The horizontal steel framing includes projecting elements that pick up the bottom edge of the glass panels. The multiple steel systems translate the pure curves of the spiral ramp through the arches of the ribs and to the simple facets of the glass dome. The spacing of the ribs is such that the glass panels can be sized to span between. The welds on the triangular ribs have been neatly done and remain as natural evidence of fabrication.

## *LATTICE SHELL CONSTRUCTION*

Curved systems have traditionally required a visual and functional separation of the structure and the glazing system. Traditional aluminum curtain wall-type glazing systems do not have the load-bearing capacity required to also be the structural support system. Curtain wall systems are normally supported by a steel beam or truss system, whereas a full integration of the steel structure and the glazing requires eliminating the deep truss or support system. Advances in computer systems for structural analysis and also for cutting permit the creation of complex structural steel shapes — lattices — that can simultaneously act as structural spanning members and provide direct support for the glass.

The glazed roof over the Great Court of the British Museum in London uses a steel lattice to cover the courtyard. At the same time, it mediates between the geometry of the round pavilion in the center of the court and the rectangular boundary of the existing courtyard. To create the strength required to limit the dimensions of the steel profiles and at the same time provide an adequate slope for drainage, the lattice shell is formed by overlapping radial curved elements. The ensuing lattice frame supports the 3,312 double-glazed roof panels. The insulating glass roof panels are set in shallow aluminum frames that sit directly on top of the lattice beams. The structural members were fabricated in Austria by Waagner Biro from Grade D steel, which has an increased ductility and ability to respond to snow loading when compared to standard carbon steel. The steel box sections are 80mm/3.15in across and vary in depth from 80mm at the center to 180mm/7.08in at the perimeter. The change in depth is imperceptible when viewed from below. All joints were fully welded to star-shaped nodes fabricated from steel plate. Although the geometry of most roof elements was unique, some economies were possible due to robotic welding.

The steel lattice skylight of the Great Court of the British Museum in London, England, designed by Foster + Partners from 1994 to 2000, creates a remarkable lightness of space given its ability to eliminate the secondary structure.

A close view of the welded connection at the intersection of six steel box beams of the glazed roof of the British Museum. The ends of the hollow box sections have been tapered to fit into the star node to provide for more surface connection for welding.

The glazed canopy over the DZ Bank courtyard in Berlin, Germany by Frank Gehry uses a lattice shell structure. The perimeter of the rectangular courtyard is used to define and brace the lower edges of the vaulted shape.

The curvature of the vault of the DZ Bank courtyard varies along its length. At its most constricted end and at midspan, a system of tension braces is used to partially restrain the forces. The shape of the central connecting plate mirrors the shape of the vault.

Additional reinforcing is provided midway along the vault, the sectional characteristics hiding discreetly in the lattice. This provides the tieback to the structure of the adjacent building.

The technology of the lattice has seen more widespread adoption for projects that seek to provide curved glazed roofs of varying geometries. The curved surfaces are again resolved into flat frames to allow for the attachment of glass panels. For exterior, non-conditioned applications it is not necessary to accommodate insulating glass. A precedent for numerous installations was the Milan Trade Fair lattice roof designed by Massimiliano Fuksas from 2002 to 2005. It uses an innovative adaptation of the lattice shell to create an undulating roof plane that transforms to include numerous vortex-like elements. Two recent projects completed in 2010 in Shanghai illustrate smaller-scale interpretations of the geometry made famous by the Milan Fuksas project.

The canopy at the Shiliupu Docks at the Huangpu River in Shanghai, China, engineered by RFR of Paris, modifies the lattice structure to create an irregularly curved system that does not require a perimeter support system to provide stability. This lattice canopy is unusual in its exclusive use of rectangular shapes – even for the vortex.

The loads of the lattice canopy are resolved at the column supports through the use of tapered members in order to provide more steel to resist shear loads at the transfer point. The rectangular steel lattice members are welded to a round connection node that is in turn connected to the top of the round HSS support column. The placement of the lighting conveniently conceals the connection.

Top: The curved roof resolves the rectangular/diamond-shaped lattice grid that holds the glass into inline-welded cross-shaped steel connections.

Right: The Shiliupu Docks lattice canopy runs the full length of the dock area, using an undulating shape that is supported on irregularly spaced columns. The curvature of the roof structure provides some of the required stability to the overall structure.

The roof of the Expo Axis pavilion at the Expo 2010 Shanghai, China by SRA Architects creates a dynamic interplay of fabric and lattice structures. The axis contains six vortex-shaped glazed lattice structures. Triangulated geometry is used which makes the creation of the smooth curved shapes much simpler.

The strength of the glazed steel lattice structure is sufficient not only for self-support but also to provide restraint points for the large fabric canopy roofs adjacent in the Expo Axis pavilion. The tension connectors for the fabric roof have been welded to the face of the steel lattice.

The vortexes of the Expo Axis pavilion are secured at grade and rise freestanding to their height above the platform level. The structural rigidity of the steel shape is fully provided by its geometry. The nodes of the Expo Axis pavilion structure are resolved by welding the straight segments to the ends of star-shaped connection pieces. Service conduits run along the face of the rectangular steel lattice sections to provide power for lighting.

The curved, triangulated plane of the lattice grid can lighten the structure and allow the reduction of the depth of the carrying members. The glazed elements need not be directly attached to the steel lattice frame. An alternative type of application can be seen in the design of the shade covering for the Yas Hotel, located at the Formula One Race Track in Abu Dhabi. The separation of the glazed panels from the grid permits hot air to escape and improves the microclimate on the terrace.

The fritted glazing panels for this shade cover at the Yas Hotel in Abu Dhabi, UAE by Asymptote Architects are connected to diamond-shaped steel frames that are in turn attached to a diamond-shaped grid that bears on major curved beams, whose load path is transferred to diagonal columns.

The underside of the Yas Hotel canopy shows the integration of the glazed components with the diamond grid of welded rectangular beams. The continuous beam sections have been curved to form the shell. The Grid-Shell Building Information Modeling (BIM) Consultant was Gehry Technologies with Front Inc. as façade consultant.

Custom connections transfer the load from the curved steel edge beam, which is also tied back to the building, and down through the sloped round support members. The spherical covers at each node conceal the physical connections, removing some aesthetic considerations from the detailing of the joints.

The sloped column loads are resolved in cast custom-made bases. An attempt has been made to create a seamless connection between the tubular column and the base.

The systems and examples described in this chapter only scratch the surface of the possibilities when steel and glass are combined. There are numerous applications that are unique and do not fit neatly into any predictive category. Each variation must always address the initial list of criteria set forth in this chapter, and resolve the technical differences of material, function and climate.

*CHAPTER 13*

---

# *ADVANCED FRAMING SYSTEMS: STEEL AND TIMBER*

---

*CHARACTERISTICS*

*DETAILING ISSUES*

*FABRICATION AND ERECTION ISSUES*

*FINISH ISSUES*

*HIDDEN STEEL*

*PROCESS PROFILE: ADDITION TO ART GALLERY OF ONTARIO (AGO) / FRANK GEHRY*

*PROCESS PROFILE: RICHMOND SPEED SKATING OVAL / CANNON DESIGN*

The glass-and-timber façade of the Addition to the Art Gallery of Ontario, Toronto, ON, Canada, designed by Frank Gehry, relies on exposed steel framing to support and tie the sculptural element back to the building. The design and erection of such an articulated piece requires an integrated approach to coordinating the structural benefits and limitations of the two materials.

Heavy timber framing systems have long relied on structural steel in the creation of connections. From a purely structural perspective, in terms of load-transfer mechanisms and paths, heavy timber framing acts in a similar fashion to steel framing. Both systems are created from a series of discrete elements (beams, joists, columns) that are hinge or pin-connected. Steel is efficient in transferring loads as well as able to create a unique aesthetic in combination with the wood. In hybrid structures, the added strength of steel can allow for a more economical structure or one that would physically not be possible in all wood.

The Brentwood Skytrain Station in Vancouver, BC, Canada by Peter Busby and Associates used a combination of steel and wood to respond to the material requirements in the competition design brief. The composite ribs were fabricated and erected by George Third and Son, a steel fabricator. The steel fabricators were required to change their fabrication and handling techniques to prevent damage to the wood.

## *CHARACTERISTICS*

When iron and steel systems were first invented, they borrowed much of their structural language from pre-existing timber design, as both materials were constructed as frames and shared a tensile language that was quite apart from the compressive language of stone buildings. However, their structural properties and characteristics are quite different, and combining the materials in a structure can present challenges.

→ The tensile strength of regular carbon steel is 400 Mpa, which is 10 times greater than for timber, so hybrid structures normally use timber elements for their compressive strength.

→ Steel is a manufactured product with highly predictable strength and qualities, whereas wood is a natural material with inherent and sometimes hidden natural defects that affect its detailing and load capacity.

→ Steel expands with heat and contracts with cold, while wood varies almost imperceptibly. In heavy timber systems the steel elements themselves are quite small, so the differential properties of the materials are not of great issue. In more complex systems, however, differential movement due to heat can be a large problem.

→ Both materials need to be protected from moisture, as wood is prone to rot and steel to rust. However, humidity itself, unless accompanied by condensation, is not a problem for steel, while wood is described as a heterogeneous, hygroscopic and anisotropic material that attracts water molecules from the air. As dry wood reaches its equilibrium moisture balance with its surroundings, it may shrink or swell. This results in tightening or loosening of connections.

→ Wood is a cellular material. The length of the cell aligns with the long axis of the tree. As wood's moisture content is reduced and free water eliminated from the middle of the cell, the tissues shrink differentially. There is little shrinking in the length (typically 1%); however, radial shrinkage can be as much as 2% and tangential 3%. Drier wood will shrink even more. It becomes critical, when combining steel and timber, to ensure that the wood has reached its equilibrium with the conditioned space prior to the setting of the connections. It is also important that the temperature is stable to prevent movement in the steel.

→ Steel is infinitely recyclable; therefore, connection design can allow for eventual disassembly of a hybrid structure, which will also permit the reuse of the timbers.

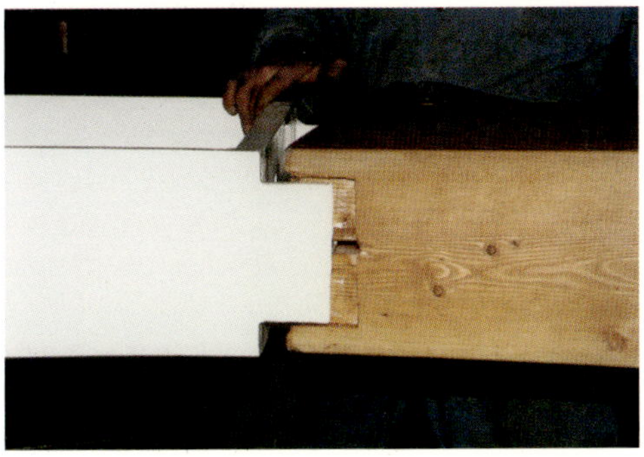

This view of the fit between the steel and wood sections on the Brentwood Skytrain Station in Vancouver, BC, Canada shows how much of the interface between materials is hidden inside the wood member. The timber has to be carefully cut to fit the steel insert.

## *DETAILING ISSUES*

The detailing of hybrid structures must reconcile the differentiated movement of steel and wood due to temperature and moisture. There are analytical programs available now to help set up the structure needed when combining the materials. A fabricator that accepts a hybrid timber and steel project should be familiar with this software, as it assists greatly in detailing.

Some detailing will require that movement is accommodated in the connection itself. In some cases, slotted holes in the steel can allow for some movement of the wood. This runs counter to most AESS work, where the tolerances are half standard and a high level of precision is required in the sizing of the holes. The expansion and contraction of the wood must still allow the connection itself to remain aligned. As the steel connections themselves will not move, it is critical that the connectors do not span the full depth of the timber members, as the timber will change shape over time and a restrictive connection could result in the splitting of the wood at the connection.

It is paramount in creating a hybrid structural system to work with the strengths of each material and to appreciate the context in which each functions optimally. For example, if designing a simple truss where the individual web members, as well as top and bottom chords, are to take either compressive or tensile axial loading, steel would be a more appropriate choice for the tensile members and wood for the compressive members. This will allow the tensile members to be very thin — able to be fabricated as slender as rod elements. The timber can be heavier in cross section, thereby expressing its resistance of compressive loading.

Left: The Gene H. Kruger Pavilion at Laval University in QC, Canada, designed by the consortium Les Architectes Gauthier Gallienne Moisan, uses light steel rods as the bottom chords of the wood trusses. The compression members have been constructed from timber.

Right: The detail of the connection shows how the steel connection plates have been inserted to slots in the wood and bolted. The tension members connect to a rectangular steel ring that is simply bolted to the bottom of the truss post. This provided a means to neatly resolve the connection of the six rods to a single point. The wood members are free to expand independently of the steel.

The hybrid trusses that clear-span across the wine production area at the Jackson Triggs Estate Winery in Niagara-on-the-Lake, ON, Canada, designed by KPMB Architects, illustrate a balanced combination of steel and wood. The steel members, more slender in nature, provide the tensile forces in the truss. This contrasts with the relative roughness and bulk of the sawn timbers.

As wood tends to expel and acquire moisture over its life, unprotected steel cannot come into direct contact with the timber or oxidation is likely to occur. The steel can be protected by being galvanized or through the application of moisture-resistant paint systems. It will help to use dry wood in the first place, which also assists in limiting differential movement. From the perspective of aesthetic balance in a hybrid AESS design, there should be enough of each material to result in a complementary use where the tectonics of each contributes to the overall design appearance.

# FABRICATION AND ERECTION ISSUES

From a fabrication perspective, a hybrid project can be carried out in the steel fabricator's shop. There are concerns about damaging the wood in the shop either through handling or by welding or heating steel too close to the wood in the structure. The use of a heat shield can protect the wood from scorching during adjacent welding. The wood needs to maintain its protective covering until it arrives on site, and then the covering should be peeled away only from the areas requiring work. The wood should not be walked upon, as is customary in working large steel, as damage can result. Covering sawhorses with wood and carpeting and using nylon slings to move the wood beams, rather than the chains and hooks usually used with steel, will minimize problems. In selecting a fabricator it is important to make sure that everyone in the shop is aware of the differences in the materials.

The staging and erection of a hybrid system is similar to regular AESS construction, with the exception that the wood must be handled more gently. Depending on the size and complexity of the members, the physical connections between the materials can either be done in the fabrication shop, then shipped, or combined on site in the staging area. Precision in fit is even more important, as wood members cannot be fit forcibly or cracking will occur. Padded slings need to be used to lift the members so as not to damage the wood. Protective wrappings need to provide weather protection until well after the erection is complete.

Most important, someone has to take charge of the project from start to finish. This is the only way to ensure a proper fit between the materials and to ensure coordination. It is possible to have the steel fabricator coordinate shop drawings, delivery schedule and erection.

The National Works Yard in Vancouver, BC, Canada, designed by Omicron Engineering and Architecture, manages the combination of wood and steel by effectively separating the two systems. Engineered wood is used for the beams and purlins, steel for the primary structure and some specialized connections. Steel is also used to cap the ends of the wood beams to protect them from moisture.

# FINISH ISSUES

Finishing concerns are different for interior and exterior structures. For interior members, fire protection of the hybrid system will be the primary concern. Heavy timber, glue-laminated timber or engineered wood members are normally used in situations where a fire-resistance rating of 45 minutes or less is required. Unprotected steel conforms to this requirement. This means that neither material requires additional fire protection in the form of a special coating. Some jurisdictions may additionally require the use of suppression systems.

The steel that is used on interior hybrid applications is normally pre-finished, in order to protect it from moisture transfer from the wood within the joint. It is also easier to finish the steel before it is combined with the wood, to prevent overspray or drips onto the wood. Where touch-ups or refinishing occurs over the life of the building, care needs to be taken to prevent marring of the wood finish.

Many types of wood that would be used in hybrid projects arrive at the fabrication shop pre-finished. Wood members are not normally stained or sealed in situ, as it is often difficult to access the material to apply finishes. It is necessary to protect the finish during fabrication to reduce the need for repair. This extends to shielding the wood from heat from adjacent welding or steel fabrication operations.

Exterior applications will require the use of finishes that are weather- and UV-resistant. UV-resistant steel finishes will reduce the need for fade remediation. UV-resistant finishes for timber will prevent differentiated fading due to varying exposure conditions. Galvanizing is often chosen for the steel due to its durability. Paint finish must be highly weather-resistant and applied in sufficient coats to ensure that the finish is not compromised during erection. Unlike coatings on steel that are waterproof, finishes on the wood must still allow the material to breathe. If non-breathable coatings are used on the wood, this can trap moisture behind the coating and result in cracking and peeling of the finish.

## *HIDDEN STEEL*

The steel used in hybrid structures may not always be apparent. Interior steel connectors and even a steel structural support element might be concealed from view for varying reasons, including giving the impression that the wood is doing the work.

The 2008 Serpentine Pavilion in London, England, designed by Frank Gehry, used an innovative hybrid of steel and exposed timbers. As the pavilion was designed to be a temporary structure, long-term durability was not a requirement. Although the initial impression is that the wood is providing most of the support, a closer look reveals that concealed steel is actually doing the work.

Left: The large wood columns and beams have steel at their center, providing both the support for the wood and the means of attachment between members.

Right: A view of the top of the glazed canopy shows how the wood is actually used as cladding over the white-painted steel structure.

Larger and more complex projects that use steel and timber, either as parallel systems with their individuality expressed, or as hybrid construction, require additional engineering and specialized fabrication and erection methods. Such is the case in projects where the size and weight of the members approaches or exceeds the ability of traditional carpentry trades and lifting and erection procedures are better handled by ironworkers.

# *PROCESS PROFILE: ADDITION TO THE ART GALLERY OF ONTARIO (AGO) / FRANK GEHRY*

Architect: Frank Gehry
Engineers: Yolles Halcrow
General Contractor: EllisDon
Steel Fabrication and Erection: Benson Steel (structure), Mariani Metal (stairs)
Glue-laminated members: Structurlam

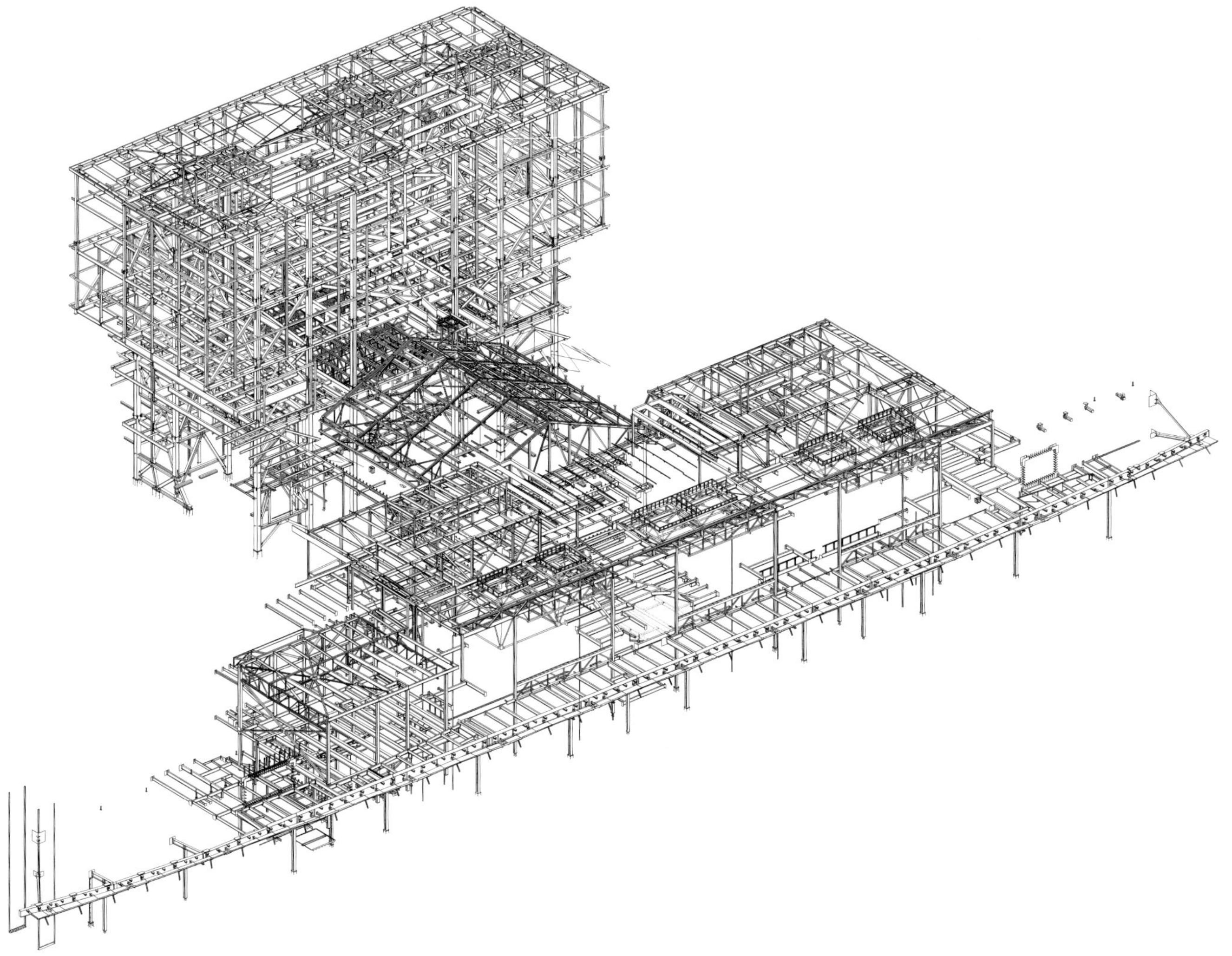

The renovation and addition to the Art Gallery of Ontario might be considered to be a very "un-" Frank Gehry-like building. The final design for the glazed arcade gallery that dominates the new north façade is one of the first high-profile projects by Gehry that does not use a highly contorted structural steel frame for its support system. "Transformation AGO" is largely a renovation to an existing building, extending the floor area by approximately 20%. The site itself imposed severe constraints on the possible scope of the design of the addition, as well as restricting the staging area for all aspects of the construction. One lane of the major street on the north face of the building was closed to traffic for the duration of construction to provide for staging. This constricted space did not allow the crane operator much, if any, view of the erection, necessitating full reliance on visual and audio communications with the erection crew for the construction of the glazed arcade.

Although the featured architectural element along the front façade of the Addition to the Art Gallery of Ontario (AGO) in Toronto, ON, Canada by Frank Gehry would have the building appear to be constructed primarily of glue-laminated wood, this structural axonometric prepared by the steel fabricator and erector, Benson Steel, reveals otherwise. Drawings such as this are prepared by the steel fabricator to account for each piece of steel that is used in the project. The glue-laminated ribs that dominate the north façade are not included in this drawing, but would be located all along the front edge.

The new front façade features a curved glass gallery framed on an angled splay of curved, glue-laminated timber ribs. Although the wood appears to be the primary structure, there is in fact a significant amount of structural steel working behind the façade to maintain the complex geometry.

Top: A look behind the curved glass "tear" at the building's east end reveals an elaborate structural steel framework that provides support for the timber system.

Bottom: Two types of finish are used on these exterior elements. The darker steel section is galvanized and the lighter, more complex section finished in heavy zinc-based paint. Most observers would not notice the difference, given the location of the material. Difficulties in galvanizing the more detailed members led to the decision to use an alternate weather-resistant finish. The galvanizing bath heats the steel and would have resulted in irreparable distortion to the member.

The fully glazed north façade is formed by a series of glue-laminated timber arms, subtly supported by and connected with structural steel components. The steel arms perform like marionette strings, working from behind, giving the appearance that the glulam is acting on its own. What made this glulam gallery so challenging to construct was that every arm was unique. Each arm is aligned at a more severely reclining angle, resulting in highly eccentric loads and necessitating steel connectors at the top and the base that were different for each member. The first arm to be erected set the singular vertical alignment datum and required significant erection time to ensure precision, as all of the other arms would be positioned relative to the datum arm.

The construction of this hybrid project was the largest of its kind to date in the Toronto area. It required much innovation in terms of creating a new working relationship between the ironworkers and carpenters on the site. The expertise of the ironworkers in lifting and setting large elements was aided by the carpenters, who understood the more delicate nature of wood. Unlike steel, wood cannot be forced into position without risking damage to the finished surface or cracking the member.

The curves were translated from Gehry's hand-drawn sketches, via Catia, to digital drawings, to the glulam manufacturer and then to the job site. While technology permits such translation in contemporary representation methods, it does not yet answer the ultimate challenge of ensuring that the members are properly aligned at a job site. The combined curve, rotation and slope of each of the elements had to fit perfectly or the subsequent couple of dozen would not align. Although the ironworkers and carpenters can perform some minor adjustments when placing the pieces, these are practically limited.

Translating steel erection practices to glulam has other challenges. During the erection process, steel and timber require different handling. Forceful practices that may be used in structural steel erection (use of chainfalls or come-alongs) would be too rough and could possibly result in visual or structural damage to the large glulam elements. Methods of "encouragement" for large glulam structures are more akin to those used on Architecturally Exposed Structural Steel. Lifting straps must be carefully padded to prevent surface damage, particularly to the crisp corners of the members. The workers used the same cloth-based belts and straps that were employed for lifting the pieces to manually pull the pieces into position, with direct one-on-one force.

When the glue-laminated members arrived, each truck would typically contain five curved arms and the large horizontal top beam that tied them together. The arms would need to be rotated in the small staging area to allow the attachment of the steel connection elements. The majority of these connectors had a galvanized finish to provide enduring corrosion resistance. Art galleries are typically kept at 50% relative humidity, and this, along with large expanses of glazing, creates conditions of higher humidity that may result in corrosion. Galvanizing is less expensive than using stainless steel connections and is more durable than a painted finish.

Working on a geometrically challenging project also translates into working without aid of the natural force of gravity to position the pieces. During a site interview Mike Jackson of Toronto Ironworkers Local 721 said that he had to visually assess each unique piece and select the lifting points entirely by experience. He used two points along the curved arms to initially lift them off the truck and flip them over so that they were "curve down" for the final lift. For this final lift, a single strap was placed by eye about a quarter of the way from the top. As with lifting steel, a rope was attached to the bottom end to guide the piece into place. The steel connections, in keeping with current AESS practice, used half the standard tolerances for structural steel. Each base element had to resolve the unique geometry and orientation of the arm with the steel supporting beam.

Top: The central arm is the only vertical member along the entire façade. The green protective wrap is still in place. Additional white reinforcing is added to more vulnerable corners to prevent erection damage.

Bottom: The glulam beams are lifted off the truck and rotated to allow for the installation of the end connectors.

The base is inserted into the end of the arm. The wood has been pre-tooled at the wood plant to fit the connector. Some minor modifications can be performed on site if the fit is not good. Connectors pass through the wood and holes in the internalized steel plate to finalize the connection of the base to the arm.

Once the arm has been fitted with its connectors, it is lifted into position. The green wrapping is left in place to reduce damage to the wood. The removal of wrapping indicates the presence of a steel connector. The base connection was secured before the top end was fixed.

The galvanized base support of the rib is attached to the transfer beam through a bolted connection.

For the long top beam member, the steel connector made the 7,000-pound piece substantially heavier at one end than the other, so the two strap-lifting points were adjusted accordingly. The horizontal glulam beam connected to the five supporting arms as well as the end of the adjacent beam. This required a precise alignment between the previously erected arms and the top beam in order for the steel connecting plates to match.

Although less apparent in the middle section of the gallery, the glulam system is reliant on some key AESS elements for its general stability. At either end of the gallery, where the reclining curved arms extend beyond the building, highly articulated arched steel ribs and struts provide support for the wood. This is true also of the twisted glulam-framed planes that form the external termination to the gallery at its east and west ends. Given the unbalanced geometry of the glazed sections, the wood is insufficient in strength to be self-supporting. These sections of the façade are subject to wind loads from both front and back and the steel is needed to limit deflections that would damage the glass.

The top beam is guided into position using a rope. In addition to ensuring that the end connection aligns, ironworkers are positioned at the other four connection points to make certain that these also fit. The galvanized steel fins that can be seen along the lower edge of the beam will provide attachment for incoming wood members along the rear face of the gallery.

Inside the main section of the gallery, the steel structure supports the wood. The steel ribs are tied back to the main structure of the building with steel struts.

Bolted connections are used to allow for easy erection, to provide slotted holes for alignment and to prevent the use of site-welding that could result in fire damage to the wood.

Left: The steel connections for the smaller wood members that support the glass have a substantial gap between adjoining members. This is to provide for better fit as well as to create the intended curve through the use of straight members. These connections needed to be designed to allow for small rotations to suit the curve, while also being identical in order to be economically mass-produced.

Right: As one looks down the interior of the gallery space, the faceting of the glazed façade and wood support system can be seen to be set against the curved ribs. In the distance, the steel struts support the west end of the space. The base connection detail of the glulam ribs is concealed beneath the flooring.

Although much of the supporting and connecting steel and associated detailing are not in the forefront in the final rendition of the interior space, their presence is still, if subtly, evident. In the instance of much of the interplay of steel and wood, there is significant independence of the two systems. Alternatively, they can be designed to allow for expansion and contraction through some spatial separation of the systems, or joints that can accommodate movement. This is not always possible in the case of larger installations, where the steel and wood must act in complete unity to resist the forces.

## *PROCESS PROFILE: RICHMOND SPEED SKATING OVAL / CANNON DESIGN*

Architects: Cannon Design
Engineers: Fast + Epp
Contractors: Dominion Fairmile Construction
Steel Fabricators and Erectors: George Third and Son

The design of the Richmond Speed Skating Oval for the 2010 Olympic Games that were held in Vancouver, BC, Canada was a complex problem. British Columbia's primary natural resource is wood, and there was much pressure on local organizers to showcase this material. However, the sheer size and span requirements of the Oval were too large to be achieved by a pure timber solution. The resultant design of the primary spanning members for the Oval creates a unique hybrid structure that takes advantage of the structural capabilities of both materials. The steel fabricator, George Third and Son, had previously been responsible for the fabrication and erection of other hybrid structures of several Skytrain Transit Stations in the area. The net result was the fabrication of the longest-spanning hybrid steel-and-wood arches in the world.

The structure of the Richmond Speed Skating Oval, Richmond, BC, Canada, was clearly a marriage between steel and timber.

The interior of the skating oval would seem to be a showcase for wood. Although the use of wood in this building is innovative, it in fact owes much to the steel that is discreetly integrated into the design to achieve structural rigidity.

This view during construction shows the role of the steel in supporting the edge condition and geometry of the wood roof. The roof panels have been fabricated from small-dimension lumber, salvaged from forests that have been ravaged by the Western Pine Beetle.

In addition to working the hybrid design, the fabricators also had to design for transportation to the site. The 100m/340ft long arches could neither be fabricated nor erected in one piece. Each was created from four elements 26m/85ft in length, weighing 17 tonnes that needed to be connected in such a way as to make them act as a single piece.

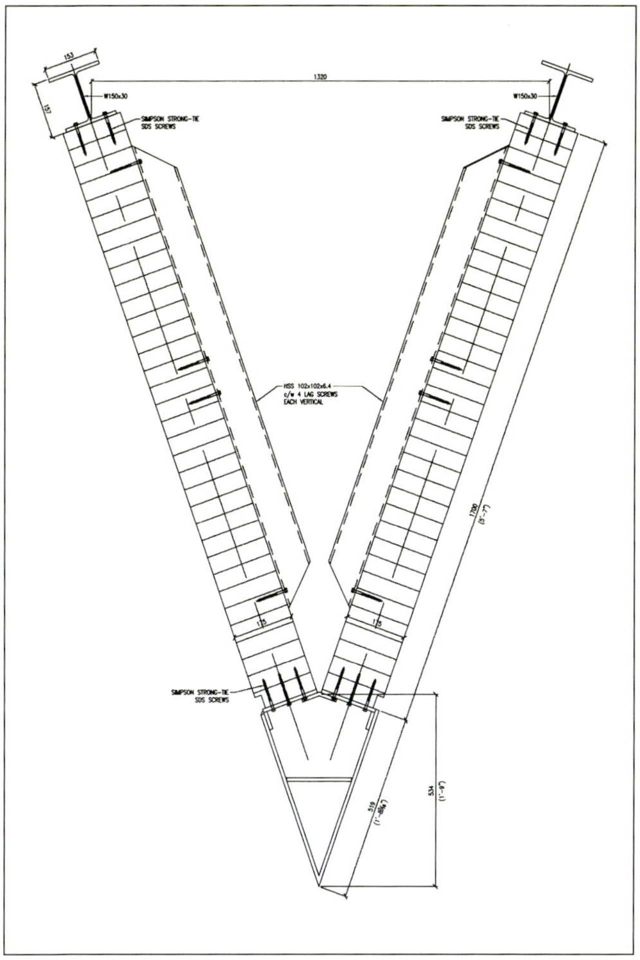


Left: The interior of the curved truss is formed by a welded curved triangular truss, created from HSS material.

Right: This sectional drawing through the V-shaped arch shows how steel elements are used at the top and bottom of the glulam sections to define the edges of the member. The glulam side pieces had to be sized to create sections that would assist in carrying the load without being too heavy, thereby creating unnecessary dead load, or too thin, creating the potential for warping.

Left: The shop view of the large arch under construction shows the immense scale of the project. It was necessary to have adequate room in the fabrication shop to accommodate the processes, to be able to lift and turn the members, and to ensure that the wood was not damaged during any of the fabrication processes. The wrap was left on the wood to assist in damage control.

Right: It was also a requirement of the arches to conceal the mechanical systems. This required additional coordination with the trades and consultants.

View of the finished arch end, showing the terminal steel connection. The wood exterior is wrapped for protection during the lift.

Following the construction of the concrete abutments, the steel framing for the end wall is erected to support the first arch.

Left: Two of the segments being connected on site. Bolted connections between the top and bottom steel support members eased this process. A special cover plate was positioned over the bottom-edge splice to conceal the joint. The two center sections were connected on site prior to the lift.

Right: Making the arch segments ready for erection on site.

As the top side of the arch was exposed during erection, extra care was required to protect the systems on the interior from damage due to rain, which is quite common in this region.

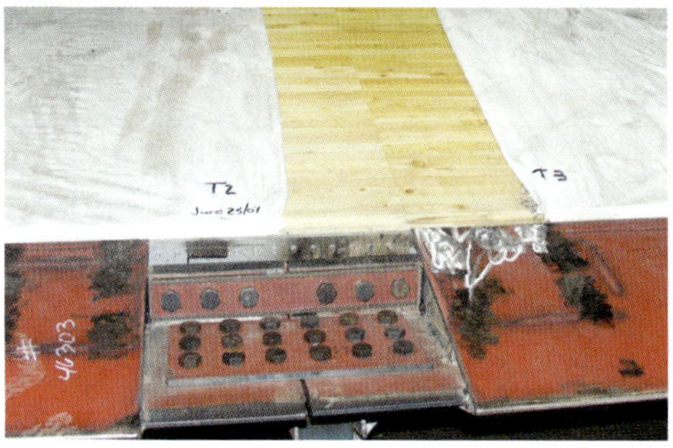

Left: The side sections of the arch were erected first and then the center dropped into place. A shoring tower supported the free end of the side sections until the segments were bolted together. A specialized sling was created to prevent stress on the splice during erection as well as balance the 51.8m /170ft long member.

Right: The type of splice used for the bottom edge connection of the arch elements. The splice was concealed by a cover plate, filled and sanded, to fully conceal the connection.

An overall view of the Richmond Oval during construction, illustrating the additional role of the concrete buttress-like columns in absorbing the thrust forces from the roof arches.

The undulating wood roof lifts away from the arches at the end condition. A separate steel truss system is integrated to support the shape. The wide-flange sections that form the top edges of the triangular arch segments are joined with curved sections that tie back down to the arch.

Left: A top view of one of the roof panels during erection. The steel fabrication shop used curved jigs to mass-fabricate these elements.

Right: The finished arch shows the integration of the HVAC supply and the support system for the wood ceiling. The splice between the arches is evidenced in the discontinuity of the glue-laminated wood pattern. The splice in the steel edge has been finished to a high AESS standard. The ceiling has been fabricated from thousands of smaller pieces of wood that were harvested from a forest ravaged by an infestation of Western Pine Beetle. This solution allowed for the use of small members, whose prefabricated panels were also supported using steel.

The sample projects featured in this chapter demonstrate that steel and wood can work very well together, from the use of steel as a connector to the creation of more complex hybrid structures. Understanding the structural and physical characteristics of the materials, as well as working with a knowledgeable fabricator and skilled erection team is critical to ensure a successful project.

*CHAPTER 14*

---

# *STEEL AND SUSTAINABILITY*

---

## *STEEL AS A SUSTAINABLE MATERIAL*

## *THE LEADERSHIP IN ENERGY AND ENVIRONMENTAL DESIGN (LEED™) GREEN BUILDING RATING SYSTEM*

## *RECYCLE VERSUS REUSE*

### RECYCLED CONTENT

### COMPONENT REUSE

### ADAPTIVE REUSE

## *SUSTAINABLE BENEFITS OF ARCHITECTURALLY EXPOSED STRUCTURAL STEEL (AESS)*

## *LOW-CARBON DESIGN STRATEGIES*

### REDUCE MATERIAL

### REDUCE FINISHES

### REDUCE LABOR

### REDUCE TRANSPORTATION

### DURABILITY

The galvanized finishes on the Calgary Water Center, AB, Canada by Manasc Issac Architects, provide the exterior exposed steel with a durable and rugged appearance that speaks to the sustainable nature of the facility design. Steel is perhaps not the first structural material that springs to mind when thinking of sustainability. However, the material here is sourced from high recycled content rather than virgin ore. The galvanized finish means less waste by avoiding repainting the structure on an ongoing basis. The exposed steel precludes the need for other cladding materials, saving embodied energy.

Construction in steel impacts sustainable and low-carbon design. At present, all material choice and even the choice to build at all, tend to negatively impact the environment. The intention here is to look at the design of steel in building to assist in reducing the negative impact on the environment through better understanding of how to use the material to its best advantage. The key to this is impact reduction.

There are several aspects of steel that must be considered when looking to design more sustainably or to achieve lower carbon impacts on the environment. First, there is the impact of the mining and production of the material itself, known as embodied energy. Second, we need to consider aspects of recycling, material reuse and adaptive building reuse. And last, we need to look at the unique inherent benefits of the material that cannot be mimicked or replaced by another material choice and see how these can best be exploited to reduce environmental impact.

## *STEEL AS A SUSTAINABLE MATERIAL*

A significant percentage of steel sold today comes from recycled, post-consumer content, rather than from newly mined ore. There is less energy required to manufacture steel with recycled content than to use 100% virgin ore, as virgin ore must undergo energy-intensive processing to remove the impurities present in raw ore. Although iron ore continues to be mined around the world, the material steel, once manufactured and put into use in buildings and as other artifacts, is capable of infinite recycling without suffering any degradation or down-cycling of its characteristics or capabilities. "Down-cycling" refers to the remanufacture of a material such as recycled plastic, a process in which the material's chemical properties or structural capabilities are degraded. Eventually, after repeated recycling, materials like plastic have no further value and become waste. The previous use of the steel is also of no importance for creating structural steel with recycled content. The steel may come from cans, automobiles or washing machines. This does not affect the final product, as the chemical composition can be refined at the mill to produce steel with specific properties.

The manufacturing process for steel is able to include significant portions of scrap steel in the creation of new structural steel shapes without drastic modifications to the production process. As the processes for manufacturing steel have changed little since 1950, meaning that the chemical composition of the steel is relatively consistent, the steel that was manufactured in the earlier part of the 20$^{th}$ century is still effectively being recycled. Since the invention of cast iron, the carbon content has been the significant focus of modification in order to alter the properties and performance of steel. Steel pre-1950 may have a higher carbon content that will make welding more difficult. If using this steel as recycled content, the final composition of the steel will be modified at the mill to reduce the percentage of carbon. If reusing the steel elements "as is", it is important to ascertain the age and age-related carbon content, as this will affect its ability to be welded. In some cases, therefore, the design detailing may require bolting.

The amount of energy required to manufacture steel varies as a function of the production process as well as by the share of recycled material. There are two mill types that manufacture structural steel shapes. Each has environmental concerns and benefits.

An integrated mill produces steel with the Basic Oxygen Furnace (BOF) method. The BOF uses 25% to 35% recycled steel in a process where oxygen is forced through the molten material to remove carbon. This creates low-carbon steel. The vessel in which the process takes place can only hold 25% to 35% scrap, the balance poured in as molten pig iron. Integrated mills are normally located near a harbor for shipping and are therefore often at increased distances from the project site, which creates increased transportation costs.

The Union Bank Tower in Winnipeg, MB, Canada is the oldest steel framed skyscraper in Canada, having been constructed in 1906. It is being renovated through an adaptive reuse for student housing and classrooms for Red River College. This involves an assessment of the load capacity of the frame as well as alternate approaches to fire protection.

Working with the existing structure and fire proofing, in this case either clay tile or no protection, is part of the challenge of reusing the building. This style of column created by separating a pair of back to back channel sections by a steel lattice is quite typical of structural design of the time. Structures of this period used riveted connections. As this column will be clad in drywall there is no need to spend energy to remediate its finishes.

The mini-mill uses the Electric Arc Furnace (EAF) method. The EAF is fed between 90 and 100% recycled steel. Mini-mills are able to be built with less dependence on major shipping routes so can be dispersed and therefore closer to project sites, reducing transportation costs. Slag or flyash is one of the byproducts of this process. It is useful as a substitute for cement in creating a more environmentally friendly concrete. Mini-mills must have a reliable source of environmentally friendly electricity in order to minimize their negative environmental impact.

If choosing steel as a recycled material in response to green rating systems such as LEED™, it is important to note that the recycled content is created using post-consumer as well as post-industrial materials. The precise proportion should be determined by contacting the mill or supplier.

Even though the EAF has lower energy costs, both BOF and EAF processes are needed for a global sustainable environment. Most North American structural steel (W shapes in particular), with the exception of some plates and coils, is produced using the Electric Arc Furnace. In many cases, however, due to shifting or increasing global demands for steel and steel scrap, particularly in Asia, there is a shortfall of recycled material, so exclusive dependence on the more sustainable EAF method is not possible.

## *THE LEADERSHIP IN ENERGY AND ENVIRONMENTAL DESIGN (LEED™) GREEN BUILDING RATING SYSTEM*

The Leadership in Energy and Environmental Design (LEED™) Green Building Rating System is an assessment tool that has been created to address the question of what constitutes sustainable design. It is currently being promoted throughout North America and other parts of the world for the evaluation and promotion of green buildings. The goal of LEED™ is to initiate and promote practices that limit the negative impact of buildings on the environment and occupants. The design guideline is also intended to prevent exaggerated or false claims of sustainability and to provide a standard of measurement. LEED™ is constantly being improved and new variants of the system added that are more scale- and program-specific. The following description refers to LEED™ 2009 for New Construction.

The structure of the LEED™ Rating System is segmented into sections, credits and points. The five key sections are identified as sustainable sites, water efficiency, energy and atmosphere, materials and resources, and indoor environmental quality. In addition to these, a sixth section is reserved for design process and innovation and a seventh for Regional Priority credits. This framework definition of sustainable design extends former ideas of energy-efficient design to include aspects encompassing the whole building, all of its systems, and all questions related to site development. Most sections include one or more basic prerequisite items. These must be fulfilled or the balance of the points in the category will not be counted.

The use of steel is mostly dealt with in the Materials and Resources section of LEED™. There will be benefits (credits) earned if it is possible to reuse the steel structure of the building with little modification. The durability of steel fits in well with this section. There are also credits available for the specification of a high percentage of recycled content in the steel. As steel is routinely manufactured with high recycled content, this is a natural attribute of the material. It will be possible to provide certificates from the mill to verify the required percentages. There are potential credits if reusing steel elements from another demolished project. Bills of sale will be required as proof of such reuse. As a function of the number of credits earned, buildings are rated Platinum, Gold, Silver and Certified. The rating system has different criteria for New Construction, Commercial Interiors and various Residential applications. For the most up-to-date information on the rating systems visit the website of the U.S. Green Building Council (www.usgbc.org).

# RECYCLE VERSUS REUSE

All of the steel scrap from the fabrication process, from the smallest shavings to the larger cut-off sections, is gathered and sent for recycling.

There is virtually no waste in a steel fabrication shop. Any material that is cut off or defective, as well as all grindings and byproducts of the fabrication process, are gathered and returned to the steel mills for recycling. The magnetic nature of steel makes it easy to salvage and even collect during building demolition processes. Steel reinforcing used in concrete construction is now routinely collected for recycling.

The general reuse of steel can be accomplished in four basic ways:

- Scrap steel can be salvaged and remanufactured into new steel components.
- Components can be salvaged during the demolition of a building, for use in another.
- New steel buildings can be designed for disassembly, so that the building can be taken apart into elements at the end of its life for reuse.
- Adaptive reuse can be applied to entire buildings so that they are repurposed with minimal modifications to the structural system.

## RECYCLED CONTENT

High recycled content is an environmental benefit of steel. This is valued in most Green Rating Systems. Although almost all steel uses a significant percentage of recycled content, recycling through either BOF or EAF methods still produces significant amounts of $CO_2$ and requires that additional energy be used in remanufacturing. It is therefore preferable to reuse the material, as the primary means to reduce $CO_2$ emissions.

## COMPONENT REUSE

The reuse of components is a highly sustainable way to incorporate steel into a building. The chemical and structural properties of structural steel have not changed significantly since the early 20th century (the precise dates vary by country and as a function of local steel mills). If the structural engineer knows the date of construction of the original building, and the measured size of the section, even with slight overdesign for additional safety, this steel is easily incorporated into a new structure. Still, even with reuse there is additional energy required to erect the steel and modify connections. There are also differing strategies that can be effectively integrated into the design process to incorporate reused steel into the structural design.

Issues with reuse lie less in the structural capabilities of the product and more in the finding or sourcing of salvaged materials. At present there is no substantial and reliable source through which to purchase used materials. Often projects will be able to source steel as a function of the involvement of one of the team members with another project that is undergoing demolition or renovation.

For concealed structural reuse it is often not necessary to remove existing paint finishes. This saves labor and related energy. If using the steel in an AESS-type application it may be necessary to remove the existing paint. However, many current projects are choosing to reuse exposed steel and expressly maintain the original finish as a means to highlight the sustainable reuse of the material.

Tohu, the permanent circus bigtop in Montreal, QC, Canada, designed by the consortium of Schème Consultants inc., Jodoin Lamarre Pratte et associés architectes and L'Architecte Jacques Plante, made a point to use large salvaged beams from some demolition work at the Montreal docks. As the project was looking to achieve LEED™ Gold certification, the architects left the existing finish in order to showcase the reuse of the steel.

Reuse can support Cradle-to-Cradle practices, as described by environmentalist William McDonough and chemist Michael Braungart, through the Design-for-Disassembly approach. This design method previsions a closed loop for steel that avoids contributing to the waste stream. In basic terms, Cradle-to-Cradle combined with Design-for-Disassembly works on the premise of the simple reuse of the material without additional energy added to remanufacture the product. In DfD, member sizes, lengths and connection methods should be selected that will be easily disassembled without excess force or the twisting or deformation of the members. This will work best with more modular designs, as the reuse of the components will fit with a greater number of future solutions.

Although it might be natural to assume all-bolted connections for this type of construction, as was done with Joseph Paxton's Crystal Palace of 1851, opinions are still mixed as to the ease of disassembling bolted connections. Difficulty in unbolting steel structures may arise from ceasing of the bolts due to layers of paint or as the result of corrosion. As a crane will be required for the process, regardless of the type of connection, to support the piece as it is being detached, both bolted and welded connections can be quickly cut, resulting in slightly shorter but structurally uncompromised lengths that will be easy to reuse. The leftover sections can be recycled. Labor costs are significant as qualified ironworkers are required for the demounting process, so speed is an economic issue. DfD is already in practice for many temporary structures, such as those used for international exhibitions. Extrapolating this for regular structural steel construction should not be a difficult task.

## ADAPTIVE REUSE

In adaptive reuse the entire building, including its durable steel structure, forms the basis for the generation of a new program and use, without significant alteration to the structure, or with simple reinforcing of an existing structure. In these instances, the age of the original structure is important in informing the design of any steel structure that might need to be added or altered. The historic age of the steel may have implications on the carbon content of the steel and its ability to be welded. Where the steel is unable to be welded, and may also have originally used rivets, bolted connections using Tension Control (TC) bolts can aesthetically combine new and reused steel structures; the round head of the TC bolt resembles a rivet head and makes a more seamless transition possible.

Even the remaining brick wall and partial steel frame of the Angus shops were able to be retained as an innovative enclosure for the parking and loading areas for the retail portion of the project. The tectonic nature of the enclosure adds greatly to the architecture of the project.

Angus Technopole in Montreal, QC, Canada, designed by Ædifica Architecture + Engineering + Design, reused historic locomotive shops to create a new office complex. They made a point of leaving the original historic finish at the lower level to create an interesting contrast with the new infill materials and program, and to showcase the historic origins of the building.

Another portion of the historic Angus locomotive shops was used for a grocery store. In this case, the entire building was adapted for reuse. The existing finish on the steel structure was cleaned up and repainted to give a fresh appearance, suited to the cleanliness expected at a grocery store. This is in marked contrast to the adaptive reuse in the office portion of the complex, where the existing finish was left "as is".

The AESS spaces added to the Institut de la Mode et du Design in Paris, France by Jakob + MacFarlane create a dynamic contrast to the heaviness of the reused concrete building.

**Historic steel may need a structural assessment for new increased loading conditions and also may require reinforcement. New steel can also be discreetly incorporated if the member shape, finish and connection type are chosen properly. A steel solution can also be used to give new life to existing concrete structures. For instance, aging concrete structures at the Paris Docks were given a rejuvenated, contemporary appearance through the addition of some innovative AESS walkways and exterior spaces.**

The adaptive reuse of the Gare d'Orsay into the Musée d'Orsay in Paris, France, designed by Gae Aulenti, provided an elegant solution to the creation of a new museum. The natural lighting down the center of the former platform area functions well to light the sculptures on display. The original building used riveted connections. Where additional steel reinforcing was required, bolted connections made for an almost seamless incorporation of up-to-date construction methods.

Top: Bolted angle and plate sections are used in the Musée d'Orsay to reinforce this corner connection.

Bottom: The new visitor access to the gallery cuts through the original trusswork of the train station, allowing for an enlightening view of the original structure.

The main access staircase in the Musée d'Orsay also cuts through the original wrought-iron beams and vaulted brick ceilings, again exposing the original structure in an interesting way, rather than seeking to cover it up, thus highlighting the building as a part of the exhibit.

# SUSTAINABLE BENEFITS OF ARCHITECTURALLY EXPOSED STRUCTURAL STEEL (AESS)

As one of the basic precepts of sustainable design is to use less material, AESS feeds quite naturally into this goal. By choosing to expose the steel, there are significant savings in the reduction of additional finishes, reducing the embodied energy in the project. These can include the elimination of suspended ceilings as well as wall board or other more expensive finishes that might otherwise conceal the structure. The AESS aesthetic can also complement the use of more minimal and highly durable floor finishes. An AESS design that is looking to be sustainable will also need to focus on restraint in the use of material for detailing and choose member sections that result in a net savings in the weight of material.

It will be important to be selective about finishes and fire-protection strategies when targeting an environmentally sustainable AESS solution. As addressed in Chapter 7 on Coatings, Finishes and Fire Protection, the VOC level of the finish will need to be controlled, as a low-VOC paint is desired to reduce off-gassing. AESS will require a durable finish, particularly if located in high-traffic areas, so to prevent frequent repainting the durability of the paint or finish may have to be balanced with the issue of off-gassing. Some water-based materials may not provide the best level of service. If high VOC paints must be used then adequate time must elapse before occupancy starts.

Intumescent coatings vary in terms of their VOC level as well, again whether they are water- or epoxy-based. There may be a need to examine the balance between the environmentally unfriendly nature of some intumescent coatings in light of the level of savings of finish materials and alternate methods of fire protection. Not all intumescent coatings allow for easy recycling or reuse of the steel, if looking for Cradle-to-Cradle or Design-for-Disassembly features. As the chemical make-up and performance of coatings is a quickly changing area, it is best to consult with the manufacturer regarding current specifications.

# LOW-CARBON DESIGN STRATEGIES

Basic carbon emissions associated with buildings result from embodied and operating energy. Embodied energy is the result of the manufacture, transportation and erection/construction processes. The broader definition will include carbon emissions from the use/program of the building, as well as transportation of the occupants as they commute to the building site or through business-related travel. Operating energy is responsible for approximately 80% of the carbon emissions associated with a building and as of the writing of this book, forms the primary target for impact reductions.

Net Zero Energy Design looks closely at significant reductions in the operating energy of buildings and asks that a building produce as much energy on site, via the use of renewable non-fossil fuel, as it consumes.

Carbon Neutral Design looks to use no fossil fuel or carbon-emitting energy sources in the operation of a building. It also allows for community-generated renewable energy sources or offsetting to balance the equation.

The four basic steps that are required to begin to design a building to meet a zero carbon or low-energy target are:

#1 - Reduce loads/demand (passive solar design, daylighting, shading, orientation, use of natural ventilation, site design and materiality)
#2 - Meet loads efficiently and effectively (energy efficient/effective lighting, high-efficiency/effective mechanical, electrical and plumbing equipment and controls)
#3 - Use on-site generation/renewables to meet energy needs (taking the above steps first will result in the need for much smaller renewable-energy systems, making carbon neutrality achievable.) Community-pooled resources are also acceptable.
#4 - Use purchased offsets as a last resort when all other means have been looked at on site.

At the present time, the embodied energy associated with material choice is excluded from the more typical carbon balance equations, as it requires significantly more complicated calculations that are difficult to assess, as they vary by location and manufacturer. This does not mean that material choice is not a significant factor and should not be included when making material and systems decisions for a building. But until such time as major reductions in operating energy are possible, embodied energy will seem less important. Once operating energy has been successfully reduced to balance with renewable energy, embodied energy will grow to represent almost 100% of the remaining problem.

Life cycle analysis is the most reliable means to factor in material impacts. Studies have shown that in a 50-year life cycle analysis the material choice for the structure of a building accounts for approximately 1% of the entire amount of energy consumed. Therefore, when considering steel as a structural system for a building its durability, flexibility and infinite recyclability are positive attributes. Most industry calculations for embodied energy are based on the manufacture of virgin steel. Very little virgin steel is actually manufactured, as the majority of steel includes significant recycled content.

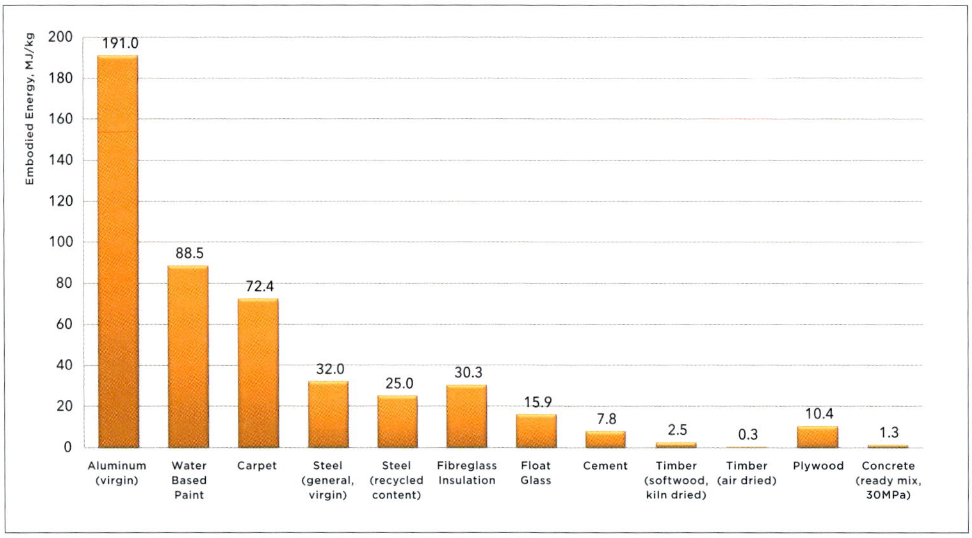


Chart showing the embodied energy of various building materials. The values for recycled steel vary as a function of the proportion of virgin to recycled content.

*Source: University of Wellington, NZ, Center for Building Performance Research (2004)*

One of the primary means to reduce $CO_2$ emissions due to embodied energy is to reduce the amount of material and, with it, the construction energy used in the creation of a building. Life cycle analysis is used to compare and rate different structural systems and their relative carbon footprints in great detail. In considering using a structural steel framing system over reinforced concrete or heavy timber, there are additional issues that must be addressed to reach a more holistic choice. Factors in the decision-making process will focus on how the structural systems compare in terms of their relationship to the passive heating and cooling systems, durability, ability to be fire-protected, recycled content as well as local availability.

Total energy breakdown of a typical hot-rolled steel retail building (approximate area less than 600m²/6,460sqft) after 50 years. The beams and columns account for less than 1% of the energy and Global Warming Potential of the structure. This will vary as a function of the building use, but the study shows that the choice of structural material is of less significance than other factors (operating energy as well as durability of enclosures, windows and doors). The calculations were created using Athena Life Cycle Software.

*Source: Life Cycle Assessment of a Single Storey Retail Building in Canada by Kevin Van Ooteghem*

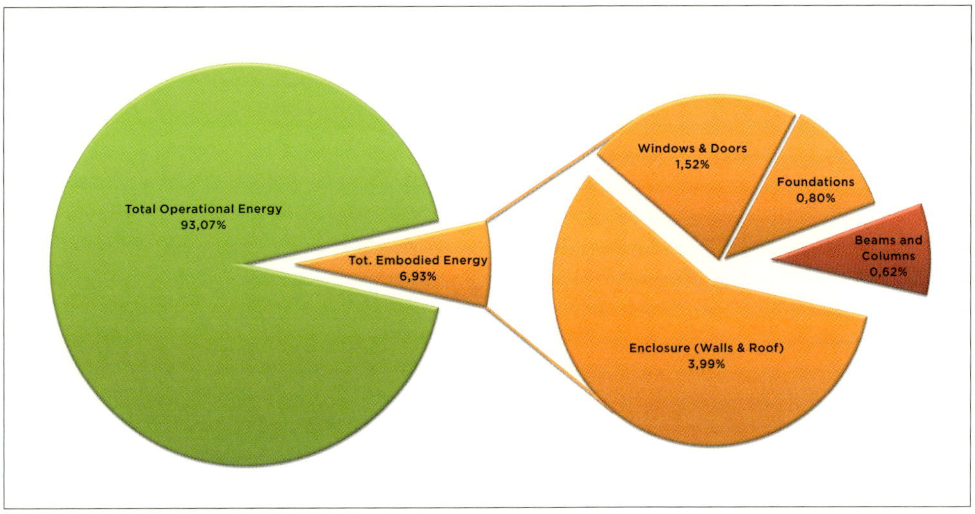


## REDUCE MATERIAL

Even between steel systems it is possible to achieve material reduction. The ability in the production of structural steel shapes to create sections that take advantage of distancing the material from the neutral axis, as in the case of W and HSS sections and OWSJ systems, allows for a streamlined use of the material that is not possible in structural members or systems that must use solid cross sections. This lightness of structure translates into less general use/weight of the material as well as reduced costs in transportation and foundation construction. HSS sections can additionally reduce the amount of coating material required, comparing the surface area of a W vs. a hollow section of equal carrying capacity (assuming that no interior finishing of the HSS member is required). This holds true for most painted finishes. Galvanized steel, however, must be coated on all surfaces, including the interior of hollow sections, to ensure corrosion protection, increasing material use. The galvanizing process is more energy-intensive, adding environmental cost.

## REDUCE FINISHES

The Lillis Business School at the University of Oregon in Eugene, OR, USA by SRG Partnership, LEED™ Silver, uses exposed steel as a means to reduce finishes. The white finish of the steel is also useful in increasing levels of reflectivity in the space to assist daylighting.

AESS buildings allow for the reduction of finish materials. Because the AESS as such is the architectural expression and requires no further covering or cladding finishes, the reduction in the use of other materials saves resources, the labor to install coverings and associated energy. Fire-resistant intumescent coating systems allow for exposed steel expression in a multitude of building types and uses.

When assessing the impact of the structure on indoor air quality, architects must select steel finishes that have low or no VOC emissions. This will be significant in choosing an intumescent fire protection, as the water-based coatings are presently applicable only to interior surface protection and tend to dry more slowly than the more volatile epoxy-based systems.

## REDUCE LABOR

The industrialized nature of the shop fabrication and construction process of steel structural systems can reduce site work and can simplify erection procedures, which translates to reduced labor and travel-associated $CO_2$ costs. If looking more holistically at steel fabrication, it will be easier in the future to source the energy supply for fabrication facilities from renewable energy sources than it will be to supply renewable energy to a construction site. Even if the end use of the project will include significant renewable energy such as photovoltaics and wind, these are not likely to be in place until closer to the completion of the project.

The LEED™ Gold Stratus Winery in Niagara-on-the-Lake uses a modular steel building system as the base for the part that houses the wine-making process. The reduction in custom fabrication reduces energy requirements. The building works toward achieving a "long life" through the choice of durable materials. All of the structural steel and exterior panels of the building (including the roof) are galvanized, thus adding to their longevity and eliminating the need for repainting or resurfacing in the future. In its quest for flexibility, the project uses a large-span steel portal-framed building with a mezzanine suspended from the frame. This design opens up the floor space and allows ease of modification for future process designs. The main steel structural frame of the building has been designed to accommodate the present structural loading as well as connections needed for future expansion plans. The pre-engineered steel building contained 49% post-consumer and 29% post-industrial recycled content, which was useful in obtaining LEED™ credits in the Materials and Resources category.

Left: The LEED™ Gold Stratus Winery in Niagara-on-the-Lake, ON, Canada by Les Andrew Architect Inc. uses a modular steel building system.

Right: From the exterior of the winery, the use of a pre-engineered system is not evident, an effect often desired for most architectural applications.

Not all exposed steel needs to be designed to use custom-produced members and specialized systems. The Semiahmoo Library and RCMP Headquarters in Surrey, BC, Canada, designed by Musson Cattell Mackey Partnership, obtained a LEED™ Silver rating and used many off-the-shelf products.

## REDUCE TRANSPORTATION

With rising fuel costs and the movement to reduce carbon emissions, it is often possible to choose a mill and fabricator to assist in limiting travel distances to the construction site, thereby also reducing the embodied energy of the material. In order to obtain green rating system (such as LEED™ ) credits for regional materials, both the source of the steel and fabricator must be located no further than 800km/500mi from the project if the material is trucked, or 2,400km/1,500mi if the material is shipped by rail or water. These distances vary by rating system and country, more densely populated countries having tighter requirements than those less densely populated with larger land areas. At this point, the distance between the source and the fabricator is not included in the calculation, but will likely be visited in the next iteration of the requirements.

Left: The library used a fairly straightforward Open Web Steel Joist (OWSJ), steel decking and W/HSS support system in an expressed fashion to create the lightness of the interior environment.

Right: The glazing system highlights the white finish on the exposed steel and uses the light color to enhance daylight levels.

## DURABILITY

Structural steel, if properly designed, detailed and coated, is a durable material for interior and exposed exterior applications. Long life of the product can positively influence the Life Cycle Assessment of the material. Durability of the coating choice is significant, particularly for exterior uses exposed to severe weathering. Corrosion resistance is an important consideration for most climates. Simple painted finishes must be refreshed frequently to maintain both the appearance and corrosion protection of the steel. Paint might certainly be the more economical choice at the outset of the project, yet over the lifespan of the building its monetary and environmental costs can mount.

For more enduring protection, galvanized steel, weathering steel and stainless steel are the better choices even if their initial costs may be higher. Of these three, galvanizing has become a popular choice, resulting in a specific aesthetic choice as well as ensuring durability for exterior applications. As previously mentioned, however, galvanizing is a protection system and not a fine finish. Hot-dipped galvanized pieces will vary in their appearance as a result of member thickness and batch.

Weathering steel also has an enduring finish but is limited in terms of the availability of section sizes and types. The target audience for the manufacture of this material is the bridge industry, and this impacts the types of sections produced.

Stainless steel is an excellent architectural choice, giving a consistent finish that is not limited to the surface of the material. However, the initial cost of stainless steel is significantly higher than that of coated structural steel and its structural capabilities require specialized engineering. Even if the embodied energy of stainless steel is high, it can be reduced when produced using bath smelting rather than electric furnaces. The increased percentages of nickel and other alloys are other factors that increase the carbon footprint of the material. On the other hand, the Life Cycle Assessment of stainless steel should address the remarkably improved finish that is capable of virtually eliminating the need for replacement coatings over the life of the building.

The Calgary Water Centre in Calgary, AB, Canada by Manasc Isaac Architects is a LEED™ Gold Facility. Durability was an important feature of many of the design decisions for the project. The use of exposed galvanized steel structure and galvanized profiled cladding contributed to the sustainable priorities for the building.

The Architecturally Exposed Steel Structure on the interior of the Calgary Water Center provided savings in embodied energy in that other finishes such as drywall were not required. The steel windbracing trusses on the front wall of the building were created from round HSS. Several "grey" finishes were able to be used that responded to specific finish issues of the various materials (including the aluminum curtain wall) yet blend together unobtrusively.

The 2009 Solar Decathlon entry by Rice University uses highly durable materials for its cladding. The choice of the galvanized finish is designed to provide a low maintenance and long life building for this prototype for low cost infill housing. The trellis that supports the green wall is also fabricated from galvanized steel components.

If properly designed, detailed and constructed, structural steel can present an enduring sustainable choice that is suited to a wide range of building types.

*CHAPTER 15*

---

# *STEEL IN TEMPORARY EXHIBITION BUILDINGS*

---

The Entry Pavilion for the Shanghai Expo 2010, China, designed by SRA Architects, exploits the innovative potential of steel in its inspirational combination of the steel lattice grid with a tension-supported fabric canopy. The project was constructed by Knippers Helbig Advanced Engineering of Germany.

The Canada Place Pavilion for Expo 86, held in Vancouver, BC, Canada, designed by Zeidler Partnership, is one of the few pavilions from this Expo designed to be a permanent structure. The theme of this Expo was transportation, and the pavilion's fabric roof used the iconography of tall ships in tune with the waterfront pier location. Today the pavilion forms part of the Vancouver Convention Center.

Playing on the transportation theme, the detailing of the sails of the fabric roof is consistent with the tensile language of the tall sails of ships.

The advantages of structural steel in the conception of temporary structures were first realized in the 19th century in pavilions designed to house the International Exhibitions. Expos are expected to represent innovation in architectural design, structure, material use and form. This is evidenced by the design for the Crystal Palace for the International Exhibition of 1851, the designs for the Eiffel Tower and Galerie des Machines for the International Exhibition of 1889, and modern Expos such as Expo 67 in Montreal, which showcased Buckminster Fuller's geodesic dome as the USA Pavilion.

Quick assembly allowing for demountability and reuse or recycling, now considered an assumption of performance, continue to form the basis for the design of contemporary exhibition buildings. Contemporary pavilion design is consistent with much of the detailing of early exhibition buildings, as the unique programmatic requirements have not significantly changed. Issues of durability impact the choice of detailing, finishing and cost for temporary and permanent varieties of innovative pavilions.

The competitions for the annual Serpentine Pavilion for Hyde Park in London have resulted in highly anticipated events with contributions by, among others, Zaha Hadid, Rem Koolhaas, Daniel Libeskind, Tadao Ando, Frank Gehry (see Chapter 13: Advanced Framing Systems: Steel ans Timber) and Peter Zumthor. Most of these temporary buildings use steel-based design and assembly methods to respond to the short time frame for construction and disassembly.

Left: The 2006 Serpentine Pavilion in London, England was designed by Rem Koolhaas of OMA and Cecil Balmond of ARUP. This team was also responsible for the CCTV Headquarters in Beijing. The balloon was secured with winches and raised or lowered in response to the weather.

Right: The galvanized steel-framed base of the 2006 Serpentine Pavilion. Many pavilions use innovative ballasting methods to avoid the use of foundations, as to neither disturb the site nor incur extra cost. Typically these installations do not have to endure freeze/thaw cycles or heavy frost conditions that would necessitate a more permanent approach to foundation design. Lightweight materials complement the temporary nature of the exhibit.

Left: This pavilion constructed for the London Festival of Architecture in England, 2008, designed by Tonkin Liu with Adams Kara Taylor, was to move several times during the festival. The heavy feet to which the HSS sections attach provide both stability and ballast.

Right: The concept of mobility entailed that petals were designed to rotate and nest to make for compact transportation. The light weight of the HSS tubes allowed for easy bending and tight radii at the tips of the petals. As the tubes were covered in fabric, deformations from tight bending would be concealed.

Steel structural systems often provide a level of durability that exceeds the length of the event, while simultaneously responding to the differing requirements of the temporary nature of the building. Even if international exhibitions as such are far from sustainable in their use of resources, the use of steel and the ability to recycle or reuse the structure is less environmentally damaging than many alternatives. Even though temporary, many of the pavilion designs have set precedents and inspired designs for permanent structures.

The Shanghai Expo 2010 employed a variety of steel-based pavilion designs to house a full range of programs and country budgets. Characteristic of most pavilions was a tubular steel frame with bolted plate connections for quick assembly. Given that much of the steel framework would be hidden by fanciful cladding treatments, a decreased level of precision in the jointing could be allowed, which also resulted in savings for the fabrication and erection budgets. These same connections maximized off-site fabrication and facilitated the division of the structure into modular elements suitable for shipping.

The Shanghai Expo pavilions fell into several types, whose complexity of structure corresponded to the budgets of the clients. The primary structural material was steel. The nature of the connection methods and finishings of the steel varied with the choice to conceal or expose the system. Even exposed steel tended to have lower-quality workmanship, which reflected an acknowledgment of the temporary nature of the structure. The generic pavilion of the Shanghai Expo provided a set prefabricated structural frame, permitting the nations to choose levels and types of finish suited to their combinations of theme and budget. These typical pavilions created a single large rectangular interior space; they also included the option of a corner tower element and were flexible enough to facilitate individualized expression.

The standard pavilion type at the Shanghai Expo 2010, China, as seen here for Croatia, Slovakia and Lithuania, included a tower element that permitted customization of the regulation steel frame. Often these "signposts" used more elaborate steel tension members to add to the architectural expression.

Left: The façade of the Kazakhstan Pavilion at the Shanghai Expo uses an irregular grid of steel cables that are pushed out from the façade with small tubular struts. The cables are wrapped with a zig zag of fabric.

Right: The bolted steel framework of the Hungarian Pavilion at the Shanghai Expo, designed by Támas Lévai, supported numerous light wood members to create a dense grid.

Pavilions for countries with larger budgets used similar tubular framing and connections, but broke from the rectilinear mode and often included odd geometries or curves.

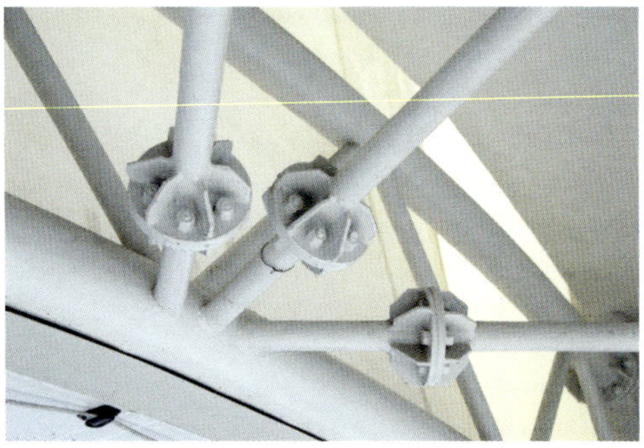

Left Top: The Finnish Pavilion at the Shanghai Expo, China, designed by JKMM Architects, used tubular steel trusses to create its doughnut-shaped form.

Left Bottom: The bolted connections relied on plate fins to reinforce the connection between the plate and tube.

Right: The cylindrical form of the Finnish Pavilion used a spiral ramp system that channeled the participants between the exterior and interior walls. The interior and exterior truss framing was connected using round HSS members with bolted plate connections.

The form of the Spanish Pavilion at the Shanghai Expo, designed by Benedetta Tagliabue, is highly irregular. Like the Finnish Pavilion, it used round HSS trusses and bolted connections. The exterior was finished in custom-fabricated woven panels that allowed some view of the tubular steel truss frame behind.

Left: The Spanish Pavilion at the Shanghai Expo had a highly articulated tubular frame, whose assembly was made more efficient by breaking the building into smaller sections that were simply bolted together. As with most buildings, full advantage had been taken of shop fabrication. The irregular form added rigidity to this very light structure.

Right: This connection in the Spanish Pavilion consisted of a round plate that had been welded to the end of the tubular frame members. The lightweight woven cladding panels added nothing to stabilize the structure, and the weathering of the panels in combination with a polluted environment led to more staining seen on the structure.

More cleanly detailed steel framing systems were found in high-profile pavilions where the steel was architecturally exposed or used to support significant areas of glazing. Proximity to view and touch also influenced the detailing. In these cases, the level of finish, workmanship and detailing came closer to that of permanent AESS structures, and although the standards never reached that of permanent AESS structures, some of the innovation can more easily be transferred to use in permanent structures. The true benefit of the steel system here lies in its demountability.

Left: The German Pavilion at the Shanghai Expo, designed by Schmidhuber + Kaindl, used a more articulated steel frame that was not only expressed on the interior of the pavilion but also, due to the transparency of the skin, revealed at night. Higher-quality detailing was used in response to the expressed nature of the steel on the interior of the building.

Right: The Nepal Pavilion at the Shanghai Expo used an exposed steel frame to create the centerpiece of its exhibit. The majority of the HSS grid is welded. The basket at the top was attached to the ribs of the middle section via slender bolted connections. The diamond grid at the lower section had been created as a series of horizontal rings that were broken into segments for shipping and then site-welded to conceal the connections.

Left: The Israel Pavilion at the Shanghai Expo, designed by Haim Dotan, used a modified lattice grid structure to create this elliptoid form. The odd geometries required the customization of most of the connections, thereby increasing the cost.

Right: A view up into the top of the glazed shape of the Israel Pavilion highlights the wide variety of connection geometries that had to be accounted for in the fabrication and erection.

The connections for the Israel Pavilion maintain clean lines by recessing the bolts and plates within the diameter of the tubes. Adequate distance must be maintained to allow for insertion and tightening of the bolts. For use in a temporary structure, these modified lattice grid connections work well to complement the clean lines of the glazed façade, while also answering to requirements for speed of assembly and lowered cost.

**The use of steel and other materials for some of the pavilions fell well outside of the typical situations. These designs responded to certain exhibition constraints and other challenging factors. For some, the circulation path that must process thousands of visitors a day became the basis of more technically elaborate design responses. For others, steel was used as an expressive cladding material and quick assembly systems had to be designed that would facilitate speed of erection and disassembly, while still remaining durable for the duration of the exhibition.**

The Danish Pavilion at the Shanghai Expo, designed by BIG, used a complex spiral ramp system to take participants on foot and bicycle up and down the building. The exterior and floor material was painted sheet steel. Unlike the heavy concrete construction of the New York Guggenheim, whose circulation system it somewhat mimics, the use of steel allowed for a speedier erection and reduction in cost.

Left: The South Korean Pavilion at the Shanghai Expo, designed by Mass Studies, used a lightweight system of steel rods to clip the thin painted metal cladding to the building. The cladding design was done by Axis Façades and the structural engineering by ARUP.

Right: The rear of the South Korean Pavilion façade. The panels were simply clipped to slender horizontal steel rods for quick mount and dismount. This image was taken about two weeks before the end of the Expo and shows some environmental wear, given the reduction in durability of the coating system chosen as a result of the temporary nature of the exhibition.

The Latvian Pavilion at the Shanghai Expo, designed by Mailitis A.I.I.M., combines the rigidity of a steel truss frame with the simplicity of a semi-transparent floating tile finish.

Contemporary exhibitions make good use of fabric structures as the means to cover large spaces. These systems provide support-free cover that simultaneously permits protection from the heat of the sun and from rain while promoting air circulation and a daylit space. The canopies are also able to host the theatrical requirements of night lighting. Newer membrane cladding systems are also used for their speed of assembly and minimal structural weight.

The Entry Axis Pavilion at the Shanghai Expo by SRA Architects showcases steel tension fabric structures to provide a light yet effective canopy for visitors. A series of glazed steel lattice funnels provide daylight to the lower level of the boulevard.

The unusual shape of the Japanese Pavilion at the Shanghai Expo, designed by Nihon Sekkei, combined an exposed steel structure with an ETFE double-layer pillow for its exterior cladding. Photovoltaic panels were incorporated into some parts of the cladding. The tubular steel frame on the interior was elegantly exposed.

The AESS tubular steel frame towers of the Japanese Pavilion were detailed to a higher level of finish than the standard demountable framing used in many other pavilions. The prefabricated sections used welded connections to increase the finish and aesthetic of the structure. The plate connectors were only partially concealed and provided both for a better speed of erection as well as a cleaner look.

Left: The Taiwan Pavilion at the Shanghai Expo, designed by C.Y. Lee & Partners Architects/Planners, combines an Architecturally Exposed Structural Steel frame with a high level of glazing and multimedia displays.

Right: The aftermath of the Shanghai Expo 2010 saw the demolition of a large number of temporary steel frame structures, here the former Taiwan Pavilion. The majority of this steel will be recycled rather than reused. Either way, the steel will feed back into the construction stream.

Temporary pavilions will continue to challenge the technical and imaginative capacity of their designers, due to the added requirements of speed of erection, disassembly and often a reduced budget, while simultaneously being charged with creating a high-profile display of "national" expertise. In this they form a concise summation of the benefits and attributes of contemporary steel construction.

## BIBLIOGRAPHY


General Technical References

Allen, Edward, and Joseph Iano. *Fundamentals of Building Construction: Materials and Methods.* Hoboken: John Wiley and Sons, Inc., [5]2008.

Blanc, Alan, Michael McEvoy, and Roger Plank. *Architecture and Construction in Steel.* London: E & FN Spon/The Steel Construction Institute, 1993.

*Detailing for Steel Construction.* American Institute of Steel Construction Inc., 2005.

Drucker, Carol. "30 Good Rules for Connection Design." *Modern Steel Construction*, May 2004.

Eekhout, Mick. "Design, Engineering, Production and Realisation." *CWCT Meeting.* Bath, 2004.

Hamburger, Ronald O., Helmut Krawinkler, James O. Malley, and Scott N. Adan. "Seismic Design of Steel Special Moment Frames: A Design Guide for Engineers." *National Earthquake Hazards Reduction Program.* National Institute of Standards and Technology, U.S. Department of Commerce. June 2009. http://www.nehrp.gov/pdf/nistgcr9-917-3.pdf.

*Handbook of Steel Construction.* Toronto: Canadian Institute of Steel Construction, [10]2011.

Lawson, Mark, and Peter Trebilcock. *Architectural Design in Steel.* New York, New York: Spon Press/The Steel Construction Institute, 2004.

Reichel, Alexander, Peter Ackermann, Alexander Hentschel and Anette Hochberg. *Detail Practice: Building with Steel: Details, Principles, Examples.* Basel: Birkhäuser, 2007.

"Steel Construction." *Detail: Review of Architecture and Construction*, Sept./Oct. 2007.

*Steel Construction Manual.* Chicago: American Institute of Steel Construction, [13]2006.

*Structural Steel Construction.* City University of Hong Kong, Division of Building Science and Technology, e-learning, Building Info Package. http://bst1.cityu.edu.hk/e-learning/building_info_pack/BST20317/3.1-StructuralSteelConstruction.pdf.

Websites

*American Institute of Steel Construction.* http://www.aisc.org

*American Iron and Steel Institute.* http://www.steel.org.

*ArcelorMittal.* http://www.arcelormittal.com.

*Australian Steel Institute.* http://steel.org.au/.

*Canadian Institute of Steel Construction.* http://www.cisc-icca.ca.

*Carbon Neutral Steel Building Systems (CN-SBS) Research Project.* http://cn-sbs.cssbi.ca/.

*European Stainless Steel Development Association.* http://www.euro-inox.org/

*International Iron and Steel Institute.* http://www.worldsteel.org/.

*Japan Iron and Steel Federation.* http://www.jisf.or.jp/en/index.html.

*Steel Construction Institute.* http://www.steel-sci.org/

*Stainless Steel Institute of America.* http://www.ssina.com.

*Stahl-Zentrum.* http://www.stahl-online.de.

*Steel: Fun is in the Details.* http://www.architecture.uwaterloo.ca/faculty_projects/terri/steel.html.

*Steel Recycling Institute.* http://www.recycle-steel.org/

*Steel Tube Institute.* http://www.steeltubeinstitute.org/

*Tata Steel (formerly Corus).* http://www.tatasteeleurope.com

*World Steel.* http://www.worldsteel.org/

History and Theory References

Benevolo, Leonardo. *The History of Modern Architecture.* 2 vols. Cambridge, Mass.: The MIT Press, 1977.

Buddensieg, Tilmann, and Henning Rogge. *Industriekultur: Peter Behrens and the AEG, 1907-1914.* Translated by Iain Boyd Whyte. Cambridge: The MIT Press, 1984.

Condit, Carl W. *American Building.* Chicago: The University of Chicago Press, [2]1982.

Frampton, Kenneth. *Modern Architecture. A Critical History.* London: Thames and Hudson, 2007.

Le Bris, Guy. *Les Constructions Métalliques.* Paris: Librairies-Imprimeries Réunies, 1891.

Levine, Neil. "The book and the building: Hugo's theory of architecture and Labrouste's Bibliothèque Ste-Geneviève." In *The Beaux-Arts and nineteenth-century French architecture*, edited by Robin Middleton, 138-173. Cambridge, Mass.: The MIT Press, 1982.

Mainstone, Rowland J. *Developments in Structural Form.* Cambridge, Mass.: The MIT Press, 1983.

Otto, Frei. *Tensile Structures.* Cambridge, Mass.: The MIT Press, [5]1982.

Steiner, Frances H. *French Iron Architecture.* Ann Arbor: UMI Research Press, 1984.

Turak, Theodore. *William Le Baron Jenney: A Pioneer in Modern Architecture.* Ann Arbor: UMI Research Press, 1986.

High Tech and Contemporary Architecture

Abel, Chris. *Renault Centre: Swindon, 1982: Architect, Norman Foster.* New York: Van Nostrand Reinhold, 1991.

Aiken, Ian D., A. Parry Brown, F. Jeff. Jafarzadeh. "Buckling Restrained Braces Provide the Key to the Seismic Retrofit of the Wallace F. Bennett Federal Building." *Modern Steel Construction*, August 2001. http://www.reaveley.com/pdf/tech/Bennett%20Bldg%20article%20-%20final%20PE.pdf

*Architectural Review.* "High-tech ice rink [Oxford Ice Rink]." May 1984: 38-45.

*Architectural Review.* "Inmos in Gwent: factory, Newport, Gwent, South Wales." December 1982: 26-33.

ARUP, ed. *Solutions for a Modern City: ARUP in Beijing.* London: Black Dog Publishing, 2008.

Banham, Reyner. "Art and Necessity: Inmos and the Persistence of Functionalism." *Architectural Review*, December 1982: 34-38.

Boake, Terri Meyer. "Constructing a Gehry: Transformation AGO." *Canadian Architect*, June 2008.

—. "Ordering Chaos: Building Libeskind's ROM." *Canadian Architect*, January 2006.

Buchanan, Peter. "Essay: High-Tech." *Architectural Review.* June 6, 1983. http://www.architectural-review.com/home/ar-archive/ar-july-1983-essay-high-tech-by-peter-buchanan/8604479.article

"Expo 2010 Shanghai." *A+ U* 478 (July 2010).

Foster, Norman. *Foster and Partners: Catalogue.* New York: Prestel USA, 2008.

—. *Foster Catalogue 2001.* London: Prestel, 2001.

—. *Rebuilding the Reichstag.* Weidenfeld & Nicolson, 2000.

*Global Architecture: Piano + Rogers Architects, Ove Arup Engineers, Centre Beaubourg, Paris, France. 1972-1977.* Tokyo: A.D.A. Edita, 1977.

Jodidio, Philip. *Piano: Renzo Piano Building Workshop 1966 to today.* London: Taschen GmbH, 2008.

LeCuyer, Annette. *Steel and Beyond: New Strategies for Metals in Architecture.* Basel: Birkhäuser Verlag AG, 2003.

Lin, Lorraine, and Bruce Danzinger. "The Imaginative Engineer: Peter Rice (1935-1992)." *Structure Magazine*, January 2007: 54-57.

Meade, Martin. "Piano Machine: Menil Museum, Houston, Texas." *Architectural Review*, August 1983: 26-31.

*Nicholas Grimshaw.* http://www.greatbuildings.com/architects/Nicholas_Grimshaw.html.

*Norman Foster.* http://www.greatbuildings.com/architects/Norman_Foster.html.

Peckham, Andrew. "Foster Associates' Sainsbury Centre." Edited by Haig Beck. *Architectural Design Profile 19* (Wiley-Academy), August 1979.

Piano, Renzo. *Renzo Piano: Buildings and Projects, 1971-89.* New York: Rizzoli, 1989.

Powell, Kenneth. *Richard Rogers Complete Works.* 3 vols. New York: Phaidon Press Inc., 1999.

*Renzo Piano.* http://www.greatbuildings.com/architects/Renzo_Piano.html.

*Richard Rogers.* http://www.greatbuildings.com/architects/Richard_Rogers.html.

"Richard Rogers: 1978 - 1988." *A+U*, Extra Edition, December 1988.

Subramanian, Dr. N. "Olympic Structures of China." *The Structural Engineer.* 2008. http://www.thestructuralengineer.info/library/OlympicStructures08.pdf.

Sudjic, Deyan. *Norman Foster, Richard Rogers, James Stirling: new directions in British architecture.* London: Thames and Hudson, 1986.

Architecturally Exposed Structural Steel

Boake, Terri Meyer. "Architecturally Exposed Structural Steel: How Is It Defined?" *Advantage Steel*, Spring 2005.

—. *CISC Guide for Specifying Architecturally Exposed Structural Steel.* Canadian Institute of Steel Construction. May 2011. http://www.cisc-icca.ca/publications/technical/codes/aessguide/.

Boulanger, Sylvie, and Terri Boake. "The Canadian Matrix: A Category Approach for Specifying AESS." *Advantage Steel*, Summer 2008.

Boulanger, Sylvie, Terri Meyer Boake, and Walter Koppelaar. "A Categorical Approach: Specifying AESS." *Modern Steel Construction*, April 2008.

Eekhout, Mick. *Tubular Structures in Architecture.* Geneva: CIDECT and TUDelft, [2]2011.

Kloiber, Larry. "Designing HSS Connections." *Modern Steel Construction*, November 2001.

*Modern Steel Construction.* "Architecturally Exposed Structural Steel: A Design Guide." May 2003.

Bending Steel

Alwood, Todd. "What Engineers Should Know About Bending Steel." *Modern Steel Construction*, May 2006.

*Modern Steel Construction.* "Bending Steel: Questions Answered." June 2002.

Casting Steel

Baddoo, Nancy R. "Castings in Construction SCI Publication 172." *Online Information Center for Stainless Steel Construction.* February 2008. http://stainlessconstruction.com/ss_info_cntr/pdfs/Castings%20in%20Construction.pdf.

Boake, Terri Meyer. "Branching Out." *Modern Steel Construction*, July 2008.

de Oliveira, Carlo, and Tabitha Stine. "Convenient Connections." *Modern Steel Construction*, July 2008.

„Non-Expendable Casting Techniques." *Castings and Forgings News.* http://www.castings-forgings-news.com/castings/ShowPage.aspx?pageID=1572.

Oliveira, J.C., S. Willibald, J.A. Packer, C. Christopoulos, and T. Verhey. "Cast steel nodes in tubular construction - Canadian experience." *Proceedings of the Eleventh International Symposium on Tubular Steel - ISTS 11.* Quebec City, 2009.

Schober, Hans. "Steel Castings in Architecture and Engineering." *Modern Steel Construction*, April 2003.

Stuart, D. Matthew. "Wrought and Cast Iron Structures." *Architectureweek.* June 15, 2011. http://www.architectureweek.com/2011/0615/building_2-1.html.

Elliptical Tubes

Packer, Jeff. "Elliptical Hollow Sections Part One: Properties and Applications." *Advantage Steel*, Fall 2009.

—. "Elliptical Hollow Sections Part Two: EHS Member Design." *Advantage Steel*, Winter 2009.

—. "Elliptical Hollow Sections Part Three: EHS Connection Design." *Advantage Steel*, Spring 2010.

—. "Going Elliptical." *Modern Steel Construction*, March 2008.

Coatings, Finishes and Fire Protective Design

Alfawakhiri, Farid, Christopher Hewitt, and Robert Solomon. "Fire Protection: Common Questions Answered." *Modern Steel Construction*, December 2002.

"Bird's Nest - China." *http://www.galvanisationzinga.com.* http://www.galvanisationzinga.com/pdf/realisations/autres/Bird%27s_Nest_en.pdf.

Burgan, Bassam. "Guidance on the Use of Stainless Steel in Construction." Edited by U.K. The Steel Construction Institute. *Symposium Structural Applications of Stainless Steel in Buildings and Architecture.* Brussels: Euro Inox, 2000.

Ferguson, Anthony, and Barbara Lane. "Arup Fire." *Swiss Re - structural fire engineering for the newest tall building in London.* http://www.mace.manchester.ac.uk/project/research/structures/strucfire/CaseStudy/steelComposite/swiss.htm.

*Fire Protection of Plain Concrete Filled Hollow Steel Structural Sections.* Bulletin No. 21, Toronto: Canadian Steel Construction Council, 1994.

Gewain, R.G., N.R. Iwankiw, F. Alfawakhiri, and G.S. Frater. *Fire Facts for Steel Buildings.* Toronto: Canadian Institute of Steel Construction, 2006.

"Hot Dip Galvanizing for Sustainable Design." *American Galvanizers Association.* 2009. http://www.galvanizeit.org/images/uploads/publicationPDFs/Galvanizing_for_Sustainable_Design.pdf.

Kodur, V.R. "Solutions for enhancing the fire endurance of HSS columns filled with high strength concrete - NRCC- 47362." *National Research Council Canada.* January 2006.

http://www.nrc-cnrc.gc.ca/obj/irc/doc/pubs/nrcc47362.pdf.
Parker, Arthur J., Jesse J. Beitel, and Nestor R. Iwankiw. "Fire Protection Materials for Architecturally Exposed Structural Steel (AESS)." *Structure Magazine*, April 2005.
Pollack, Beth. "Fire Protective Coatings: An Overview." *Modern Steel Construction*, March 2005.
"Zinc Coatings." *American Galvanizers Association.* 2006. http://www.galvanizeit.org/images/uploads/publicationPDFs/Zinc_Coatings.pdf.

Diagrid Buildings and Towers
Ali, Mir M., and K. Moon. "Structural Developments in Tall Buildings: Current Trends and Future Prospects." *Architectural Science Review*, 2007.
Baker, William F., D. Stanton Korista, and Lawrence C. Novak. "Engineering the World's Tallest - Burj Dubai." *CTBUH 8th World Congress.* 2008.
Carroll, Chris, et al. "Case Study: CCTV Building - Headquarters & Cultural Center." *CTBUH Journal*, no. III (2008): 15-24.
Chandler, Graham. "Encana's Bow Building; the making of an icon." *Alberta Oil Magazine.* June 7, 2010. http://www.albertaoilmagazine.com/2010/06/encana%e2%80%99s-bowbuilding-takes-its-cues-from-iconic-towers-in-new-york-and-chicago/.
Charnish, Barry, and Terry McDonnell. "'The Bow': Unique Diagrid Structural System for a Sustainable Tall Building." *CTBUH 8th World Congress.* 2008.
McCain, Ian. "Diagrid: Structural Efficiency and Increasing Popularity." *e-book exchange.* March 27, 2011. http://e-boook.blogspot.com/2011/03/diagrid-technolgy-structural-efficiency.html.
Moon, K. "Design and Construction of Steel Diagrid Structures." *NASCC.* Phoenix, 2009.
Moon, Kyoung Sun. "Sustainable Selection of Structural Systems for Tall Buildings." *5th Civil Engineering Conference in the Asian Region and Australasian Structural Engineering Conference 2010.* Sydney, 2010.
Munro, Dominic. "Swiss Re's Building London." *http://www.epab.bme.hu/.* 2004. http://www.epab.bme.hu/oktatas/2009-2010-2/v-CA-B-Ms/Free-Form/Examples/SwissRe.pdf.
Proctor, Don. "Bending the Bow." *Building.* February 2008. http://www.building.ca/news/bending-the-bow/1000219897/.
Scott, David, David Farnsworth, Matt Jackson, and Matt Clark. "The Effects of Complex Geometry on Tall Towers." *Wiley Interscience.* November 2, 2007. http://onlinelibrary.wiley.com/doi/10.1002/tal.428/pdf
Seica, Michael. "A New Urban Giant: The Bow Tower." *Advantage Steel*, Fall 2010.
Soo, Kim Jong, Kim Young Sik, and Lho Seung Hee. "Structural Schematic Design of a Tall Building in Asan using the Diagrid System." *CTBUH 8th World Congress.* 2008.
Steel Institute of New York. "Hearst Tower." *Metals in Construction*, Spring 2006: 21-27.
"Tall Buildings in Numbers." *CTBUH Journal*, No. I (2010).
"Tall Buildings in Numbers." *CTBUH Journal*, No. II (2010).

Steel and Glass
Leckie, John. "Steel and Other Materials Part One: Steel and Glass." *Advantage Steel*, Summer 2007.
Mazeika, Aaron, and Kieran Kelly-Sneed. "Getting Started with Cable Net Walls." *Modern Steel Construction*, April 2007.
Rice, Peter, and Hugh Dutton. *Structural Glass.* London: E & FN Spon, ²1995.
Ryan, P., M. Otlet, and R.G. Ogden. *Steel Supported Glazing Systems.* SCI Publication, Vol. 193. Berkshire: The Steel Construction Institute, 1997.
Schittich, Christian, ed. "Glass Construction." *Detail: Review of Architecture and Construction* 2007 - 2 (March - April 2007).
Schittich, Christian, Gerald Staib, Dieter Balkow, Matthias Schuler, and Werner Sobek. *Glass Construction Manual.* Basel: Birkhäuser, ²2007.
Wigginton, Michael. *Glass in Architecture.* London: Phaidon Press, 1996.
Wurm, Jan. *Glass Structures: Design and Construction of Self-Supporting Skins.* Basel: Birkhäuser, 2007.

Steel and Timber
"Heavy Connections." *Canadian Wood Council.* 2010. http://www.cwc.ca/NR/rdonlyres/AB3D54E7-BE30-4B85-8608-397FC8721B95/0/HeavyConnections.pdf.
Leckie, John. "Steel and Other Materials Part Two: Steel and Wood." *Advantage Steel*, Winter 2007.

Sustainable Design
Architects, OWP/P. "Structural Steel Contributions Towards Obtaining a LEED™ Rating." *Modern Steel Construction*, May 2003.
Boake, Terri Meyer. "The 3Rs of Steel: Reduce, Reuse, Recycle." *Advantage Steel*, Summer 2006.
—. "The Leap to Zero Carbon." *Journal of Green Building* (College Publishing), Fall 2008.
Boake, Terri Meyer, and Caroline Prochazka. "LEED™: A Primer." *Canadian Architect*, January 2004.
Boulanger, Sylvie, and David MacKinnon. "Recovery Strategies to Bypass the Grave." *NASCC.* Montreal, 2005.
Boulanger, Sylvie, and Sylvain Boulanger. "Steel and Sustainability: Integration." *Canadian Architect*, January 2004.
—. "Sustainability and Steel II: Recovery." *Canadian Architect*, March 2004.
Boulanger, Sylvie, Sylvain Boulanger, Mark Gorgolewski and David MacKinnon. "Sustainable Steel Issue." *Advantage Steel*, Summer 2004.
Gorgowleski, Mark, and Carmel Sergio. "The Development of the Angus Technopole Building in Montreal, Quebec." *Advantage Steel*, Fall 2006.
Hewitt, Christopher. "The Real Deal: Sustainable Steel." *Modern Steel Construction*, September 2003.
Hewitt, Christopher, Michael Pulaski, Michael Horman and Bradley Guy. "Design for Deconstruction." *Modern Steel Construction*, June 2004.
Van Ooteghem, Kevin. *Life-Cycle Assessment of a Single Storey Retail Building in Canada.* Waterloo: University of Waterloo, 2010.

*All internet-based references were valid as of July 2011.*

## ILLUSTRATION CREDITS

Unless otherwise noted, all photographs in this book were taken by the author Terri Meyer Boake.

Les Andrew Architect Inc.
Stratus Winery Construction, 226

Benson Steel
Isometric of Art Gallery of Ontario, 208

Brian Boake
Dubai Metro Station interior, 35;
Watercube interior, 177

Sierra Boake
Image of Terri Boake, 248

Cast ConneX® Corporation of Canada
Earthquake resistant brace, 147, 148;
Universal pin connectors, 148;
Quantum Nano alternate, 151

Jean Gu
Taiwan Pavilion demolition, 235

Vincent Hui (with assistance of Sam Ghantous):
Fair Store Rendered Detail, 28
Chapter 3, all technical illustrations
Chapter 5, all technical illustrations of Sainsbury Centre, Renault Centre, Inmos Microprocessor Factory
Rose Center 3D rendering, 94
Curved steel typology illustration, 118
Chinese National Theater detail illustration, 123
Tall building typology diagram, 127
Reliance Building Rendered Detail, 180
Reagan International Airport illustrations, 186
Serres technical illustrations, 187
Serres spider connection, 189
Newseum technical illustrations, 191

Taehyung Richard Kim
Image of Vincent Hui, 248

Mike Kowalek
Baltimore Convention Center, 40, 82

Walters Inc.
Bow Encana: BIM model, 25; technical drawings, 136, 137
OCAD: isometric, OCAD rendered overlay, 41; OCAD detail, 91; transportation and construction photos, 100, 101
ROM: Cover drawing; Chapter 4, all technical drawings; "Owl" shop photo, 48
Leslie Dan: Chapter 4, all technical drawings
Guelph Science Building: digital renderings, 153; all images, 154, 155; final casting images, 156

Ziggy Welsch (George Third & Son)
Brentwood Skytrain Station detail, 205
Richmond Speed Skating Oval, all construction photos, 212-215

# INDEX OF TECHNICAL SUBJECTS

## INDEX OF APPLICATIONS

## INDEX OF BUILDINGS

# INDEX OF ARCHITECTS AND STEEL FIRMS

## INDEX OF LOCATIONS

## ON THE AUTHOR

TERRI MEYER BOAKE, BES, B.ARCH, M.ARCH, LEED AP
Terri Meyer Boake is an Associate Professor and Associate Director of the School of Architecture at the University of Waterloo, Cambridge, Ontario, Canada. She is the Past President of the Society of Building Science Educators – an international group of academics that teach in the area of sustainable design. She is President-Elect of the Building Technology Educators' Society, a group dedicated to vitalizing teaching in the areas of structures and construction. She has been teaching in building construction and structures since the early 1980s and launched an effort to expand the environmental core curriculum at the School of Architecture at Waterloo during the mid 1990s.

She works with the Canadian Institute of Steel Construction and the Steel Structures Education Foundation of Canada to develop interactive multimedia case studies to promote the teaching of steel construction in schools of architecture across Canada. She is active on the CISC Architecturally Exposed Structural Steel task force and has published the "CISC Guide for Specifying Architecturally Exposed Structural Steel" in 2011.

Terri Meyer Boake holds a professional degree in Architecture from the University of Waterloo and a post-professional degree in Architecture from the University of Toronto. She is a LEED-Accredited Professional in sustainable building. Actively engaged in researching carbon-neutral building design, with an emphasis on architectural and passive solutions over a reliance on system and energy sources, her current research project involves the creation of resource materials to assist educators and practitioners in the better understanding of how to create Carbon Neutral Buildings. She has presented on Low Carbon Strategies in Canada, the U.S. and China. She is authoring a web site for The Carbon Neutral Design Project, an initiative funded by the American Institute of Architects to assist their members in designing more sustainable buildings (www.aia.org/carbonneutral-designproject )

She is an avid photographer and has spent significant time traveling to document and bring noteworthy buildings to the attention of the community. Noting a deficiency and lack of critical construction process information available in current publications, her goal has been to document and present buildings with a "construction eye".

## ON THE TECHNICAL ILLUSTRATOR

VINCENT HUI holds several degrees including Masters degrees in Architecture (University of Waterloo, Canada) and Business Administration (Schulich at York University). He also holds a Certificate in University Teaching and is a LEED Accredited Professional.

He currently divides his time serving as a partner with the design firm Atelier Anaesthetic and teaching a variety of courses at Ryerson University's Department of Architectural Science in Toronto, including studio, structures, and digital tools. He has cultivated an extensive background of research in Computer Aided Design, Building Information Modeling, parametric design, advanced simulation and rapid prototyping. As the head of Ryerson's Architectural Design Lab, RAD | Lab, Vincent has overseen the design, fabrication and exhibition of innovative design work around the world.

With professional experience from projects in Asia, Europe, the Middle East and North America under the auspices of firms around the world, Vincent has tempered his pedagogy within an accessible, real-world context. Some of his current research initiatives stem from his interests in architectural pedagogy and media including the integration of ubiquitous computing, advanced simulation and gaming technologies in design education. He is currently working on interactive, multimedia tools for the Steel Structures Education Foundation of Canada as well as an augmented reality database for architectural projects in Toronto.

As a colorblind designer, Vincent has been passionate about leveraging technology as a tool to empower everyone with creative desire and improve design communication.

Steel: A History of Strength. A Future of Possibilities.

express it

use architecturally exposed structural steel categories

British Columbia
Alberta
Central Canada

cisc icca
CANADIAN INSTITUTE OF STEEL CONSTRUCTION

Ontario
Québec
Atlantic Canada

www.cisc-icca.ca/aess

RAMS HORN SCULPTURE
CALGARY, AB

ROYAL ONTARIO MUSEUM
TORONTO, ON

WALTERS GROUP
DEFINE | BUILD

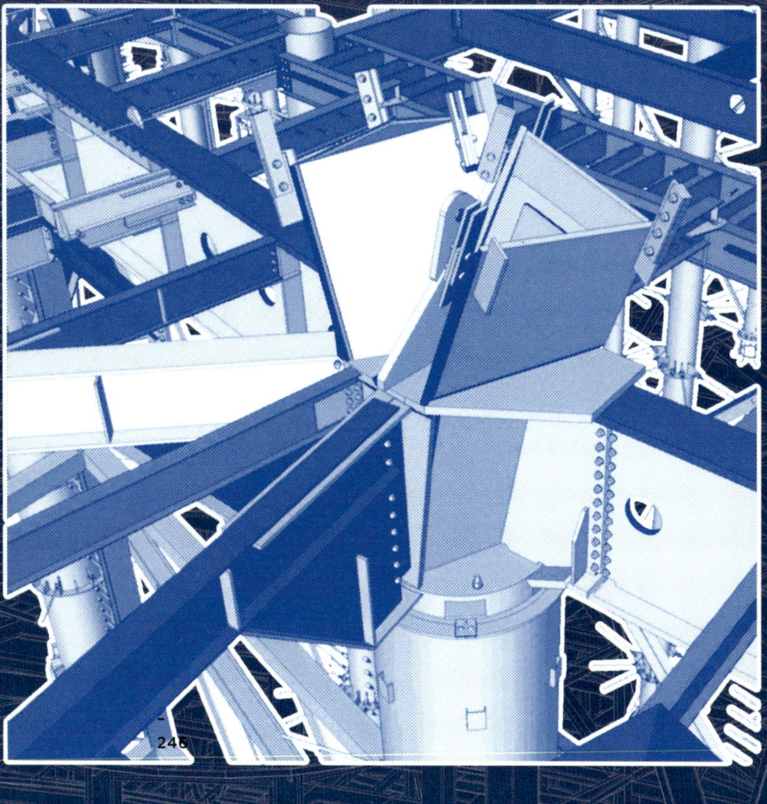

ONTARIO COLLEGE OF ART AND DESIGN
TORONTO, ON

WWW.WALTERSINC.COM

318 RYMAL ROAD E, HAMILTON, ONTARIO, CANADA | L8W 3N1 | 905.388.7111

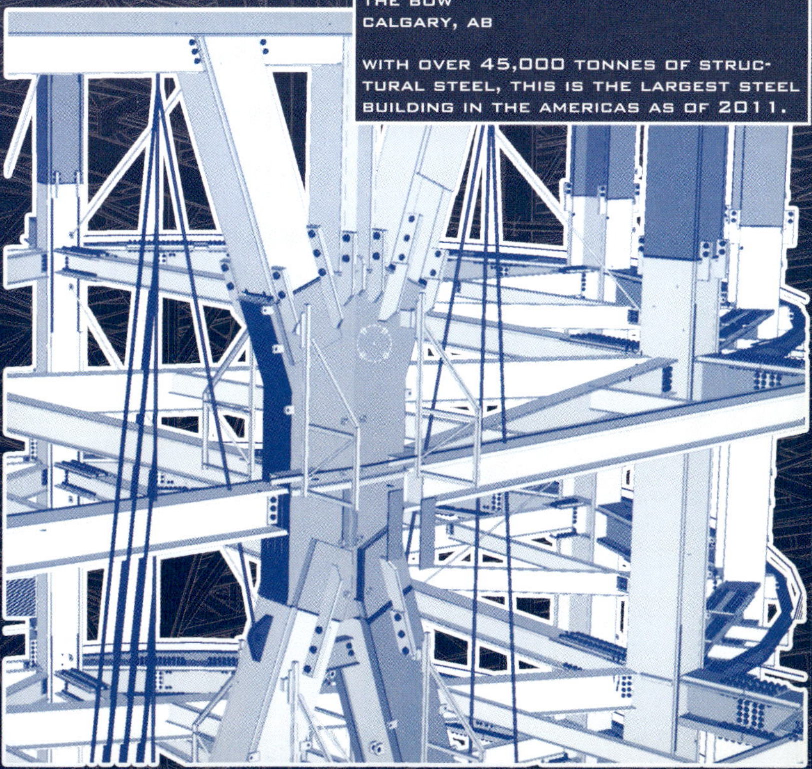

THE BOW
CALGARY, AB

WITH OVER 45,000 TONNES OF STRUCTURAL STEEL, THIS IS THE LARGEST STEEL BUILDING IN THE AMERICAS AS OF 2011.